Free as a Bird

BOOKS
10 East 53d St., New York 10022
(a division of Harper & Row Publishers, inc.)

Published in the United States of America 1974
by Harper and Row Publishers, Inc.
Barnes & Noble Import Division

© Philip Wills 1973

Printed in Great Britain

ISBN 06-497736-6

Free as a Bird

Philip Wills

To
The Igguldens of Australia
The Georgesons of New Zealand
The Laschs of South Africa
The Orsis of Italy
all fellow Romantics of the Air

Contents

PART TWO

WHAT IT'S ALL ABOUT

PART THREE
APPENDICES

Illustrations

FIGURES

MAPS

Acknowledgements

Some of the historic source material in the first part of Chapter 1 is from Ann and Lorne Welch's excellent *The Story of Gliding* (John Murray, 1965), and my thanks are due to them for having done all the hard work to make it readily available.

Many of the flight descriptions, and some of the other material, have appeared before in various journals: *Country Life*, *The Times*, *Guardian*, *Flight*, and *Sailplane & Gliding*. I am grateful to the Secretary of the British Air Line Pilots Association; to Mr Walter Tye; the Editors of the *Daily Telegraph*, *Evening News*, London, and *New Scientist* (whose article first appeared on 14 August, 1969), for the courtesy of allowing me to reproduce their copyright material.

'Altitude in Undress' was published in *The Beauty of Gliding* (Max Parrish), which has been out of print for some years. I have included it in Chapter 9 because it rounds off this chapter.

Rika Harwood has combed out many mistakes, but memory being what it is I will have made others, for which I remain responsible.

I also have to thank Alex Aldott for permission to use one of his many extraordinarily beautiful colour photographs for the dustjacket of this book.

P.W.

A summer day

Summer is the season for gliding. Many people still have the idea that gliding depends on hills for upcurrents, but this is not so. The main (though not the only) source of energy in the rising air used on most cross-country flight comes from the sun. Warm air is lighter than cold, as anyone who has made a hot-air balloon will know. When the sun shines on a dappled earth, ploughed fields and the roofs of towns, the tarmac of an airfield runway, the slope of a hill facing the sun, these and a hundred other 'thermal sources' will get warmer than surrounding green fields, forests and lakes, and the air above them will tend to rise. In certain weather conditions, this rising air will entrain further volumes of the surrounding atmosphere, and coalesce into vast rising bubbles that can go on climbing until, as they cool, they form the cumulus 'woolpack' clouds of summer and sometimes develop even further into the towering cumulo-nimbus clouds of the thunderstorm, rising 30,000 ft or more into the sky.

It took a surprisingly long time for man to discover this daily cycle of the dynamic air. How often have you noticed the clear blue sky of an early summer's day? Then, as the sun climbs and the earth begins to warm up, comes the first hint of a fluffy cloud; later on the sky is dappled with bulging pincushions of white cumulus; finally, as the sun sets, these clouds begin to topple and die, until with the last light the sky is again a clear and possibly dusty blue. During the night, the dust that has been carried up during the day by the marching fountains of rising air slowly settles, and so by dawn the air is again clear and visibility unhindered to the horizon. The same sequence is to be repeated.

If you are wise you will jump into your car and get to your gliding club as quickly as you can, because in such weather the queue of members eager to fly starts early. As soon as you arrive you get your name on the list, and then join with your fellow-members in the hundred and one tasks involved in getting the aircraft into the air. For in gliding nearly all the work is carried out voluntarily by club-members; this is part of the fun and keeps the cost of flying to the minimum.

The gliders have first to be assembled (unless the club has enough hangar space to store them fully rigged) and then checked for air-worthiness. The tow-cars, launching winches or towing aero-planes have to be serviced and checked; pilots and drivers allotted parachutes and barographs (for recording heights achieved during flights) installed. The gliders have to be towed to the launch point, the winches towed to the downwind end of the site, and the winch wire run out for perhaps 3,000 ft to be connected to the nose of the glider.

At last your turn arrives. Parachute on, barograph ticking, you are strapped in, check your controls, shut the cockpit cover, check the launch-wire on the hook. A batman at your wingtip signals to the distant winch, the wire tightens. 'All-out'; with a jerk your aircraft trundles forward, you ease back the stick, and in a steepening climb you leave the earth. Just before you started you looked around the local sky, and to one side you saw a couple of sailplanes circling serenely. They had found a rising thermal and, like the rooks, had put their machines into a circle in order to stay within it. They are marking the course for you.

At 1,000 ft on the wire you are nearly over the launching winch, and you pull the release knob. As the wire falls away, your glider jumps up as if for joy. Instantly you turn towards your lucky friends, who by now have climbed well above you. But as you reach the air beneath them your aircraft suddenly comes alive. The wings trem-ble, the controls twitch under your hands, the needle of the rate-of-climb indicator (variometer) moves from a steady three down to zero, up a bit, down, up again. The starboard wing has lifted, so the rising air is probably to that side. You thrust it down and turn into the lift. The variometer needle, after various hiccups, settles to a quiet two up and, as you circle round, the earth starts to recede below you. You have made contact, you have latched on to the lift, you are away, with no sound about you other than the rush of the wind over the wings of your aircraft.

You are now no longer a man; you are an intellectually advanced bird. You have not the instincts of a bird (although as the years go by you take an increasing number of decisions instinctively), but you have a considerably better intelligence. To keep aloft you have to continue to find rising air, and you know a good deal about the natural laws that create it. In order to avoid the trouble and expense of an away landing and a retrieve by road, you have decided to fly a triangle of, say, 100 miles, round turning points you have already declared before you took off. The first thermal takes you, in circling flight, up to the fluffy base of a shallow cumulus cloud. You are still not far from your take-off point, and it is not permissible to go into a cloud so near to home, for if this were done by everyone the collision risk would be too high. So you straighten up on course and set off in the direction of your first turning point. At 60 knots, the gliding site is left behind you, and the green and brown chequered country-side slides quietly past beneath. Ahead, below, and somewhat to starboard, is a small country town; slightly to port, and above, is another cumulus. Over the first, or under the second, is likely to be another column of lift. Which to try?

The problem is solved by the sight of two buzzards peacefully circling, ahead and slightly to port. You fly over and join them in their gyrations, and immediately the variometer swings to 'climb'. The three birds swing round in space amicably together, then once more at cloudbase you straighten up on course and leave the pair to their meditations. And so the flight continues. It is a summer's day. You are not trying to race, to break records, to take risks; you are just enjoying yourself. The glory of the earth and the freedom of the air are, for two or three hours, all yours. Towards evening, as the rising thermals carry up myriads of insects from the fields below, they become full of darting swallows, not circling for pleasure like the soaring buzzards or seagulls, but jerking to and fro with beaks agape to pick up their suppers on the wing.

The evening clouds are building up to their climactic height, before the setting sun drains their lives out of them and they topple and die. If you felt like it, you could switch on your gyroscope and circle up inside, in milky silence, to 10,000 ft or more. But, five miles ahead, the club-house on the edge of the airfield glints pinkly in the setting sun. The faithful two-seater is still taking off, circling and landing with its pupil aboard. One or two sailplanes are approaching to land;

others are being towed across the field towards the hangar. Tea and buns call, and the chatter of exchanged experiences of the day. You put the nose of your sailplane down and strike for home. The airfield boundary sweeps below, you pull out your airbrakes, the grass beneath leaps up, the skid kisses the field; a bump or two, and the life fades out of the aircraft. You are down, once more an earth-bound gregarious biped. One wing slowly drops and touches the ground. One of your friends comes up. 'Nice fly?' A typically British understatement.

ᴗ   ᴗ   ᴗ

You have just had a day of freedom in excelsis: yours has been the sky and all that therein is. It will seem in retrospect as harmless and as natural a glory as man could aspire to. This book will try to show how that freedom has been won and retained and to fore-shadow the work and struggle that lies ahead to preserve it. For if it is taken for granted, it will stage by stage be worn away and like the evening cumulus will die.

The first six chapters of this book in the main attempt to show the work and the philosophy behind it, and from Chapter 7 onwards I try to paint the picture of what it is all about: why we have done, and must continue to do this basically dull work, so that the air can remain available to us within the limits of other and more severely practical demands on it. The philosophy roots back to one statement made long ago: Man does not live by bread alone.

So if some of my readers find that parts of the first six chapters are hard going, be very glad that others are prepared to carry the burden.

PART ONE

∞

Getting airborne

I

∞∞

The Pioneers

A short history of British gliding

For the first several hundred years of the history of gliding, the
design of motorless aircraft was attempted simply because these
were, in the absence of any conceivable engine, the only possible
devices through which the secrets of controlled flight by human
beings might be discovered. In this chapter I do not propose to
record any of the doings in this field. For, as one of the most unexpected outcomes of the first World War, gliding was reborn in the
shape which developed it as it is today, as the greatest sport of all
time, involving the use of the energy stored in the atmosphere to
maintain sustained flight.

Although, in the modern jargon, gliding produces a considerable
'fallout' in the fields of meteorology, aerodynamics, structures and
materials, and even sociology, it is now regarded all over the world
as a sport—and possibly the only true aerial sport—and it is the
development of gliding in this country in this sense that I propose to
cover briefly.

In 1922 world records stood at six minutes' duration, 6 miles
distance, and 1,000 ft climb. In 1972 duration records have been
abandoned as mere pole-squatting, having been raised in 1952 to
56 hr 15 min; the world distance record is 633 miles (over 1,000 km),*
and the world height record 46,266 ft, while speed records round
triangular courses, of 100, 300 and 500 km, exceed 65 mph. During
the 1965 World Gliding Championships, held at RAF South Cerney,
86 pilots from 28 nations flew 48,500 miles over six competition
days. While they were flying about half the air traffic over the
British Isles consisted of gliders, and there were nearly three times

* At the time of going to press, a flight of over 1400 kms has been made and is awaiting
homologation.

as many gliders flying in uncontrolled air space as there were powered civil aircraft flying in controlled air space.

It was in 1922 that gliding in its modern form first appeared in our country. Fired by the rather vague tales of motorless goings-on coming from Germany, the *Daily Mail* offered a prize of £1,000 for the longest glide exceeding 30 minutes, and the Royal Aero Club organised a meeting at Itford, on the South Downs. Thirty-five gliders were whipped into existence within eight weeks, many of them fantasies which never left the ground.

There was, indeed, a curious element of fantasy over the whole meeting. Harold Perrin, the Secretary of the Royal Aero Club, who organised it, was a figure somewhat larger than life. I recall him as a large, energetic, red and rude man who charmed all who knew him well by occasional bursts of gruff kindness. Many of the aircraft came straight from cloud-cuckoo land: they included an ornithopter of 54-ft span; a two-seater helicopter, and a biplane 'powered' by a fan, to be driven by the wind and turning an airscrew. There was the warping-wing glider that warped its wings right off, fortunately without hurting its pilot, and the biplane rigged in a tent too small to extract it from, whose owner's problem was solved when the wind blew the tent down and destroyed his brain-child.

At the end of the meeting Maneyrol, flying a glider with two identical wings fore and aft, with the pilot sitting between them, won the prize with a duration of 3 hr 21 min, and after the tumult and the shouting had died, everyone packed up and British gliding went into cold-storage for another eight years. In fact, the only gain to the future of gliding achieved from this curious and isolated explosion of interest was that Gordon England, in spite of a crash which fractured an ankle, was sufficiently interested to become one of the leading figures in the next revival in 1930.

Late in 1929, *The Aeroplane* published an article on the recent dramatic developments in Germany, as a result of which Douglas Culver arranged a 'gliding lunch' at the Comedy Restaurant in London on 4 December. Thirty people promised to come and fifty-six turned up. A committee was formed which later gave birth to the British Gliding Association. Two German experts came and demonstrated slope soaring, and one of them, Robert Kronfeld, flew 50 miles along the South Downs from Firle Beacon to Portsdown Hill. Dozens of clubs were formed, primitive gliders were rapidly built or bought, and as rapidly destroyed. Within two years British gliding was once more on the verge of extinction.

Apart from the British Gliding Association, kept alive by a magnificent donation of £1,000 from Lord Wakefield, there were two main survivors, doggedly hanging on.

The Aeroplane, flushed by the success of its first article, had started a small paper *The Sailplane and Glider*, price 3d, with Thurstan James as its Editor. When the movement collapsed, it offered this magazine to the British Gliding Association, who took it over and appointed Frank Entwhistle, of the Meteorological Office, as its Editor. In January 1933 he in turn had to give it up, and Dr A. E. Slater took on the job. In Doc Slater's brilliant and devoted hands this magazine, now *Sailplane & Gliding*, is today acknowledged as one of the best gliding publications in the world, bought in about 60 countries, and turning in a small, but regular, profit to its owners, still the BGA.

The other survivor of note was the London Gliding Club, hanging grimly on to a series of sites near Dunstable, and eventually acquiring freehold and settling for good at their present world-famous site under Dunstable Downs. There is a curious law of gravity about certain human beings: if by chance three or four get together, they attract others of the same general type. Although the pioneers of the London Club were each individualists in the extreme, they all exhibited the same characteristics of energy, enthusiasm, ingenuity, perseverance, and the love of a challenge and a fight for an apparently hopeless cause.

But no cause is hopeless, no problem insurmountable, when it attracts men like Graham Humby, Toby Ashwell-Cooke, Dudley Hiscox, Sebert Humphries, Mungo Buxton, Eric Collins, Louis Desoutter, and a host of others to its solution. There were moments of black despair, when luck stepped in to save the day. Turned off their last possible launching site on top of the Downs the members assembled in Turvey's Farm at Totternhoe. Hearing their problem, Mr Turvey told them one single spur of the hill running up from his field belonged to him and they could use it. They erected a simple wooden hangar. It was blown down. They put it up again.

On 21 February 1931, Humby and Gerry Smith each held the air for over five minutes in an open Primary glider; the first ab-initio British pilots to win the C certificate. On 24 May, Henry Petre broke Maneyrol's British record of nine years before with a flight of 3 hrs 28 min.

In 1932, two British-designed sailplanes appeared which were to open up the sky to dozens of future pilots. Corporal Manuel designed and built the Wren, and L. Baynes designed the Scud which was produced by Abbotts, a firm of motor-car body builders at Farnham. Mungo Buxton bought a Scud II for £100, including trailer, and later invited me into partnership. Forty years later a Scud II is still flying at Dunstable, and a rebuilt Wren at Redhill.

In 1933 Collins for the first time was prolonging his flights by the use of thermal lift, first with a flight of 6 miles, reaching 950 ft, and then with one of 22 miles, gaining 2,300 ft. The whispers of those maintaining that these thermal things were only exotic happenings in foreign countries were gradually stilled.

Right through that winter, and on into the following spring, a band of fanatics rushed to Dunstable whenever the wind had a westerly component. No one knew exactly what caused these thermals, or when they might be expected: at last, on 18 March 1934, in the showery north-westerly air behind a cold front, Humphries in a Crested Wren gained height and tore off downwind, to land 19 miles away. Collins, in the Kassel two-seater, broke the two-seater record with a flight of 46 miles, and I, arriving late, jumped into the Professor and landed two and a half hours later at Latchington, near the river Blackwater, 55 miles away, with the single-seat record.

The British gliding movement was off the ground.

From now on, we were over top dead-centre, although it did not seem like it at the time. In October 1933 we had had a week-end meeting at Sutton Bank, in Yorkshire; miraculously after a cloud-bound Saturday we had a fine westerly Sunday and put in so much flying from this dazzlingly beautiful site that a committee was set up, consisting of Norman Sharpe, Fred Slingsby and myself, to attempt to build a gliding centre there. After some years of difficult negotiation we achieved a lease, and today the Yorkshire Gliding Club own the site, with its fine club-house and equipment.

In 1934, Espin Hardwick, a wealthy Birmingham stockbroker,

erupted on the scene. Espin had the heart of a lion in the body of a gnome, a wizened little hunchback for whom many of us would willingly have died. He advanced the London Club the money for their site, then found the Long Mynd in Shropshire, and began a long battle which produced the Midland Gliding Club; also Gerry Smith and Louis Slater found a site in the Pennines, which led to the present Derbyshire and Lancashire Gliding Club, at Camphill, where many of our later National Championships were held.

Above all, in 1934, Major Jack Shaw met Fred Slingsby, who had been building gliders in his tiny works at Scarborough, and the outcome was Slingsby Sailplanes Ltd, Kirbymoorside.

So by now we had a number of well-founded Clubs, our own magazine, and a source of British-built aircraft. We were a viable unit. The BGA having been through some distressing birth-pangs, had been battered into its present shape by the pressure of the offer of a Government subsidy of £5,000 per annum which was withheld until an agreed new structure had been worked out. By 1935 this had been done.

The next crucial year proved to be 1937, when we sent a British team to the first International Gliding Competitions, held on the Wasserkuppe in Germany. We did not do very well, but we learnt how important, as a means of measuring pilot ability, was a marking system. We came back just in time to go to our own Nationals at Camphill, and the day before ran up a marking system of our own. For the first time our 1937 Nationals became a competitive event enabling the pilots to measure their individual skills against each other. The result was 43 cross-country flights with an aggregate of 1,489 miles: an unbelievable advance on anything which had happened before.

1938 brought a golden harvest of records. We had installed aero-towing hooks on a number of aeroplanes, including the Avro 504 of Captain Phillips, and an Avro Cadet of Heston, and thus were no longer bound by the soaring westerlies. In the spring north-easters there were remarkable happenings. On the 17th of March, Kit Nicholson beat my 1936 distance record of 104 miles in his Rhonsperber with a flight of 120 miles from Huish to Bigbury-on-Sea; he held it for one day. For on the 18th, Sylvan Fox in his Rhonadler beat it with a flight of 145 miles from Huish to Fowey. Twelve days later I flew my Minimoa 209 miles from Heston to St Austell. On 3 June I climbed in a small cumulo-nimbus cloud to 10,180 ft near Dunstable. On 9–10 July, Murray and Sproule gained the two-seater duration record with a flight lasting 22 hrs 14 min over Dunstable Downs; and on 18 August Young won the single-seater duration record with a flight of 15 hrs 47 min from the Long Mynd.

On 22 April 1939, Geoffrey Stephenson flew across the Channel from Dunstable, in his Gull I. On 22 June, McLean broke my height record with a remarkable climb of 10,350 ft in an open Grunau Baby in the Helm Wind at Hartside in Cumberland, the first big wave flight in this country, but nine days later, on 1 July, I won it back again in the Minimoa, with a flight of 14,170 ft from Dunstable.

Over the next six years the only event worthy of brief record was one curious sideline to the Battle of Britain, when the air over the Channel, so full of hurrying and noisy adversaries, also contained a few of us oddly floating about in our gliders at 35 mph while boffins on the Swanage cliffs peered at their rudimentary radar screens to see if they echoed the reflections of wooden gliders.

As soon as possible after the war we got back to our passion again. The drawings of Hans Jacobs' pre-war Meise (Olympia) were available, and Dudley Hiscox persuaded Chilton Aircraft to build one. Horace Buckingham of Elliots of Newbury took it over and built over a hundred. They formed the core of club and privately-owned sailplanes over the following years. Fred Slingsby and I were sent on a tour of Germany and brought back a number of the more interesting types, including two Weihes. The handling and performance of this wonderful 18-metre was such that Slingsby was spurred to beat it—and the result was the Sky, which put British aircraft at last in the lead. For the Sky was followed by the Skylark series, which won competitions and records all over the globe, and then by the Dart, which proved a worthy successor.

In 1948 we sent three teams to compete in the first post-war world contests, at Samaden in Switzerland. The outcome was stark tragedy, Kit Nicholson and Donald Greig lost their lives in two fatal crashes on one day.

Then came 1952, when at last we came to the top. In the World Championships in Spain, in the single-seater Class, we won 1st, 3rd, 9th and 11th places, flying Slingsby Skys, and Skys also took

4th, 7th and 14th places. At a reception held by Alan Lennox-Boyd after our return, attended by four previous Ministers of Aviation and many distinguished heads of the Ministries, we received a telegram of congratulations from Winston Churchill.

Perhaps the next vital question to be answered was whether or not the first band of pioneers would find a second wave to carry on the torch. The 20 years since the end of the war provided an affirmative answer. People like Ann and Lorne Welch (although Ann overlaps back into the first era), Frank Irving, Nick Goodhart, Walter Kahn, David Carrow, Peter Scott, Ken Wilkinson, and many others show that there are still challenges sufficiently difficult and enticing to attract people of the calibre required.

The final critical year was 1965, when in June we held the World Gliding Championships at RAF South Cerney. With the support of that Service these were the largest, and we are told the best organised, of the whole series. They attracted an unparalleled public interest and paved the way for a further dynamic expansion of British gliding. The Slingsby Dart won the International prize for the best Standard Class glider, and its various marks kept our flag flying for some years after.

Since 1970, however, there can be no doubt that the Germans have overtaken us in the field of glider design, by their skill in the development of resin-bonded glass-fibre structures, which has made previous advanced designs virtually obsolete.

Faced with this enormous gap, Slingsby's have done the only possible thing, and have taken a licence from one of the leading German manufacturers to build their Kestrel.

As a convinced European, I hope that over the years ahead we shall see a fruitful interchange of ideas which will keep first one country, then another, in friendly rivalry. This in fact is what has happened in the field of civil aeroplanes, where the sums of money involved are relatively gargantuan. But even in gliders, the development of an entirely new material such as glass-fibre, to the highly sophisticated standards required for such a purpose, could easily require a sum of the order of £1 million, over a period of ten years or more. So it would be crazy to duplicate such a programme, and immensely wasteful in both time and money.

As for the future, the main problems are twofold: the sites necessary for the formation of new clubs, and the constant battle to retain freedom of the air. If we fail in this, our cause will have been finally lost. Experience up to the present gives grounds for hope, for we take some beating.

Aeroclub of Nice, 1934

My own experience of gliding only spans the period from 1933 to the present day, but the following two stories may show the strides we have made even in that time.

In 1934 we went on holiday to Cannes, and whilst there we were invited to a meeting of the *section vol-à-voile* of the Aero Club of Nice. The following is a free translation of the subsequent report of this function in the local newspaper, describing about fifty seconds of flying in a primary glider.

La sortie de l'Aéro Club de Nice et de la Côte-d'Azur

'The Aero Club of Nice, etc., made an expedition to Caille on Sunday to visit its Sailplane Section, whose training ground is in this picturesque region.

This visit also had as an object, to go and thank the Mayor, the Municipality, and the population of Caille for the well-wishing amiability (*la bienveillante amabilité*) with which the section had been received and for the way in which it had been offered on their part the greatest possible facilities to enable them to organise usefully the training of their members.

The caravan arrived at Caille at 11 hrs 15.

At 12 hrs 15 an aperitif was offered to the Mayor and the Municipality. M. Francis Teisseire, the President of the Administrative Commission, in the name of the Club and of the Sailplane Section, uttered in well-chosen words a charming speech which was much applauded (*prononça une charmante élocution très applaudie*) and thanked the Mayor, the Municipality and the population of Caille for the precious assistance and help offered by them towards the accomplishment and pursuit of the work to which the Aero Club of Nice and its Sailplane Section was so irrevocably attached (*inlassablement attachés*).

At 12 hrs 45 the members set themselves to lunch. We noticed

. . . (here follows a long list of members, mayors, corporations, and population of Caille).

At dessert, the *doyen* of the pilot aviators, the Capitaine Pugnetti, rose to thank the committee of organisation of these so united and agreeable festivities; which he did with his usual gusto.

In a delicate gesture, M. Paul Scoffier presented the ladies with some magnificent carnations.

The feast over, the delegation repaired to the training ground of the Sailplane Section, to help at the trials which had been organised.

In spite of great difficulties on account of a recent accident, the courageous party of sailplaners (*la courageuse équipe de vélivolants*) had not hesitated to spend part of the night effecting the necessary repairs. This work accomplished, the machine had been installed in its trailer (*l'appareil fut installé sur sa remorque*) and the party in full order launched itself towards Caille. The *appareil* and its personnel had arrived at 3 o' clock in the morning.

On the following morning the party proceeded to the assembly of the glider, and in the presence of the delegation and the local authorities, the machine landed the first time in an impeccable manner at the end of a trial flight made by the director, Robert Guillot.

Then, the excellent pilot Coli, member of the section, executed a magnificent flight, and held the air during several seconds (*tint l'air pendant quelques seconds*), from about one hundred metres, to the repeated applause of all the spectators, demonstrating at once the courage (*cran*) and the *finesse* of the pilot, the quality of the machine, and the numerous attractions, both of utility and of a seductive sport, which is Gliding.

After having congratulated M. Guillot, director of the Sailplane Section, and all the young sportsmen composing it . . . who were drilled and disciplined around their chief and attentive to his orders, for their perseverance and the technical skill of each of them, the members of the delegation quitted with regret the picturesque village of Caille, silent and dreaming, hidden in the midst of grandiose mountains which dominate and encircle it like a rampart, jealous that it should not be discovered.'

Thirty years later: Camphill, 1964

For nine days we had suffered what seemed the only wretched patch of weather in the British Isles, which elsewhere were basking in a heatwave. Day after day low cloud, drizzle and high winds swept our Pennine moor at Camphill, while friends at Dunstable and Dunkeswell were steadily flying in semi-tropical sun. We had squeezed three days' contests out of the nine allotted to the 1964 Northern Regional Championships, and those of us able to fly twenty-or-so miles out of the hills had found ourselves in a different, warmer and sunny world.

Camphill, the site of the Derbyshire & Lancashire Gliding Club, is on top of a 1,300-ft plateau, with steep 600-ft slopes on the western and southern boundaries; from these a beautiful view of the fields and hills of the Peak National Park can be seen—when weather permits.

On our last day we awoke once more to a low grey sky, and a strong north-west wind bore a slight mist of rain. But five miles to the east of Sheffield, a line of silver running north and south marked the eastern slopes of the Pennine Chain, and occasional breaks in the cloud to the west also gave an idea of a similar area of fine weather in that direction. It seemed almost certain that the Pennines were covered with a tablecloth of low cloud, formed by a standing wave. Those who have seen the cloud called the 'Tablecloth' hanging down over the top of Table Mountain will have seen a small edition of this precise cloud—but ours was presumably 150 miles long running north and south and 20 miles from west to east covering the Pennine Chain from Matlock up towards Scotland.

The standing wave is an aerial phenomenon which gives rise to large smooth areas of rising air, in which sailplane pilots have climbed to immense heights. If only therefore we could get airborne and navigate ourselves forward from the hill, flying blind in low cloud, it seemed almost certain that an unusual, exciting and even dramatic flight was on the cards. We had been set the task to fly a race to Husbands Bosworth, an airfield 12 miles south of Leicester and 66 miles away. In a standing wave it might be possible to achieve sufficient height over Camphill itself to do the flight in a single glide, for with the upper winds nearly behind us, we should achieve a gliding angle of around 1 in 40. Thus from a height of say two miles (around 10,000 ft) a single glide could take one 80 miles to sea level.

Was it safe? The skill, experience and equipment of the field in a Regional Championship cover a wider spectrum than in the Nationals, for the former act as a training and proving ground for pilots wishing to qualify themselves for the latter. A brief clearance in front of the hill had enabled five aircraft to be launched, and these had reached cloudbase while still on the wire, only around 300 ft above our field, but had flown forwards towards the sunny patch and then been lost to view. Fortunately I was equipped with radio, and had had a good deal of experience of wave-flying, so it was decided to send me off so that I could report back on what things looked like from the air. There was little hazard for four or five aircraft, but to launch up to 25 into what might be a restricted area of lift in low cloud was clearly unwise.

I was strapped into the cockpit of my Skylark 4, the winch-wire was attached. I switched on the radio and my turn-and-bank indicator (an instrument enabling one to fly accurately when out of sight of the ground), and we were off. No point in climbing steeply, I only needed 300 ft over the edge of the hill. At this height I was brushing cloud-base, released, and went forward towards the brighter sky ahead. For half-a-minute or so I was blind, climbing strongly on a westerly course, then emerged into a patch of clear air, with rags of broken cloud ahead through which the sun shone down on to the green fields of the valley, fields bounded by stone walls, stretching west towards Tideswell.

I turned right, and above me on my right was the typical swelling bank of the leading edge of a wave cloud. I flew north, climbing steadily, and at 3,000 ft reached the top of the wave-cloud. On my left, the clear patch had closed in, and I was flying in dazzling sunshine above a rolling cloudscape, the top of which was indented with cloud valleys echoing the configuration of the valleys below.

At 6,000 ft I could clearly see the eastern, western and southern boundaries of the tablecloth, but to the north it extended to the horizon. And below there were now no gaps, the one through which I had ascended seemed to have filled in. Soon I saw, floating dreamily around me, the beautiful shapes of four of the five aircraft which had taken off before me. The uncanny silence and smoothness of a typical wave enmeshed us all, the Skylark was flying several knots below its usual speed, the only sound a gentle susurration of the air sliding silkily over its wings.

'Philip to Kitty. It's really wonderful up here, but to get up through the cloud is a bit of a trick, and on the whole I recommend that launching should be suspended until the cloud breaks up a bit more in front of the hill.'

This was rather awkward, as it meant that the five of us already airborne might have a considerably easier task to reach our goal than our remaining competitors, but it couldn't be helped. The air is a stern disciplinarian, and its rules have nothing to do with contest marking systems.

For the next three quarters of an hour all thoughts of racing to our goal were expunged by the delight of exploration. Below, the sheet of cloud looked like an endless field of dazzling snow, ploughed by a drunken giant. The furrows were a mile wide, and instead of running parallel, north and south, they curved in sympathy with the invisible valleys beneath. Lift over the upwind crest of each furrow was wide and smooth, and at 6,000 ft we were each effortlessly suspended some 3,000 ft above the cloud sheet.

At length, reluctantly, I turned south on course. 'Philip to Kitty: Am setting off on course, please follow. Afraid I shan't be able to tell you where I am for a bit, but I should go fast, with the wind behind me.'

Ten minutes later: 'Philip to Kitty: There is a small hole through the cloud beneath me, and exactly in the middle is a glider on the ground.'—'Kitty to Philip: Yes, I think we know about that one.'—'Philip to Kitty: If you can tell me where it is, I shall know where I am.'—'Camphill base to Philip: The glider is a mile south-east of Bakewell.'

So that was that, and a minute later a momentary extension of the hole showed the western end of the formal gardens of Chatsworth. And now ahead and above, suddenly the most marvellous sight: suspended in the sky the solid-seeming outline of a classic lenticular cloud. It looked like a gigantic heap of inverted plates, piled closely on top of each other. It was roughly circular in plan, and lens-shaped in elevation. In spite of the strong wind, it was stationary in space, the wind blowing through it. Its edges were milky, but its body seemed as firm as a cardboard cloud on a stage: a dazzling white miracle, suspended in a deep blue, dazzling sky.

Under its upwind edge I found the expected lift, and quickly climbed in the clear air in front of it. And now came the crowning glory, when, drawn as by a magnet, I was joined by my three remaining friends, and together the four of us, in our brightly coloured beautiful craft, weaved our way up against the backcloth of blinding white, until at over 8,000 ft we had conquered the cloud, and, breathless with the beauty of the world, were looking down on its rounded perfection.

The scene ended like a conjuring trick. Momentarily I turned away from the cloud, then swung the nose of my machine back towards it. It had vanished. Some minute change in temperature, humidity, or pressure had within 30 seconds altered the wavelength of the system, and it had dissolved into the thin air which was its sole constituent. The remaining evidence of its brief life lay in four sailplanes suspended improbably in the high air.

I landed an hour later, the flight only marred by a last minute error which delayed my landing for a few minutes. For I started my last glide to earth from a height which would have been adequate had Husbands Bosworth been at sea-level, and only just in time realised it is 500 ft up.

Ten minutes after my landing two of my companions in glory hove into sight—but two miles down wind and too low to make the goal. They landed together in a field. An hour later my son Christopher arrived in a Skylark 3, and news of other landings, some fairly near, came in; for around 3 o'clock the sky at Camphill had partially cleared and the rest of the field had got away.

I received a clear impression that many, if not most, of us, behaved on landing exactly as if we were slightly drunk. We were possessed by an imperative urgency to try to communicate, as well as we were able, the glories we had seen.

Many people have, of course, seen wonderful cloudscapes from the windows of powered aircraft; and if I were to try to explain how different was our experience, I can only suggest that whilst in an aeroplane one is a mere spectator, protected from the vast nothingness outside by the underlying tension of mechanical business, we in our silent sailplanes were integral to the scene, we were as much a part of it as the glorious lenticular cloud which had etched it indelibly in our memories.

2

∞

Running the Show

On structures

In the last chapter I wrote that the early troubles and arguments in the BGA arose from defective structure. The older I get, the more I am convinced that in correct institutional restructuring lies one of the main solutions to many of the major problems of our time.

I am sure that history will declare that Jean Monnet, the architect of the Treaty of Rome, was a greater man even than Winston Churchill. This rather distinguished-looking civil servant of a man enunciated a law as follows: 'Human nature does not change, but when nations and men accept the same rules, and the same institutions to make sure they are applied, their behaviour towards each other changes. *This is the process of civilisation itself.*' For this process Monnet coined the word *'engrenage'*, roughly translated as the putting of gears into mesh.

One day in the early '40s I was sitting at lunch in the Mess next to an Army Major who had just returned from the Desert War campaign in North Africa. We were at the time experiencing a strike of Welsh coal miners, and I was indignantly critical of their lack of patriotism and their self-interest. My companion replied 'Don't you believe it: I have just been in command of a battalion of those very same men in the desert, and they were absolutely magnificent.' They were simply the same men in different structures.

The basic fact is that most men *want* to work together, *want* to contribute, and *want* to know the people they are working with, but in too many instances are locked in a structure which makes it impossible for them to do so. The result is they start blaming 'the other side' instead of the structure.

Now in our own small world of British gliding, let us look at the structural problems which we faced and overcame in 1934. The Association at that time consisted of individual members, and obviously the total membership of the very small clubs, although they were all the time forming and rapidly destroying themselves, outnumbered those of the exceedingly few 'large' ones—in fact the London Club of Dunstable was almost alone in having more than 50 members.

At that time the Chairman of the BGA was a pioneer of British gliding, and a gallant one. He and his colleagues, observing the sport as it then was, saw it confined to bungey-launches in elementary Primary gliders (looking much like five-barred gates sprouting wings suspended on piano-wire) and leading at its best to slightly less elementary contraptions beating along the tops of suitable hills facing the prevailing winds.

They therefore concluded (and given this premise they were no doubt correct) that gliding *per se* would develop as a cheap introduction to 'real' (powered) flying, and foresaw large numbers of young people being introduced to aeroplane flying in this way

But out in the field, one or two of the larger clubs began to acquire members with quite different horizons—of gliding becoming a sport in its own right, with immensely wider possibilities and fascinations; although in those days even the most far-sighted visionary could not possibly have foreseen the extraordinary advances that were subsequently to take place. This meant developing the BGA in quite a different way, and applying its limited funds to quite different purposes. Basically this meant that, instead of encouraging large numbers of small clubs using a small site and equipped with one or two Primaries (costing £45 each!), the way ahead lay in encouraging necessarily fewer but larger and better equipped clubs, which could develop more advanced flying.

Before we knew where we were, the BGA was accusing the larger clubs of promoting the cause of the rich against the poor, and the larger clubs riposted by accusing the BGA of promoting boys' brigades instead of a 'he-man' movement. We were all very young, and each party believed it was right. Alas for *homo sapiens*, who rapidly reverts to his cave in these circumstances.

The BGA '*engrenaged*' itself by changing from an Association of individual members to an Association of clubs, with those clubs which had achieved some degree of viability (security of tenure of sites and so forth) in control. Thus control passed from a large number of individuals of whom the majority at that time must clearly hold the 'poor man's training for powered flight' idea, to clubs dominated by those believing in gliding as an end in itself.

The main credit for this should go to Toby Ashwell-Cooke. He was a short, square, argumentative, one-hundred-percent political animal, no doubt infuriating to his opponents. He was a quite un-skilful glider pilot. But he was in his element in argument, unlike the rest of us political simpletons, and we were lucky that he was caught up in ours, and on our side, for he had the instinct to be right. Without him, we should probably have lost.

In 1937 he experienced the early symptoms of Parkinson's disease, it took thirty-four years to kill him, inch by dreadful inch, and he died in 1971, his essential guts still unbroken. But, as it turned out, he had more influence over the future of British gliding than almost anyone else. We should not forget him.

I recall the Extraordinary General Meeting which I chaired, at which this rebirth was finally achieved. Prior to that, the office of the BGA Secretary had fallen vacant (because no one wanted to put themselves in the crossline of fire which was going on), and I persuaded a friend of mine, Walter Briscoe, to fill the temporary gap. We could not both together get into the tiny office, it was so full of files, so we went through them and threw away the larger pro-portion so that we could both sit down and get to work.

Before the Meeting, I had read up a book on the art of Chairman-ship, and threw out lofty rulings about substantive motions and the like, and eventually our reorganisation was agreed. But not before I had been accused by a very worthy gentleman indeed of having (a) sabotaged the BGA records, and (b) pinched the petty cash. Fortunately—or unfortunately—the BGA cash in those days was so petty that this was laughed off. Then we went on to discuss at length a very worthwhile project which we had to reject because we couldn't raise the necessary £5.

So at last the BGA became an Association of Clubs, and we were granted our £5,000 subsidy, which we limited to those clubs which could apply it to stabilise themselves—as part-contributions towards the purchase of sites, hangars, and similar capital assets, and not as a subsidy towards reducing the actual cost of flying-fees. This produced miracles, as even though £5,000 in those days went a lot further than now, it was not a large sum.

But another vital feature of structures: they attract to themselves people worthy of them. What able and ambitious young man today would select his career in one of our strife-torn industries? There is a kind of Gresham's Law in this situation, where unhappy and inefficient organisations can only attract the less efficient managements, and so spiral downwards, whilst happy and efficient ones attract the best. You may think you know men who would make better Prime Ministers than the ones we get. But if you think of it, none of your choices would be prepared to go through the structure which acts as a sieve through which a man has to pass to get to the top of the political tree.

The 1935 structure of the BGA, however, stood the test triumphantly, attracting to it a succession of competent enthusiasts whose work has earned for it the delegation of all those functions which in other countries are carried out by Ministries.

The most prestigious recognition of the respect for our work which we have achieved came in 1955 when we gained our most noteworthy adherent.

By great good fortune I had during the war a good deal to do with Alan Lennox-Boyd (now Lord Boyd), which stood us in good stead when later on he became Minister of Civil Aviation. In the summer of 1954 he was, alas, posted to the Colonial Ministry, and before taking up his new post came to Camphill, in the Pennines, and stayed in his caravan with his wife, Lady Patricia, to attend the World Championships which we held that year.

One evening, sitting in his caravan in the endless rain which nearly washed away the representatives of 19 nations—and which ever since has internationally earned for the site of the Derby & Lancs Club the name of 'Damphill'—he asked me if there was any final service I felt he might render us, which is the sort of thing few Ministers bother about when on their way to a new and senior appointment. I asked him if he could approach the Duke of Edinburgh and ask if he would become our President.

Six months later I was in New Zealand, and the day after a height record flight in the Mt Cook wave, I received a letter from Alan saying that if I wrote suitably to Buckingham Palace and asked if His Royal Highness would consent to become our Patron, I might get a favourable reply. I did, and it came.

I suppose few people outside our country, and few even within it, will realise what this means. It is simply that in our Patron we have a man of extraordinary ability and distinction, who is prepared to act immediately, and without red tape, in supporting a cause in which he believes. Far from being a mere figurehead, he has unfailingly supported us whenever we have asked for his assistance in any matter within his scope. British gliding would not be where it is today but for the help he has willingly given us in a number of critical moments—sometimes when he was in the midst of handling great affairs of State.

My last act as Chairman of the BGA, after the enormous success of the 1965 World Gliding Championships at South Cerney, was to initiate a revised structure to fit it for the tasks of the 1970s and beyond. The Association had by then grown so large that Council exceeded 40 members, and hence it was obviously necessary to change it in some way to achieve a smaller executive body with the minimum loss of democratic control.

I should not like it to be thought that the structure adopted by the BGA is automatically applicable in other countries: indeed in the USA the Soaring Society of America has exactly the reverse set-up —it is an association of individual members. The reason is simply geographical.

In Britain we have a small country with official control concentrated in the centre—London. So it is desirable and possible to have an Association run by highly competent people, all of whom are in reasonable reach of the capital, near enough to the Ministries to create confidence in their ability to accept delegated control, and close enough to their clubs to exercise it.

The US gliding movement is not very much larger than ours, but spread over an immense area. So it is impossible to have a central body to whom nearly every competent individual can have physical access for regular meetings, nor can the SSA have the same close relationship with Washington that we have with our Ministries in London. So in fact they exercise no delegated powers, and most of the matters controlled by the BGA are, in the USA, kept in the hands of the Federal Aviation Administration.

However, gliding in the United States has been able to latch on to the much greater freedoms given US sporting flying generally, and so has not suffered as much as might be expected. But they are much more restricted in the field of altitude-flying than we are, because this is a freedom only needed by the sailplane pilot. So here we get no help from powered light aviation; whilst gliding in their country is a much more expensive sport than it is here.

Another basic structural feature of the BGA is that at its formation the Royal Aero Club delegated it full powers in all matters to do with gliding. In few other countries has the National Aero Club been so far-sighted. Usually it has retained control, and its members being predominantly interested in powered flying have ignored or over-ridden the special requirements of motorless flying.

These are, therefore, in my view, the fundamental rules which should apply to any organisation, whether it be a nation state, a business, or a central Gliding Association:

1　Analyse as clearly as possible what the organisation is set up to achieve.

2　Define as closely as you can the kind of people most likely to be able to produce the required results.

3　Set up a structure, or alter the existing structure, so as to attract precisely this kind of man or woman to its service, and design it in a way likely to expedite his or her progress to its summit.

4　Get each committee chairman to draft his Terms of Reference —then check them across, and amend them if necessary to ensure there is no overlapping in responsibility between any committees. Nothing leads more inevitably to friction than people treading on each other's toes because their jobs are ill-defined and overlap.

5　See that committee decisions are minuted and copies sent to committees working in adjacent fields.

6　If the wrong men seem to be coming to the top, or if the right men don't seem to be producing the required results, don't blame them: suspect the structure. It is easier to change structures than men.

The structure of the British Gliding Association which has grown biologically from its duties, and the Terms of Reference of its constituent committees form Appendix 1.

This has for nearly 40 years given us a machine to control our own affairs, attracting to its service people who have shown themselves competent to do so.

A fundamental tip: members of Council, once elected, are not delegates of their individual clubs (with their hands tied by their individual club policies) but representatives of the whole gliding movement. Competent people must have powers to exercise their own initiative, on the latest facts available to them. If you lay down a structure for puppets, that is what you will get.

Let us look, therefore, at the different fields in which the British Gliding Association has been given responsibility, and how they have exercised it.

Almost alone amongst the nations of the World, the British gliding movement is not subjected to governmental control, but itself handles all matters connected with (a) aircraft registration, (b) Certificates of Airworthiness, (c) pilots' licences, (d) pilots' medical standards, (e) instructors' categorisation, (f) instructional standards, (g) pilots' qualification standards.

In addition to this formidable list, accidents/incidents are reported to, and analysed by the Safety Panel (serious accidents are in addition reportable to the Ministry), and airworthiness requirements have been established by the Air Registration Board, in closest consultation with the Association's Technical Committee.

The most difficult field is that of Air Traffic Control. Here we disseminate all official regulations, and endeavour to see that they are observed. Simultaneously we are involved in an endless battle to ensure that each regulation is not only necessary, but can be seen to be necessary. Here we are up against very big guns indeed, and although our success is not absolute, it is, I am sure, better than in any other country.

Member clubs of the Association (who control it through an Executive Committee) bind themselves to abide by the Operational Regulations of the Association, and in this lies the core of the self-imposed discipline on which our safety record has been established and our good name founded.

The battle to achieve and hold this good name has been long and arduous, sometimes involving just dull hard work, sometimes moments of quite high drama. It has all had to be waged in the spare time of a large number of highly competent and dedicated enthusiasts. It will, of course, never end: it can never be wholly won, but may indeed be wholly lost.

The Fédération Aéronautique Internationale

The FAI is an association of National Aero Clubs, and is the International body which controls world records and world championships in all fields of aviation, from model aircraft to astronautics. At present it has 44 active members.

To fulfil this task involves two functions, which it carries out rather well: and it has adopted a third, which it does not—because structurally it cannot—cope with very successfully.

To control world records and championships involves first the necessity to define them and impose detailed controls and regulations, so that everyone knows exactly what to do and what paperwork is required. So for each different branch of aviation there is a corresponding FAI committee—the gliding one is the Commission Internationale de Vol à Voile, or CIVV. Each committee draws up a sporting code covering its particular field—the gliding code is called Section D, and is the small green booklet that most people carry around with them in case the chance of a record crops up.

A glance through Section D will at once indicate the vast amount of detailed work that has to go into its compilation—and from time to time its amendment, as the sport develops and new possibilities evolve. Meetings of CIVV are held once or twice a year, usually in Paris, and it is astonishing how delegates come from all over the world to assist in its work, and how ideas from many different nations fit together to expedite the development of motorless flight. For instance, the idea of competition speed flying originated in Switzerland; the definition of the standard class glider in the UK; while Germany is taking the lead in powered gliders.

CIVV has been fortunate in having Pirat Gehriger as Chairman (or President) for the entire post-war period; his firm and multilingual leadership has immensely eased its work.

So at the committee level FAI does a really excellent job, ably assisted by a tiny secretariat in Paris, consisting at present of the Secretary-General, Charles Hennecart, and Sandra Prodrom, a most helpful, charming and efficient Secretary.

The Committees all report to a Council, who formulate the General Policy of FAI and in turn report to the General Conference.

The main task of the General Conference is to award the annual medals and certificates of merit in a suitably dignified way. This is a very different sort of job, and requires a different sort of person, and sometimes the two kinds don't see eye to eye. The sort of chap who is prepared to go to committee meetings to thrash out the definition of a turning point is quite different to the man who can go to a distinguished jolly and lend it distinction. In fact there are all too few Prince Philips and Lord Brabazons in the world, men who truly confer honour on those they meet. But one can't award a gold medal to the first man to land on the moon, in a small back room, so General Conference meets in some salubrious spot, usually at the invitation of a national government, and has a gay and interesting week giving and receiving hospitality on a more or less lavish scale, and awarding its medals in the maximum light of publicity. I suppose most such international bodies suffer from this same problem, but the member national aero clubs of FAI have always been pretty mean in their subscriptions, so delegates to FAI meetings have to pay most of the expenses involved. Most nations no doubt subsidise this, but not the UK. So when Kitty and I went for the first time to the 1969 General Conference in Helsinki we found ourselves out of pocket for the week to the tune of some £400. We met some enchanting people, went for some fascinating expeditions, and listened to 14 speeches telling us what wonderful chaps we were. Then the 1970 Conference was in Delhi, which was out of the question.

The basic structural problem of a body such as the General Conference is bound to be that it may become inbred, and conservative.

The final speech of the retiring President at Helsinki praised us for being as fixed as the constellations: the same people met year after year in different parts of the world. I could not help feeling that this was not a matter for congratulation, but a weakness.

The third task FAI attempts is an attack on unnecessary restrictions to sporting flying, which abound in every country. One or two of the committees are devoted to this task, but to attack bureaucracy is too big and complex a job to be handled by a loosely-knit association of aero clubs backed by a tiny and overworked secretariat.

As an example one of the committees set up for this third task is the Medical Committee, its obvious function being to try and procure the abolition of unnecessary medical restrictions in the various fields of sporting aviation, which abound in many countries. In fact, it is useless for British pilots to attend gliding courses in some countries, since it takes them most of their holiday to get through the local medical examinations and acquire the necessary certificates.

Unfortunately, its terms of reference are altogether too vague. They read: 'Commission Internationale Médico-Physiologique duties relate to all medico-physiological matters affecting private flying, sporting aviation, air touring, astronautics and air rescue, and parachuting.'

The result of this is that each succeeding chairman can go off in almost any direction he likes, and can accidentally start treading on other people's toes. The first chairman after the war decided on drafting a complete set of recommended Medical Requirements for Sporting Pilots. When we came to one of these recommending abstinence from sexual intercourse for at least 48 hours before a record attempt, I asked innocently how the FAI intended setting up a body of official observers to ensure compliance. Alas, few laughed. But the code was dropped.

A recent chairman, without quite realising what he was doing, started running this committee on the lines of the General Conference. Instead of short, hard-working meetings in a central spot, he summoned meetings at various delectable places and laid on long social functions interspersed with short sessions. At the Dublin meeting in 1970, $3\frac{1}{2}$ hours work was done in three days, with intervening hospitality from President de Valera down.

Thus the attendants to the committee became mostly those with the time to make a leisurely holiday of their meetings, young busy men with new ideas could seldom participate, and conservatism became the order of the day. For a while—for I think it has now been put right—the chairman, though an admirable man, made a structural mistake, and it produced an inevitable result: the shape of the structural sieve made it difficult for the very men most needed by the committee to attend it.

When I produced a paper (Appendix 3) proving that state-issued Glider Pilots' Medical Licences were unnecessary, but that this matter was perfectly controlled in some countries (including the UK) by the sporting body concerned, it was greeted with a blank inability to comprehend, and everyone got very cross in the ensuing arguments. I eventually persuaded the FAI officially to adopt my formula for freedom (Chapter 3, p. 47), but alas they do not yet understand how to apply it. I hope one day someone will take it from there.

But to sum up, for the money its member national aero clubs are prepared to spend on it, FAI does a quite essential job, in which the UK, as one of the founder nations some 60 years ago, has always taken a leading part. It is one of the organisations which must be supported, for as an international body it is facing in the only direction which mankind can take if it is to survive.

In 1965, the British Gliding Association held the FAI World Gliding Championships at South Cerney, a giant undertaking, involving over 200 of us in an organisation of intense complexity.

One of the most worrisome episodes was our effort to permit the participation of the Democratic Republic of Germany. One of the rules of FAI is that all world championships held under their aegis must permit the participation of all member states. When the East German entry arrived, we were advised by the Foreign Office that they could not give entry permits to members of a state not recognised by NATO. They would give them to any competing team as individuals, but if East German pilots took part, they would not be permitted to display their flag or have their national anthem played. Try as I might, I could not get them to budge.

There followed a most distressing exchange of correspondence between myself and the East Germans. Technically, by insisting on coming, and then being refused entry, they could have invalidated the whole championships: and then if their allied communist countries had cancelled their entries, they could have ruined us financially.

Finally, their secretary wrote an angry letter asking what I would have done if, in a championship held in another country, I had been faced with a similar indignity. I replied that the first sentiment I would have held would have been one of sorrow and sympathy with my colleagues of another country, who although infused with an identical spirit of friendliness based on our mutual enthusiasm for our common sport, were being forced by powers beyond their control to behave in a manner entirely in conflict with their convictions.

The East Germans cancelled their entry. The Russians sent a last minute telegram to South Cerney threatening nemesis: but they didn't carry it out: the Russian team had already arrived and flew with us. The championships took place, and another small bond of international friendship was forged. The stupidity of politicians was overcome by the powers of a correct structure, however fragile: for we ended up with a perfectly amicable relationship with all concerned.

On being Chairman

Looking back over my nineteen years as Chairman of the British Gliding Association, I suppose much of it was a long hard slog, enlivened by the fact that one was working with a band of exceptionally nice, able and interesting people all inspired by the same selfless enthusiasm. Each added expertise in his own particular field, and I suppose my main contribution was as a businessman—I had a very lively belief that we must maintain financial independence, and so build up our assets by our own hard work that we would never have to kowtow to anyone for money. We welcomed financial support, but never had to agree to any strings. This added immensely to the respect accorded to the Association.

This tends to be eroded by the appalling Treasury convention that the State cannot support any organisation that is 'making a profit'. Quite rightly, since we do a lot of work which if we were not there would have to be undertaken by the State, and since, done by enthusiasts, it costs a fraction of what it would cost the taxpayer if done by a Ministry, we ask for and get a small reimbursement. But if on top of this we work ourselves to death selling books, ties, scarves, and so forth, and show a 'profit' at the end of it, our State contribution is reduced or withdrawn. On the other hand, if we make a loss, the Ministry cannot *guarantee* it will be made up. So the temptation is to slack off, and then approach the Ministry on our hands and knees to save us. What a way to undermine the independent spirit! However, I doubt if it will succeed—we are a pretty tough lot.

There was another very interesting feature of the job. Lord Acton's dictum 'Power corrupts, absolute power corrupts absolutely' has had a great effect on people's thinking, but unfortunately it is off the beam. What *is* true, and all in positions of responsibility must always bear in mind is, 'Power *isolates*, absolute power isolates absolutely.' Hitler reached such absolute isolation that he was in an even worse case than the lunatic who maintains he is Jesus Christ, for unlike the lunatic he was surrounded by people who assured him he was right. All the others had either retired discreetly or had their heads chopped off: an intrinsic fault of the structure of any dictatorship.

But the BGA Chairman is hardly isolated at all, because he is in the inverse position to that of a prostitute: he has responsibility without power. None of the people working with him is paid, so they can only be held together by a common enthusiasm and mutual respect. If he starts throwing his weight about, he will be out in a jiffy. It is an extraordinarily valuable bit of training for the exercise of authority in the more usual spheres of life, teaching one the imperative need for communication at the human level.

In the BGA, apart from the slog, there were moments of high drama, and others of intense worry, but there were also moments in retrospect which were really rather funny.

How not to open an AGM

It was Chris Riddell who started it. We had decided to have our Annual General Meeting for a change at Harrogate. 'Now', said Chris, 'I would like the Chairman to land in a sailplane, on the Stray, on the Friday afternoon; I could arrange for him to be met by the Mayor, the Press and TV.' Cries of horror from the Chairman at the prospect of adventuring the air in the frozen North early in British March were rapidly steamrollered.

So Friday, 11 March, saw Kitty and me in the Standard motoring up to Doncaster, where Jack Speight and partners were to put at my disposal my old Skylark 4, and Jack Tarr was to tow me in his Auster most of the 36 miles from there to Harrogate, for release and landing on the Stray, a large open common nearly in the middle of the town.

It started off a nice sunny spring day, but when we reached the M1 and let her out, the tendency of the car to pull right was so pronounced that we stopped to check the tyres. As soon as I got out I realised the tyres were all right; the trouble was due to the gale, blowing from the north-west on the ground, but up above almost from the north—in the teeth of our forthcoming Doncaster–Harrogate track.

As we went on north, we started to run into local rain and even snow storms. At one moment the sky was grey and ragged and overcast to the horizon: five minutes later the storm would have blown past and overhead was blue again.

Arrived at Doncaster airport, we found the Skylark 4 team huddling in the shelter of their trailer, in the lee of the hangar, and unanimously decided it wasn't on. We repaired to the club-house and rang up Chris at the Crown Hotel. He was quite adamant. 'I've got the Mayor and nearly 200 people here, and it's quite good outside—surface wind moderate, upper wind 30 mph, sunny.'

The red blood of the British Gliding Association aroused, we went back to the trailer, almost crawling against the gale on our hands and knees, lined it carefully up and down wind, and with infinite precaution extracted the bits of the Skylark from it. Twenty minutes later, we had successfully kept all the bits in the same county, and she was rigged minus a safety-conscious wing-tip.

We were all chattering-toothed with cold, emphasised by about a hundred small boys in football shorts with goose-pimpled legs who suddenly arrived to watch the fun. I crept into the cockpit, the missing wing-tip was hitched on, and Jack Tarr cautiously taxied up the Auster; we were hooked together, and set off into the teeth of the gale.

The Skylark took to the air almost before the wheels of the Auster started to turn; I dropped my own wheels, and about ten minutes' hard grinding brought us over the far edge of the aerodrome. We were off.

We levelled off at 1,500 ft, in order to keep some semblance of forward movement, and set off for Harrogate. At 70 knots on the clock Doncaster crept slowly backwards, but the tug ahead was leaping up and down as if it was a float signalling the onset of a giant fish. And about ten miles north of the town the fish took the bait good and proper. With a frenetic surge the tug ahead disappeared far below, out of sight. I banged open the airbrakes, but a rapid look down showed the Auster nearly vertically below, the rope just tightening to put its tail straight up. Consigning the Mayor, the entire British Press and all other organs of publicity to a determined secondary role, I pulled the release. The rope fell away. At least we weren't going to get into the papers in the wrong way.

I turned round to see if there was any hope of getting back to the airfield—there wasn't. So I selected a ploughed field beside the main road running north from Doncaster, and descended vertically onto it. The Auster had turned with me, and spent a few minutes circling round overhead, then disappeared to the south. Blessing the detachable tips of the Skylark, I waited for the first helpers from the road, took one tip off and laid it up-wind on the ground, then set off for the 'phone.

I didn't have any idea how to sort out the situation. By now the party would have left Doncaster airport—there would be no one there. Alas, the reception party would have left the Crown Hotel at Harrogate and even now would be freezing to death waiting for me on the Stray. I could only 'phone the hotel and implore them to send a messenger in arctic furs out to summon back the waiting crowd before they died of exposure.

I hadn't gone 50 yards before, with a toot of its horn, the trailer drew up beside me. They had hooked up and set forth through Doncaster to Harrogate, and to their amazement saw the Skylark in a field 20 yards from the road. Two minutes later Kitty arrived in the Standard, with Peter's wife. She had been driving north along the by-pass when she suddenly saw the Auster, trailing a forlorn unoccupied rope behind it. Then she watched it fly off to the east and circle round and round. Realising the form, she drove towards the centre of the circle.

The logistics of the situation were now simplified, but quite complicated enough. The glider, its trailer, two cars and five people were together in a field five miles north of Doncaster. The Auster had disappeared southwards; probably Jack Tarr would take it back to safety at Yeadon Airport, Leeds, since Doncaster airport would be empty. Chris, the Mayor and the Press were still presumably on the Stray. But the glider wheels? Where were they? 'Oh' said Jack, 'Peter set off ahead of all of us with those, in a fast car, so he could get to the Stray in time to help you get the Skylark off the field.'

Only the few who have had to get a Skylark 4, which has dropped its wheels, out of a ploughed field in a gale and into a trailer designed to take it with its wheels on, will know what we went through in the next half hour—but we did it.

Then, exhausted, we agreed that Kitty and I should dash on to Harrogate in the Standard, to see if we could arrive in time to defrost the Mayor and the Press, whilst the trailer and team set off for Doncaster. Peter's wife said: 'When you find him, tell him to come back to Jack's where we will stay the night.' But we never did.

For Peter-with-the-wheels was rushing north along the by-pass (quite unnecessarily—he could have kept up with us on a bicycle)— when one of those things happened which make all gliding enthusiasts so dislike the internal combustion engine. For these devilish devices stop as soon as they run out of fuel, which is what happened to this one.

He got out and started running for the nearest garage. Then he trotted. Then he slowed to a walk. By the time he reached the first garage he was just able to gasp out that he wanted two gallons of petrol in a tin. They gave it to him. Then he found he had no money. In spite of his utmost pleadings they took it back.

By the time he reached the second garage his plight was so pitiable that they gave him his two gallons, on condition he left his watch as a pledge. So by the time he reached the Stray he didn't know how late it was, but it was dark and all the houses locked up, so he deduced it was too late, and disappeared into the night.

Meantime, about an hour and a half late, Kitty and I had reached the Crown Hotel to find, to our enormous relief, Christopher, Mayor and Press all thawing out over cups of tea. Jack had 'phoned the Crown, who had sent a page complete with St Bernard out to the Stray and passed our message.

Never have we been photographed so much for not doing something. And never have I stood up so nice a Mayor.

But one has to confess that only in gliding can so much confusion be produced in so short a time. Next year we agreed we should walk.

When to start

I joined the Council of the BGA in 1934, just at the time it was beginning a period of exciting metamorphosis and growth.

It is terribly important to start a new job at the right time—and almost always sheer luck if you achieve it, for it is frustrating and useless to be too far ahead of the conventional wisdom.

I record one instance of this in Chapter 4, where on a matter of Air Traffic Control we were up against a blank wall of incomprehension for years, until suddenly and without any apparent reason the authorities caught up with us and accepted our contention.

Nearly forty years ago I and some friends became associated with a remarkable man called Henri Coanda, who had the most fertile mind I have ever encountered. He had discovered a trick of the air, or, more accurately, of fluids, which he called '*l'effet Coanda*', with vast implications for the future, and a wealth of possible applications. Unfortunately, like most such men, he was really only interested in the process of invention, and never persisted long enough to bring to the commercial stage a single application.

Over the years his backers put up what in those days was a large sum of money, and arranged for a number of outside technical experts to investigate his principles. In the very early days I remember discussing the subject with our last BGA Chairman, Ken Wilkinson, Chairman of BEA.

During the pre-war years I achieved one government contract for the development of an exhaust system for an aero engine, which was under test at Heston when the war broke out, and Coanda, whose works were in Paris, disappeared under German occupation.

Five years later, after the liberation of France, I was in my Air Transport Auxiliary office at White Waltham when I got information by a circuitous route that Coanda had been arrested and was in Drancy prison as a suspected collaborator. By this time he was in his sixties, and unlikely to survive in an unheated prison with bad food. I got permission to fly to Paris to try and search him out and investigate what he had been doing during the war.

Paris just after its liberation was an extraordinary experience. The town electricity had failed, the street lights were off, and one walked around under a cold brilliant moon with the Parisians perambulating arm in arm in the traffic-less streets, no longer constricted to the pavement, free at last.

With the assistance of the security officials I got my permit to visit Coanda, and found my information was correct: he was indeed ill. Without anyone to pull special strings, it was unlikely that his case would come up for examination in time for his survival, for there were thousands of people in like case, but we cross-examined him on the spot and satisfied ourselves that he was blameless. He had strung the Germans along, to keep his works going and staff employed, but produced nothing of any value. So we secured his release, and took over his latest idea, for a water-pump using his Effect, which Miles Aircraft tried to develop. Once again, however, it failed to gel.

Then the problems of peace took all my time, and I forgot all about it for ten years, when I happened to mention his name to Nick Goodhart during the 1954 Nationals at Camphill. Nick expressed great interest, and was astounded to hear Coanda was still alive. It appeared that *l'effet Coanda* was now recognised as of immense importance, and was being applied in several fields.

We traced Coanda to a farm in the south of France, where he was growing fruit on land aerated by a superabundance of worms, having discovered a method of producing a vermicular population explosion. But by now all our patents had expired, we had lost our money, and the world uses *l'effet Coanda* without any benefit to its inventor or those who kept the thing alive until it was ripe for general comprehension. I still have some Coanda shares if anyone would like to buy them. . . .

When to stop

When to stop being a Chairman of a show like the BGA can be as difficult a problem as when to start—in fact much more difficult. When you are invited to take on the job, presumably a very large number of folk think you have shown yourself competent to do so, and if they are right, you probably feel pretty sure that you can cope

—and that you have the enthusiasm, the knowledge and the time to take it on.

But if you make a good fist of it, everyone is only too pleased to leave the job to you, and the years roll imperceptibly on. Eventually you feel it's about time to hand over—the recurring worries get you down, you are getting older and busier and a bit stale. But now everyone says: 'Go on, Philip, you're doing a good job—try another year anyway.' Eventually you start feeling somewhat trapped, and more and more so when you start seriously trying to find a successor, and no one volunteers 'because you're doing all right'.

Two horrid possibilities start creeping in: as you get older gradually you begin to slow up, and so the volume of work you can get through decreases, and you have a fearful vision that in a few years' time you might have got the show into such a mess that no one in their senses would want to take over and sort it out.

The second one is worse. The world is full of honourable organisations that were started fifty years ago by young and enthusiastic men, who have remained in control ever since. As they grow up and become richer, they require a higher and more expensive standard of service. The movement becomes too dear for the young to join it, and the job of Chairing it becomes ever more complicated and time-consuming. The now old boys are still dedicated and competent folk—but they have one fearful weakness. They are increasingly apt to die. Then, since there is no follow-up, their life's spare-time work is in dire trouble—it may even collapse.

So one must keep very firmly in mind, the young may not be so competent as you are (you may think)—but they have the inestimable advantage of survival. It took the last three of my nineteen years in the chair of the BGA to find a successor, and now we have changed the Rules so that there is a maximum five-year tenure of office. This, like all changes of structure, changes the very nature of the job. It means the Secretary becomes more of a Secretary-General, and the Chairman does much more delegating. You may lose a Chairman with a few years' more good work still in him, but the risk that he may then for good or bad reasons go on for a few more years after that is avoided.

Another reason for this change goes back to the changing structure of society itself. I was lucky enough to be born into a family business, so except for the war years and my two years in British European Airways have always been my own boss. I hope I haven't let my enthusiasm for gliding affect my business life, but at least it has meant my hours of work have been flexible.

With the development of technology and size, fewer and fewer people have such freedom of action, and it is hard enough to find any competent person who can get permission to take on a demanding spare-time job for even a few years. So the period must be shortened and the job delegated as much as possible.

This loss of individual freedom and independence has much more profound consequences than one might think. My BEA career came to an end because I could not bring myself to accept a major decision which I knew to be wrong, but I stuck to my line to the bitter end because, quite subconsciously, I knew I could afford to lose my job, and it would not affect my or my family's financial independence.

The point at issue was the future of the Viscount—the one outstandingly successful post-war British civil aircraft. As General Manager (Technical) of BEA I had been responsible for ordering this aircraft from Vickers in 1946, before we had a Board to refer to. Some eighteen months later all sorts of pressures were applied to cancel this order and substitute one for the Elizabethan. The reasons were political, not economic, or technical. I felt certain that the Elizabethan, though a good aircraft, had no development future, whereas the Viscount was the first of a new generation of aircraft, in which at that time we had the lead.

For six months or more I resisted these attempts from all levels, but eventually I was defeated, had a nervous breakdown, and was forced to resign. But by then Vickers had the prototype flying, and were so impressed with the aircraft that they decided to keep it alive in the hope that BEA would eventually re-order it. This indeed happened, the major loss being that the Viscount could have been in service some years earlier, with many millions of pounds exports gained, and a technical lead established which might have kept us ahead for years.

I am not holding myself up as a far-sighted hero—to qualify as such I should have won my point and held my job. I am simply pointing out that I could afford to risk failure, because the financial structure into which I was lucky enough to be born gave me possibilities of action not available to almost anyone today, because that structure, permitting individual financial independence, is being destroyed by the current political drive towards egalitarianism.

A major error of timing

The Viscount affair was the single biggest error I personally made in being too early, and in failing to recognise when to stop, which completely altered the subsequent course of my life. Had I not been six years ahead of the conventional wisdom in my views on the Viscount, I might possibly have remained in BEA, and certainly had I done this my subsequent gliding life would not have unrolled as it did. But to be quite fair I think it probable I would have come unstuck in BEA in some other way—I had not the political wisdom to give way to pressures when they became too strong to resist at any level I happened to be at the time. I was too accustomed to being my own boss; or to make no bones about it, I had not all the qualities needed for that particular job.

When I left British European Airways in early 1948, I occupied the following year of convalescence, while recovering from the accumulated overwork of the previous eight years, in preparing a paper which included remarks on the economic future of the two nationalised airlines. This paper was eventually published in the February 1950 issue of *Aeronautics*.

Looking up my old records on this—for me—sad time I came across a later article which I wrote in *Aeronautics* issue of December 1955. Bearing in mind we had not in 1948 the benefit of computers —and even remembering that in forecasting, as in gambling, one is apt only to recall one's successes—I still feel that my 1948 prediction was rather a good effort.

The premise on which the 1948 forecast was based was that the future results of an airline (so far as they lie within its control, and hence excluding such extraneous influences as depressions and political restrictions of international travel) depend predominantly on its operating fleet and its future aircraft programme. If this programme includes the introduction into service, as first user, of a new type of aircraft, then this inescapably involves that airline in a very large, but calculable, initial loss over about the first two years of operation. After this new type becomes 'stabilised', and, if it was correctly selected in the first place and soundly developed, it becomes a profitable aircraft both for the initial user and for all subsequent users.

The reasons for this large initial loss, and methods by which it could be estimated beforehand, were analysed at length but can perhaps best be summarised as the inevitable expense associated with 'getting the bugs out of' a new type of aircraft; those bugs which only show themselves after it goes into regular service.

At that time, the future aircraft programme of the larger Corporation was too undecided to make a detailed economic forecast possible, but that of BEA was, with one major unknown, in process of crystallisation.

Figure 1 is a reprint of the aircraft programme diagram on which I based my economic forecast. It incorporated one guess, regarding the major unknown I mention, which at the time might have been considered desperately optimistic. When I left BEA the Corporation had just decided to abandon the Viscount, and purchase instead the Elizabethan. The latter machine, excellent as it was, was in my opinion (as it turned out to be) a dead end. I guessed that, although the Viscount had been shelved, it had been brought to a stage where its development would be continued outside the Corporation, to a point where it would become obviously necessary to re-order it, and I assumed that 30 Viscounts would be re-ordered in time to start service in 1952/3.

The subsequent history of how this came true would make a Nevil Shute novel, of which the dogged and persistent heroes would be Air Marshal Coryton of the Ministry of Supply and Sir George Edwards of Vickers. But the machine which had been abandoned in the time of Mr d'Erlanger and Mr Wood was in due course re-instated in the time of Lord Douglas and Mr Masefield, 20 Viscounts being ordered at first, six later.

The fact that BEA then had to go through the development ordeals of two parallel types of aircraft could obviously not be altered, nor was there any escape from the fact that the initial development losses were inevitably more than doubled, while the final delivery times of both aircraft were delayed. These considerations were taken

Free as a bird : Italian eagle

Philip Wills and the Scud II, 1933
Eric Collins and the Rhonadler, 1934

into account in my forecast. But the correctness, indeed the inevitability, of the decision to reorder the Viscount is not now in doubt.

Based on the premises I have outlined above, I produced a graph forecasting the annual results of the Corporation up to 1956/7. This graph is shown in Figure 2, with the actual results achieved superimposed.

Except for the year to March 1952, the results achieved coincided closely with those forecast. The 1952 deficit (£1·4 million instead of £0·2 million anticipated) was ascribed partly to a strike, and partly to a temporary setback in general national prosperity leading to travel restrictions. Both these causes were of a kind specifically excluded from the terms of my analysis.

The Corporation's 1952 annual report also adduced late delivery of the Elizabethan as a factor contributing to this loss, but in fact this had been assumed by me and taken into account in my 1948 calculations, as Figure 1 shows. One important conclusion can be drawn from this story. In a long-range operation such as running an airline, the praise or blame accorded to those in charge is always out by a time-scale of up to five or seven years. How much more nonsensical is it to praise or blame a new Government of a whole country for its immediately current circumstances?

On having a patron

On 5 June 1956 I awoke to a blinding blue day of early summer. It was 6 am, and the early morning chorus of birds was starting up in the garden. At first hazily, then more into focus, came the feeling that this was going to be a special day. Then it all came in sharp and clear, and I woke Kitty. This was the day we were off to Poland to fly in the World Gliding Championships. And we had arranged no mean starting ceremony.

We woke up our team, had breakfast, and went out. Already the air smelt of warm mown grass. In the drive at Kits Close was parked our Skylark 2 in its new trailer. In the garage was our brand new Standard Vanguard, with its special smell of new leather and paint.

We locked everything up, and packed in the numberless items of equipment, from sleeping bags to radio, and then were off on the road to London and Leszno.

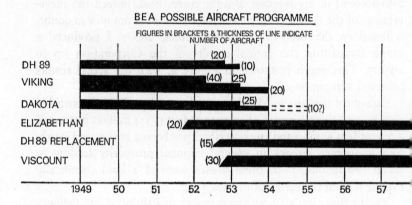

Figure 1 The aircraft programme of British European Airways forecast in 1948

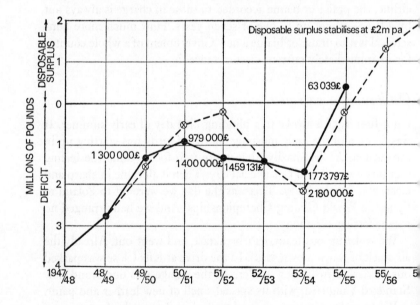

Figure 2 The forecast financial results are here shown dotted, while the actual figures achieved are shown by a continuous line

Running up Western Avenue, I switched on the BBC, and straight into a radio talk '. . . if you are in any sort of trouble,' the voice said, 'find a good strong piece of string . . .'—the rest of the sentence was drowned in laughter.

We drove through Shepherds Bush, into the Park at Marble Arch, round Hyde Park Corner and into the Mall. Here we found the other three trailers and crews waiting for us, with Ann Welch and Yvonne Bonham, everyone dressed very smartly. We waited for a few minutes, until at five to four we moved on to the first big moment of the day.

Our Patron, the Duke of Edinburgh, had asked us all to tea at Buckingham Palace. Driving in through the gates past the sentries and in front of the usual crowd of sightseers didn't seem quite real. This was not at all the sort of thing I had expected when, more than twenty years ago, I had had my first bungey launch in a primary from the top of Dunstable Downs. But we drove on, into the central courtyard, and carefully parked our five cars and four trailers in the middle. As we walked towards the steps, I was amused to see Tony Deane-Drummond hanging behind, carefully locking the doors of his trailer. System is everything!

We were shown into the central room, and the team lined up. Prince Philip came in, and it fell to me, as team leader, to effect the introductions. To my horror, half way down the line I dried up, and John Williamson had to introduce himself.

Then tea was brought in by a number of footmen, and we stood and chatted for about half an hour. Kitty was enchanted to see that the Duke had a cup twice the size of everyone else's. Then he came out to see us off, had a look inside the trailers, and wished us well. We drove out, past the cameras, and round the Park to the Horse Guards Parade.

By some magic, Nick Goodhart had got approval for us to rig our aircraft here, in front of the Press, and this we proceeded to do, in the midst of a growing crowd. Then photos and interviews, during which I incautiously let on about Tony locking up his trailer whilst in the Palace yard. Then we derigged, and set off on the Dover Road.

Half-way to Dover, we all stopped at a roadside inn for supper, and it was then that Nick Goodhart found he had lost his wallet, with all his money for the trip in it. We all cross-examined him, and finally the most likely possibility was that, whilst rigging on the Horse Guards Parade, he had taken off his coat and thrown it on the ground, and an onlooker had stolen his wallet. We phoned back to the nearest police station, but there was no news, so went sadly on to our nightstop at the Whitecliffs Hotel. Whereupon Nick found his wallet, where it had fallen out of his pocket on to the floor of his car, and we all said 'silly ass', and felt better.

Our boat sailed at daybreak, so we were just off to an early bed, when the phone rang for Ann. It takes a lot to upset Ann, but when she rang off she looked very upset indeed.

'That was the *Daily Express*,' she said. 'They rang to say they were just putting tomorrow's edition to bed, and before actually sealing it, it was correct, wasn't it, that a member of our team had had his wallet stolen from his trailer, which he had left unlocked, whilst it was parked in Buckingham Palace?' Euphoria gave way to panic. Did the Duke read the *Daily Express*? Probably not, but there must be a Press Office at the Palace, which did. 'For the love of God, what did you say?'—'I told them it was absolutely untrue, that no one had lost his wallet anyway. Whereupon they said it was too late to alter the story now, they could only pull out the whole thing. Which they have done, thank God. And they promised to try and kill the story if anyone else has got it.'

So, after all the planning, we got no Press at all about our departure to the 1958 World Championships. Nonetheless, it was a memorable, if somewhat scarifying day.

3

On Liberty and Safety

Risk

'In sports involving the use of the air, as in all other sports, an individual should be free to take such risks as he wishes, *so long as no third-party risk is involved.*

It follows from this that it is for the State to impose only that degree of regulation necessary for the reasonable protection of third parties. It should be the further duty of the sporting body concerned to lay down such further standards as are necessary to protect the good name of their sport.'

If I am ever to be remembered for anything, I should like to be remembered as the man who first defined and put forward the above philosophy. If, as I hope, it becomes accepted, it won't be long before it is taken for granted, and people will be unable to believe that anything so obvious had to be fought for. But for over thirty years, at first subconsciously, and then explicitly, this is what I have been advocating, and in the process have experienced much opposition. And if and when it is adopted, hundreds if not thousands, of bureaucrats all over the world will have to find other work to do.

Only towards the end of this time did I find that I was a hundred years late in my advocacy. John Stuart Mill, in his famous essay 'On Liberty', has said it all before.

'The object of this Essay is to assert one very simple principle, as entitled to govern absolutely the dealings of society with the individual in the way of compulsion or control, whether the means used be physical force in the form of legal penalties, or the moral coercion of public opinion. The principle is, that the sole end for which mankind are warranted, individually or collectively, in interfering with the liberty of action of any of their number is self protection. That the only purpose for which power can rightfully be exercised over any member of a civilised community, against his will, is to prevent harm to others. His own good, either physical or moral, is not a sufficient warrant. He cannot rightfully be compelled to do or forbear because it will be better for him to do so, because it will make him happier, because, in the opinion of others, to do so would be wise or even right. These are good reasons for remonstrating with him, or reasoning with him, or persuading him, or entreating him, but not for compelling him, or visiting him with an evil in case he do otherwise. To justify that, the conduct from which it is desired to deter him must be calculated to produce evil to someone else. The only part of the conduct of anyone, for which he is answerable to society, is that which concerns others. In the part which merely concerns himself his independence is, of right, absolute. Over himself, over his own body or mind, the individual is sovereign.'

I expect that so far my reader will have agreed with every word I have written in this chapter. But so ingrained has become our servitude to bureaucratic paternalism, that I have a nasty feeling that when I get down to cases, and actually indicate the sort of result which can flow from the adoption of such a philosophy of freedom, some may experience pangs of doubt.

I will give a short example here, and a longer one in a later chapter. There is conclusive evidence that a solo pilot in a glider involves no third party on the ground or in the air in any significant risk. So the State must give him (or her) freedom to do what he likes, only ensuring that he has the facilities available to enable him to be taught enough to assess for himself the risks he is taking to his own survival.

To protect the good name of their sport, the British Gliding Association requires third-party insurance. The extremely low premium is itself evidence of the smallness of the risk.

Now some—but not all—States lay down a minimum age below which a child may not become a solo pilot—usually sixteen or seventeen years. Yet there are plenty of cases of boys of lesser age proving themselves first-class pilots—and many people of all ages who cannot ever learn to fly safely.

My case is that the proper people to control the situation of the minor are (a) the parents, (b) the qualified Chief Flying Instructor, and (c) since the death by accident of a child might adversely affect the good name of the sport, the national sporting body (British Gliding Association); and that it is absolutely wrong for the State to over-rule their authority—*because no significant third-party risks are involved.*

Why should the State prevent a boy of 14 from flying a glider when it doesn't stop him underwater-swimming or mountain-climbing—which decision it is quite happy to leave to Mum and Dad? The unassailable answer is that in those countries with no minimum age limit (including the USA and Australia) there have been no accidents ascribable to the youth of the pilot.

A child riding a push-bike on a public road undoubtedly introduces a significant third-party risk. Yet the State does not lay down an age-limit—it leaves it to the common sense and responsibility of the parents.

Some may say, 'But if you crash in your glider you *might* hit a crowd or a house'. The answer to this is 'In theory you might, but we have analysed 4·5 million flights over the past 18 years in this country alone, and in *fact* the risk is many times less than others we take every day without giving them a thought.'

If the State is to protect us against risks as small as this, in logic it must protect us against all dangers greater than this one—and life would become insupportable. Certainly ski-ing would be subject to State-imposed safety standards, as would many other pleasures necessary for the enjoyment of life. We should be pushed a huge step forward towards 1984.

Appendix III presents a more complicated case, but one which should give some idea of the amount of work involved in the attempt to free sporting flying from unnecessary shackles, and of how much hard evidence is available to those prepared to give up the time required to amass and analyse it. You may find it dull, but do not underestimate its value to your future liberty.

Values

The problem of the value of a human life brings one down to the most profound questions of philosophy. What do we believe in—or, if you are made that way, what does God want? Quality or quantity? You can either believe in a world teeming with poor, underfed, uneducated and brute-like billions of unhealthy human beings, or you can believe that the human race should comprise a smaller number of higher quality people living fuller and more richly-coloured lives. Everyone faced with this question will elect the second alternative, even though many religions try to make it impossible to pursue it.

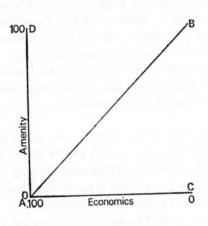

Figure 3   Amenity versus economics

But to achieve this second goal is almost unbelievably difficult, for it involves an attempt to quantify the virtually unquantifiable. Let us look, as an example, at the Roskill Committee, which was set up to decide the location of the third London airport. What it had really been asked to do (though no one seems to have crystallised it) was to measure Social Amenity versus Economics. One could graph it as follows: An airport at point A would have maximum economic advantage, and be socially intolerable. It would in fact be in Hyde Park, with the main runway extended over Hyde Park Corner through Green Park to Horse Guards Parade. It would earn us millions of pounds, and lead to a revolution. B would bring in no traffic, and upset no one. It would be on, say, an uninhabited island in the Hebrides, and income-tax would go up.

Roskill examined four alternatives, at Nuthampstead, Cublington, Thurleigh and Foulness. They each fall slightly above or below AB, Foulness being nearest B. To try and make sense out of their report, the unfortunate Committee was however bound to pretend that AC and AD could each be expressed in the same medium— money. What is the equivalent in cash of one man not hearing the song of one nightingale? An airport at Cublington will drive night- ingales out of earshot of 1,000 people, at say 5p a time, whereas at Foulness only 200 such deprivations will occur. Put it down on the bill.

You may think I am joking, but I'm not. Three of the four pos- sible sites would have brought all gliding in South-east England to an end. The cost of this to society at large was fairly exactly 'calcu- lated' at £3,600,000. But what was actually involved was a con- siderable degradation of the richness of life for a few in exchange for a slightly higher material standard of life for the many.

The Roskill report recommended Cublington, with one dissident. It turned out that the learned judge had stuck in his pin too far towards the left of the graph of social tolerance, for Foulness was finally the political decision.

Let us look at some other almost unbearable questions we will have to answer if we are to achieve our goal. Because someone asked awkward political questions, it recently became illegal to drive farm-tractors unless they are fitted with crash canopies. This will save 40 lives a year at a total cost of £4 million a year—or £100,000 a life—ten lives per million pounds. The following table (from *The Biocrats* by Gerald Leach) shows what a million pounds could buy if applied in other directions:

What could £1,000,000 buy?

Crash canopies on all UK tractors	10 lives
Artificial kidneys: five years of life	105 lives
Cervical cancer screening	720 lives
Lung-cancer X-rays for old smokers	2,400 lives
Pedestrian injury campaign	3,750 lives
Oestral screening in late pregnancy	20,000 lives
Fewer decayed teeth by fluoridation	73,500

'Mediator', the latest radar system to reduce the risk of aerial collisions, has already cost over £100 millions, and will cost about £10 million a year to run. Since there have not over the last 20 years been any collisions involving airliners in the UK it is hard to find a place for it in this table. The mere idea of aerial collision induces such horror in most people's minds that questions of cost/benefit go by the board.

But this table makes it clear that much less than this £10 millions a year applied in other directions could fairly immediately start saving more than 30,000 lives a year, and improve the health of a very much larger number of people.

I will record a few instances of the way lives are unnecessarily hazarded or even lost by our failure to think logically on the subject of safety.

1 In 1968 it was decided to give a two-year trial of an extension of British Summer Time to the winter months, which amongst other advantages put us on the same clock-times as the rest of Europe. At the end of the trial period it was left to an open vote in the House of Commons as to whether we should continue the experiment or revert to Greenwich Mean Time.

During the debate it was conclusively shown that around 1,000 lives a year, plus several times that number of persons injured, had been saved by BST, and enough electric power to save us in the future around £100 millions in new power stations. Many of the lives saved were those of children, who were more awake, and so more aware when going to school in the dark in the morning than if they had to return from school in the dark in the evening.

Nevertheless, this benefit was diffuse in relation to the hardships suffered by farm workers, milkmen and so on, and the emotional appeal of the traditional regard for dear old Greenwich Mean Time; so by a majority vote we returned to GMT: a triumph by a vocal minority of emotion over reason and even common humanity.

2 In the summer of 1969 there occurred a breakdown in Air Traffic Control coverage over an area of the North Atlantic. Two approaching airliners therefore simultaneously decided to alter course to the south, to reach an area where they would regain radio location coverage. They both thereby set up a man-made collision probability several thousand times greater than the random probability of collision if they had simply carried on on their original courses, and they did in fact manage an airmiss, evading collision because they saw each other in time to change their respective courses. This course of events was subsequently explained by a senior Airline pundit, who declared that course had initially to be altered 'because the doctrine of "see and be seen" [i.e. collision avoidance by looking out of the window] is now as dead as the dodo'. This ignored the fact that it was this very procedure which had in this case proved entirely effective!

3 The manufacturer of one of our most successful small meteorological rockets carried out his trial firings from a remote Scottish island, directing his rockets out over the empty sea. At around 100,000 ft the rocket discharged a parachute, carrying instruments, and then the remains fell into the sea.

After some months various Ministries became interested, and finally one committee pointed out the danger of this operation to any passing ship. Mathematical calculations showed that this risk was infinitesimal, of the order of 10^{-8}; this meaning that if 100 firings were carried out each year the chances were of one hit in a million years, and even then the bits were so small that it was extremely unlikely they would do any serious damage if they hit the deck of a ship. Nevertheless, it was ruled that in future no firing could take place until the area of likely fall had been searched by an aeroplane. Now the risks of fatal accident to the occupant of an aeroplane in a commercial operation is around 1 in 300,000, and clearly greater than this in a Service aircraft. So to avoid a 1 in 100 million risk five or six men were regularly put to at least a 1 in 300,000 risk, and since the weather conditions had to be exactly right for each firing, and it took some hours to lay on the preliminary air search, by which time the weather had often worsened, the development of the device was enormously slowed down and the economic cost, as well as the risk, were both increased by a very large factor.

4 Just after the last war, there was quite a strong Press campaign to require that passenger aircraft should carry emergency parachutes for all on board. We in BEA had to do a lot of study to work out that one—it would reduce the payload on a 30-seater aircraft by, say, 600 lb. How much would that cost? How many lives per year

would it have saved on the accident records of the world's airlines over, say, the previous ten years?

Making several assumptions, such as that mothers would abandon their infants in arms and grandmothers would survive a parachute descent into the midst of a jungle, the sum came out at, if I remember rightly, £29 millions a life. But in fact it would have saved more lives than we calculated, for if fares throughout the world were increased to cover this loss there would have been a reduction in the number of passengers carried, and hence a reduction in lives lost through other kinds of aircraft accidents than the very few in which parachutes could have conceivably played a part. So once again the debit side of this precaution would have involved not only a financial loss, but also a loss in the richness of the texture of living—i.e. a social loss.

5 Our Transport Minister recently announced the retention of the 70-mph speed limit on motorways. What he has *not* done is to validate it. The correct way to consider such a matter would be to obtain the actual figures, and produce a table which would look something like this: (the figures are purely imaginary).

Speed limit mph	Fatal accidents p.a.	Serious accidents p.a.	Minor accidents p.a.
No limit	1000	3,000	10,000
90	900	2,500	8,000
80	800	2,200	7,000
70	700	2,000	6,000
60	600	1,800	5,000
50	400	1,200	4,000
40	300	1,000	3,500
30	250	800	3,000
20	250	800	3,000
10	250	800	3,000
0	0	0	0

(*Note*: I am assuming that as speed-limits became so low as to be widely disregarded, the accident rate would not come down much.)

Now the Minister has to weigh these figures of benefit against the cost, both economic and social, of progressively slowing down the commerce and social cohesion of the nation, and stick a pin in what he considers is the right compromise.

Maybe he does this, but if so, he doesn't think the public is brave enough to be given the facts, and in such a case I believe he is wrong, because unless and until we can all learn to think in this way we shall go on wasting lives unnecessarily in some directions and degrading our standards of living in others without adequate benefits in increased safety.

Now we come to a much more difficult question. What right has an individual to risk the lives of a third party or parties? None at all, is the obvious answer. But wait a bit.

A private motorist goes out on the road with a few gins on board and runs down an innocent pedestrian. Easy—he should be treated with great severity by Law.

A perfectly sober private motorist goes out, and a drunken pedestrian falls under his wheels. Bad luck—but it cannot be denied that if private motoring was prohibited, that life would have been saved.

But by far the commonest accident is where both parties commit errors which, alone, would have led to no accident, but together lead to a fatality. Where do you draw the line?

Society admits that the private motorist is a desirable person as such, and hence admits that, whether or not he has a right to risk other people's lives (by merely existing), he must be permitted to do so, to however small a degree.

Applying this to gliding, the number of innocent airfarers who have lost their lives by collision with gliders is nil. But the *risk* that one day this will happen is unavoidable: though it is obviously *almost* nil, it could be expressed by a finite number. Does society accept that the value of gliding (which it certainly does not rate as high as it should) is worth this almost infinitesimal risk? The answer is that society does not think of this aspect of the matter at all, either in relation to gliding, air travel, motoring, or anything else. It leaves this aspect of the matter to Them—to the authorities—and they handle most of it in an entirely irrational way also. *But not all of it.*

An aeroplane is designed to certain safety standards—but this is exactly the same as saying it is designed to certain standards of acceptable danger. A main spar is designed to fail in not more than

1 in a 100 million cases. Engines are designed to a factor of reliability ensuring that, in a multi-engined aircraft, they will not fail simultaneously oftener than once in a 100 million times.

But the great point about this figure is that it is known—it is accepted as justifiable economically and socially. If a similar rationality applied in all other fields we should really get somewhere.

I have been to a meeting with a number of high-level aviation experts and have heard it said, 'We can make no compromise with safety'. To be as polite as possible, this is a completely muddled attitude—safety is compromised every time an aircraft leaves the ground, and every time you get into your motor-car and take it out of the garage. Each safety standard that is laid down is a compromise with safety, and should be in fact an equation between the additional safety achieved, and the financial and social cost of its achievement. Unfortunately, this complicated calculation is almost invariably done subconsciously and based on emotional and irrational feelings, so that the word 'calculation' is a misnomer.

An interesting example is inherent in noise abatement regulations. To reduce the noise level imposed on people living round airports near major cities, approach and take off tracks are laid down, and pilots taking off are instructed to reduce power after take off at a lower height than is consistent with maximum safety. A marginally increased risk is imposed for a very short time on those in the aircraft to improve the quality of life of the people living permanently in the affected zone. In my view (which is just as subjective in these intangible equations as that of anyone else), this is a perfectly justified decision. A bargain and a balance has been struck between amenity and risk, by agreement between politician and technician. *But I wonder how many people realise it?*

Oddly enough, a proposal to increase the angle of glide on the approach path from 3° to 6° has so far been rejected on safety grounds, although it might on analysis be shown that this would produce a greater enhancement of amenity versus augmentation of risk than the take-off procedures already practised.

I hope therefore that I have convinced my readers of two premises on which to base a case:

i) In a free society, an adult person should be left free to take such physical risks to his own person as he wishes.

ii) No society can survive unless it is accepted that a human life has a certain finite value.

At present this is only accepted subconsciously, and this is not good enough, because only when it is consciously accepted will we be able to apply what resources we have to reducing the risks of living to the minimum without unnecessarily diminishing the richness of the texture of living. So we are riding a tight rope in that (a) man must have a sufficiency of material welfare to make for a stable society, and (b) life must be interesting enough to make for a stable society.

In the poverty-stricken two thirds of the world the conflict does not exist, for man gets all the interest and stimulus he needs from the sheer battle for survival. But in the richer nations, the solution to this conflict is central to their future stability and progress.

A VERY SMALL DEGREE OF ACCEPTABLE RISK IS IN FACT A TRACE ELEMENT WHICH IS ESSENTIAL TO ALL PROGRESS AND TO THE VERY SURVIVAL OF SOCIETY.

In fact, we need a new word for this very small touch of risk. Minimum acceptable risk, of the order of, say, one in a hundred thousand to one in a hundred million, is a vital necessity, whilst major risk is on the whole to be avoided. But we use the same word, with its pejorative implication, for both meanings, and consequently even the most intelligent people get them mixed up.*

I recently read an article saying, 'Space flying has become too dangerous. Further flights should be suspended until it has been made absolutely safe.' Probably the writer then put down his pen, walked downstairs, and drove home in his car, taking a risk of fatal accident of the order of 10^{-6}, without it even occurring to him that he could have gone by train and reduced the risk to say 10^{-8}, still less that he could not go home at all if he insisted on being 'absolutely safe'. He willingly accepted a small degree of risk because he liked his wife's cooking.

The Federal Aviation Administration of the United States is many years ahead of the rest of the world in its philosophy. Even

---

* Our own society currently shows many of the symptoms of risk starvation: vandalism, mugging, and drug taking are some. But this could form the subject of another book!

they have not yet got around to the problem of amenity, but at least they see it in terms of cost/benefit.

The following is an extract from their basic Statement of Policy (doc. 1000.1, 5–6–1965). Many times I have tried to persuade our own Ministry to echo it, but have been told that in this country it would be politically impossible to do so.

The Agency's safety objective is to achieve and maintain a level of safety which, within the limits of national resources allocatable to aviation, is in optimum balance with the cost and efficiency of air transportation. Achieving this objective will require the Agency to develop criteria and a method for assessing and relating costs to each proposed improvement in safety.

While it may seem crass to speak of costs when considering improvements in air safety, the relationship which exists between safety and cost must be recognised. Pursuit of the goal of absolute safety, for example, would impose an economically intolerable requirement for public expenditures and an unjustifiable penalty on the air transportation system—it might become absolutely safe to fly but so expensive or so inefficient that no one would. This is simply to say that for most increments in safety, there are corresponding (though not necessarily equal) increments in cost. Having two pilots on the flight deck is safer than having one but it also costs more. Providing 2,000 ft vertical separation on the airways would be safer than 1,000 ft separation but it would result in a less efficient use of the airspace.

It is clear that a price must be paid for many safety improvements, either in terms of dollars or system efficiency. Therefore, in carrying out its responsibility to promote air safety, the Agency will judge each proposed safety improvement in light of the price to be paid for it.

The air travelling segment of the public make a similar judgment when they buy an airline ticket or a private airplane. They accept a level of safety which is less than absolute—in effect calculating the risk against the benefit. The benefit in this case is a lower priced ticket or cheaper airplane along with a more efficient method of transportation. Viewed another way, the traveller (subconsciously) calculates the risk against the cost in dollars and efficiency of less risk.

This acceptance of a calculated risk is an integral feature of daily life and by no means peculiar to aviation. There is a calculated risk

Rhonsperber (Kit Nicholson), and Hjordis (Philip Wills), Camphill, 1936
The Minimoa at Huish, 1937

Dr A. E. Slater with Kitty Wills at the World Championships Spain, 1952

The British team, Poland, 1958. L–R: Tony Goodhart, Tony Deane-Drummond, Ann Welch, Nick Goodhart, Philip Wills

factor in every mode of transportation, be it train, bus, auto, or simply walking across the street. In a larger sense, the acceptance of calculated risks is a part of a general attitude toward life. The level of risk which the traveller will accept is a complex function of many variables but the determining factor is the cost of less risk. This balancing of risk with the cost of less risk is a dynamic rather than a static process, and changes in time.

Discipline

During the war I flew in Air Transport Auxiliary, a civilian organisation with the job of ferrying all types of aircraft from factories to squadrons, and in between. All of us were trained to be able to fly any type of aircraft, from single-engined trainers to four-engined bombers, without any aid other than specially written technical handbooks and notes, which were produced by our own technical department. We had women and men pilots, grandmothers, some men with one arm, leg, or eye; we had one pilot with only one of each. There was only one type he couldn't fly, because the throttle was inaccessible to him.

As soon as the war was over, we were forgotten as quickly as possible, and I can't help thinking that this was partly because we had proved one inconvenient fact—that ordinary men and women can fly anything, if they put their minds to it, are given sensible basic training, and are not fettered with unnecessary restrictions.

Being civilians, we did not have King's Regulations behind us to enforce discipline, but had to impose our own. This did not prove too difficult, as most of us would have paid to do the job, if we had been able. The general atmosphere was a little like that of the gliding world, immense enthusiasm and a high sense of responsibility. But there were always a few who suspected our standards: certainly to the conventionally-minded we were an improbable organisation.

For reasons I never knew, it so happened that during the life of ATA we had posted to us, for general duties, one Air Vice-Marshal and one Rear Admiral. The AVM was tall and stringy and stern, and presented an air of slight disapproval. The Rear Admiral was large and pinkish and quiet. He started off in No. 1 Ferry Pool as a second-officer pilot, and I will always remember the morning he came into the Ops. room, when I was making up the day's programme, and very hesitantly asked if I could possibly let him off delivering naval aircraft in future. The trouble was, he said, that although he wore our uniform (with one stripe up), he was still a Rear Admiral, and when he delivered an aircraft to a Naval Station, they had to turn out and pipe him ashore. So I agreed.

One day, however, our Commodore, Gerard d'Erlanger, thought it might do us all good to be given a lecture on discipline, to be delivered in turn by our AVM and our Rear Admiral. So the 40 or 50 pilots of No. 1 Ferry Pilots Pool assembled in the lecture room. The AVM mounted the platform.

'To illustrate the nature of discipline,' he began, 'I will tell you a story.'

'There was a shipwreck in the Pacific Ocean, and captain and crew took to the boats. They sailed and rowed for several days, until at last an island hove over the horizon.

'They approached its shores with great relief, but the captain instructed them to alter course and row along a few hundred yards out, whilst he inspected the coast for evidence of the hospitality or otherwise of the natives. Having circumnavigated the entire island, to their great disappointment he told them to row on.

'After another day or so, a second island appeared, but after the same course of events, once again the men were told to row on, in spite of the growing shortage of food and drink in the boats.

'A third island eventually was reached, and once more the captain told the men to skirt it. Suddenly, rounding a headland, they came on a small golden beach. On the beach was a gallows, with a dead man suspended from it.

'"Row ashore men," commanded the Captain, "for there you can see that on this island there is discipline."'

There was a fairly blank silence amongst the audience whilst the AVM descended from the stage and the Rear Admiral took his place. The second address commenced in a quiet, almost dreamy voice. It was very short indeed.

'The word "discipline",' said the Rear Admiral, 'comes from the word "disciple"; and a disciple is one who follows his leader because he believes in him and trusts him.'

He stopped; we waited for him to go on, but it was the end of his address.

We were too sensible to applaud, as he stepped down from his rostrum. But from that day on we took him to our hearts. His name was Bouchier.

I don't suppose any other single sentence has so affected my way of thinking. These two addresses crystallised the opposing views of discipline, to drive, or to lead. Although the latter is much the more difficult, as our civilisation develops it is increasingly becoming the only possible way to make it work. And yet the two factions are still constantly at odds, and the result in the British gliding movement has been an endless dialogue with the authorities, who are split within themselves as to the better course.

Within our own ranks we fortunately have no option; we are given responsibility for maintaining safety, but no legal authority of sanctions. So we have had to lead, for good or ill. The results to date have been not too bad: our record is at least as good as in any other country, and better than most. But I suppose we have one over-riding sanction: if we don't keep our own house in order, They will step in and do it for us.

Self-discipline

Safety in the main relies on self-discipline. The air is too big for it to be possible for a policeman to watch an aircraft all the time.

A great deal depends on our relationship with the authorities: and this is a two-way thing—mutual trust and confidence with each other leads to enhanced safety. It takes many years to build up a system of this sort, the establishment of good channels of communication, and continued hard and selfless work to maintain it. I recall a good example. Some years ago an unfortunate glider-pilot from Lasham lost himself in cloud, and the upper wind was much stronger than he had anticipated. When he located himself again, he found to his horror that he was quite low down and in the Gatwick Control Zone. He did the right thing: he opened his airbrakes and landed in the nearest field. The police arrived, names and particulars were taken, and he trailed sadly home.

When this was reported to the BGA I rang up the then Director of Air Traffic Control Services, and told him the sad story. Then I said, 'Look, we should very much like to look after this ourselves. If his club grounds him for three months, he will accept it as just, and the other club members will do likewise because, by his mistake, he could hazard our continued freedom from official control. But we must do this quickly, whilst it's all fresh in people's minds, we can't wait for weeks to see if there is going to be an official prosecution—but if there is, then the unfortunate man can't possibly be punished twice, so we can do nothing. So could you possibly make enquiries, and if you can persuade the Ministry to leave it to us, it really will be better for everyone.'

Within 24 hours I was told we could go ahead. All went as I had hoped, except that as an additional bonus a lot of folk said, with surprise, that even the bureaucrats were sometimes human. And I am sure that many pilots took extra care subsequently to try and obey the rules.

A short while after this a very similar incident occurred to the amateur pilot of a small aeroplane. He got lost, wandered across a control zone, without seeing another aircraft, and landed at an airfield on the far side. In the absence of similar liaison, and with a long history, whether justified or not, of bureaucratic persecutions of pilots in light aeroplanes, he was summoned and fined £250—a huge sum for an error which had in fact hazarded no one. The indignation was great enough to result in many of his friends clubbing together to help pay the fine. And self-discipline—and hence safety—was the sufferer.

The first, second, and third rule of discipline is that a rule should only be made if most of the 'ruled' can be convinced that it is necessary.

This, indeed, is the distinction between 'good' and 'bad' *law*, as the police know very well indeed. If a law is passed which a large proportion of people regard as unjust, or unnecessary, the police can only enforce it at the price of great unpopularity; and in a democratic country this will make their task increasingly difficult. An unpopularity acquired by enforcing bad law will spread to a general lack of co-operation by the public and, even worse, by a tendency to break, when they please, *all* laws, good and bad. In the ultimate, this must lead to anarchy or dictatorship.

Accident prevention

As Director of Operations of Air Transport Auxiliary during the war I was for some time Chairman of the Accidents Committee, and with the assistance of many others (notably Air Commodore Vernon Brown of the Accident Investigation Department) we built up a philosophy for the investigation of accidents which then got transferred to BEA and much of which is now reflected in the world-wide system used in civil aviation.

The basic rule is not what one would expect at first sight. It is:

THE PRIMARY PURPOSE OF ACCIDENT INVESTIGATION IS THE PREVENTION OF FURTHER ACCIDENTS, OR THE REDUCTION OF THE FUTURE ACCIDENT RATE

Arising from this, the apportionment of blame or responsibility is comparatively insignificant; unless the investigator is very careful it may actually affect adversely the achievement of this primary purpose.

In wartime it was easy enough to hold rigidly to this conception, but in peacetime all sorts of pressures are brought into play to deflect it—all of which are inimical to safety. But after a serious accident, some interests will be anxious to locate blame, whilst the Airline Pilots Associations and the like quite naturally fight to avoid responsibility being attached to one of their members if there can be the smallest shadow of doubt. One sad result of this is that, whilst in ATA we expected to clear up an accident and its cause and initiate remedial action within three weeks, in peacetime it is often necessary to have a full legal enquiry which can take a year or longer to reach a conclusion.

The main thing to bear in mind is that when an accident occurs, the pilot is a very important person indeed. He can safely be left to punish himself, if he feels responsible—I know, as I have had my share. But if he has made a mistake, and will describe it fully and frankly, one can take action to see no one else makes the same error again. If however he comes to think the investigators are looking for someone to punish, he may try to cover up what actually happened, or to rationalise it in some way which will lead the investigator astray.

Before our work in ATA, accidents were split into two categories, and depending on the amount of damage were categorised as 'major' or 'minor', and there was a '48-hour rule' whereby no report had to be made if the aircraft could be repaired in that time. But our philosophy showed that in fact the amount of damage done in an accident can sometimes bear an inverse relationship to its importance. An accident leading to the loss of many lives may leave no clue to future remedial action, although subsequent technical investigation of any parts which can be recovered can produce almost miracles. But an 'incident' leading to no damage at all can if fully reported, lead to quick action which will save all possibility of recurrence. In fact, to the accident investigator there is little difference between an 'accident' and an 'incident': the fact that the latter involves no damage is irrelevant.

So clearly it is necessary to define the word 'accident' in a sense quite different to that given it by the public or the insurance companies. Sometimes the uninformed reaction to an 'accident' makes it difficult for the investigators. Many years ago I was on the investigating board of a well-known airline, and we had to consider a case of a forced landing of an airliner, successfully effected in a small field, but which we found became necessary because of an initial error of the pilot.

Before we could come to our finding, however, the grateful passengers had clubbed together and awarded a gold watch to the errant pilot for his brilliant landing, which was duly lauded by the Press. This rather tied our hands. We administered a confidential reproof to the pilot: I doubt if he ever subsequently wore the watch.

Just after the war, a number of aircraft operated by British South American Airways simply disappeared at sea, all on board being lost. These indeed were serious accidents in the ordinary sense, but quite unimportant from the accident investigator's standpoint—for no cause could ever be discovered, and no remedial action taken.

On the other hand, during the first few weeks operation by BEA of the Viking, our Chief Technical Officer by chance overheard one of our pilots in the mess discussing an odd experience whilst approaching to land at Oslo at night. His stick started to hunt in pitch, but he managed to correct it and land without further incident, and a thorough investigation of the elevator and controls could find nothing wrong.

Our CTO however, happened to have the figures relating to the Viking pitch stability in his head, and he jumped into action. It was on the edge of mathematical possibility that a quite small build-up of ice on the leading edge of the Viking elevator could unbalance it to the point of uncontrollable instability: if this led to a crash, the ice would melt before the investigator could get to the scene, and no evidence would be found of the cause.

There fell to me the ultimate responsibility which is the nightmare of all Airline Technical Managers—I had to insist that the entire fleet of Vikings be grounded. It is hard nowadays to envisage the resistance I had to overcome, for of course today pilots have much more technical training, so such an incident would be immediately and officially reported, much more is known of stability problems, and much stiffer tests are required of prototypes before they can go into service. Also the technical complexity of modern aircraft is more widely appreciated. During one of my arguments with the then Board over this crisis, I was scarred when one member said that he thoroughly mistrusted all this technical hooey—in his view running an airline should be no more difficult than running a fleet of buses. I don't think my reply to this did much good to my subsequent airline career: I said I was only prepared to leave the aircraft on service on written instructions from the Chairman. But this was a case of grounding the first and only postwar British civil aircraft in the full glare of world publicity, and virtually on a hunch, which as it happened turned out to be correct.

For some weeks we flew empty Vikings through cumulo-nimbus clouds at icing levels, and Vickers did their sums all over again and tried out various modifications. Eventually a small change to the trailing edge of the elevator produced a satisfactory variation of the errant b_1/b_2 and the aircraft went back into service for many useful years. How many lives we saved by picking up an 'accident' before it actually happened is anyone's guess.

Since the Viking was only a metal-skin version of the wartime Wellington bomber, I have often wondered if in fact we actually lost a number of Wellingtons during the war from this cause. So subtle a defect would not be likely to be picked up by war trained pilots who had not the support, as we had, of an intensive and highly expert team of development engineers; and there were plenty of other causes which could be guessed at if one or two aircraft crashed from time to time without apparent reason.

The different safety standards needed between wartime operations and civil ones in peacetime may be shown when I say that, in its first year of operation, we sorted out over 2000 defects on the Viking, each having to be classified as to urgency of modification, although only this one led to complete grounding of the fleet. This is no criticism of the Viking, for the same development problems must occur with any new aircraft (or indeed motorcar), and the number of defects then diminishes over the years as the design becomes stabilised in operation. But no amount of pre-operational testing can get all defects out of any mechanical device.

The temptation for an airline to 'buy foreign', and thus let the other fellow go through these expensive and nerve-racking preliminaries, is strong indeed. It has seemed to me that government should grant a development contract to its first national user to cover the expense of all this, which should in no sense be regarded as a subsidy, still less as a criticism of the design. This would mean that the first user of a new type would not be economically prejudiced in comparison with subsequent buyers.

Now whilst in a disciplined service such as the RAF, ATA or an airline, it is possible to impose a full reporting system from all concerned, it is obviously not possible in a widely scattered community of private pilots, many of whom will simply not bother to report an apparently unimportant incident which led to no damage; so once again everything hangs on self-discipline.

If the pilot of a private aeroplane mishandles his petrol cocks, so that his engine fails when his home airfield is just below him, he may land, curse his stupidity, put them right, take off again, and leave it at that rather than go to the trouble of reporting a ridiculous incident and being laughed at by his friends. It may not occur to him that the layout of the cocks is unnecessarily tricky and could be redesigned so no one else could again make his mistake. And later on the same thing may happen to another pilot in a less favourable position, who will be killed, and may even be held responsible for the deaths of his passengers. But who really should bear the basic blame?

Thus, once he has an accident, or even fails to report an incident, a pilot bears a terrible responsibility: for by prompt and honest reporting he may well save future lives, whilst by covering things up he may escape scot-free but achieve a dreadful secret burden on his future conscience.

In ATA I failed in this respect once myself, and what might have happened gave me sleepless nights afterwards. I had to collect a Mosquito from a Midland aerodrome which was to be ferried to RAF Lasham, but there was not time to get it through, so I took it in to our women pilot's pool at Cosford, so that they could on-ferry it the next day.

Everyone else seemed to like the Mosquito, but I found it a tricky bitch of an aircraft, very easy to swing on take-off (since it was very highly-powered for its weight) and apt to jink on touch down which took place at high speed. On this occasion no sooner did my wheels touch the runway than the aircraft swung violently to port, but I managed to correct it by rather hard application of the starboard brake. There seemed to be no damage, the green light indicating undercarriage locked down was OK, nevertheless I gave the structure a cursory inspection and could see nothing wrong. No one had seen the momentary twitch after touch-down.

I flew back to my office at White Waltham the next day, and that evening received an abrasive phone-call from the CO at Lasham, which at that time was the departure point for aircraft being ferried over to the Second Front.

'You sent in one of your damned women pilots in a Mosquito today, and she has just pranged it in the middle of the airfield. You are not—repeat not—to permit women pilots to fly into Lasham again.'

My heart fell into my boots. 'What happened?' 'The b——woman made a bad landing and the undercarriage leg collapsed.'—'What is the aircraft's number?'—'Hang on—here it is—CR442.' It was mine!

I told him the girl was as blameless as he was and—too late—reported the incident. The RAF Commander did not like me for showing up his anti-feminism, and for a different reason I never forgave myself. By my lapse, I might have killed that girl.

In hunting down cause and responsibility, the accident investigator can find himself in an endless receding spiral, and has to stop somewhere. After a fatal accident in bad weather to one of my pilots, I received a terrible letter from his wife—also a pilot. The morning of the accident they had had a bad row at breakfast, and she felt sure this had affected his flying, for they were a deeply devoted couple. I wrote back what I could, and I hope I comforted her. But there could never be any proof. The cause of the row? She was pregnant, and suffering the momentary irritability of the pregnant woman.

A few months later she too lost her life. An engineer in a moment of carelessness had sprayed paint over the filler cap of her aircraft's petrol tank and blocked the air-vent, and her engine failed over bad country. We had to see that the actual inspector concerned was traced and told the result of his momentary lapse, for if he had not been told, he might have sent another pilot to his end. He too must bear a heavy heart. But who knows? He might just have lost his wife in an air-raid, and not have been in a state of mind to spot a blob of paint the size of a large pin-head. A good accident investigator, like a good doctor, needs a clinical compassion, or he will often fail to get to the heart of the matter. But it was wartime and we were all driven very hard: we had not the time, we had not the time.

This discipline, however, etches itself into one's personality, and I carried it into my future life.

A better thing than to arrive

I dashed along the bridge at Paddington until I came to the sign: 17:37, Twyford, Henley. I ran down the steps and tumbled into the first carriage. I then looked at the station clock, and found that mine was fast, and I need not have hurried: it was 17:27.

So it was a bit worrying when almost immediately the train started, and I asked my next-door neighbour what I was in. 'The Golden Hind Express', he replied. 'First stop Taunton.'

I ran down the corridor, through a dining-car (which would have given the game away had I seen it before) and met the guard. 'Oh, dear,' he said, 'we had two ladies who did this last week. I managed to stop the train at Hungerford, but I don't know if I can succeed again.' Apparently the form is to chuck messages out as one passes the stations, and hope someone will ring ahead and get the train stopped further on. But this was a crack express, and I could well see the disadvantages. I asked him to try, saying that although I was certainly not as beautiful as the two ladies had been, it would never-theless be a kind gesture.

On the way back through the dining-car, everyone seemed to have heard of my plight. If we failed to stop the train, they would run up a specially quick meal for me before Taunton. I felt quite a hero, and decided I was going to follow the advice of the Napoleonic old lady to her daughter on the subject of rape: 'Put up as much of a fight as you can, but if you fail, enjoy it as much as possible.'

Back in my carriage, the ice had been broken, and I and the two other occupants fell into a lively conversation. One had that morning flown in from Durban, the other worked in Libya, and I had strong business connections in Rhodesia and South Africa. The time flew by.

Twice before Reading the brakes came on and I made all prepara-tions to depart. I got one of my companions to stand by the carriage door to close it if I managed to jump down on to the track. But each time just as we neared walking-speed the signal ahead changed from red, and we picked up speed again, thus probably saving me from breaking the rules. After Reading I gave up. It would be quicker now to go on to Taunton.

The dining-car attendant came along to say my dinner was ready. Would I bring my coat with me so that I could stay aboard until the last moment?

I had an excellent meal, ahead of the other diners, and as we braked to a halt in Taunton my bill came up. I paid it, and with the good wishes of the dining-car in my ears, the guard arrived and introduced me to the waiting Station Superintendent. The mes-sages he had thrown out had been wired forward to Taunton, and everyone was ready. I felt, not like a slightly dim commuter, but privileged Royalty.

At the opposite side of the platform an immensely long train of milk-wagons was drawn up with a somewhat ancient guard's van at the end of it. To my amazement and horror this had been held on its way to Clapham Junction, and was waiting for me. I was asked where I wanted to be dropped. 'Where does it stop?' I asked. 'Don't worry about that,' came the reply, 'we will stop it wherever you want.'

Slightly dazed at being presented on a plate with an entire 675-ton milk-train, I asked what time it would pass either Reading or Twyford. 'We can't be sure of that,' they replied, 'because it is out of its slot on the line now, so might get held up by the other traffic.' Even more abashed, I decided on Reading, for it would be open all night, while Twyford would put up its shutters before midnight. It would have been a sad end to my saga to have had to pass the night locked in there.

I got into the little box in the ancient guard's van. I am bound to say it was a little shabby after the warmth and comfort of the crack express: I would not have had it otherwise. It was about a six-foot cube, with a row of pigeon-holes and a stool for the guard, a let-down seat for me, a rather dim light bulb, and an extremely elderly gas-stove struggling feebly against the cold night air.

Christmas was near. Here was my pumpkin, drawn not by a team of rats, but a diesel engine and a long line of cylindrical milk-wagons. The guard, a grey-haired friendly man, came in with a piece of paper authorising him, if he wished (for the guard, I found out, like the captain of a ship, has the final say in the conduct of his train) to carry me as excess baggage as far as Reading. He shut the door, seized a prehistoric paraffin lamp and waved it vigorously out of the window. At about 20:00 hrs we rattled off back along the line towards home.

After he had finished his chores, we fell into conversation. This was the nightly milk-train from the West Country to Clapham Junction. We would stop at Castle Cary to pick up more wagons. Then he would get off at Westbury, to come back on another train to Taunton, where he lived. He had two boys. I had three and a daughter. He came from Teignmouth. My family comes from Moretonhampstead, on the edge of Dartmoor nearby. Again the time flew as we rattled on.

At about 9 o'clock we came to a halt, apparently in the open country. But peering ahead out of the window, I could see the distant lights of a station. My friend jumped down on to the line to superintend the coupling of the new load under the cold canopy of stars. Twenty minutes later we were on our way again, and soon picked up a new, younger guard. In no time we were once more in companionable chat.

Once we stopped so long that he left me to go forward to the signal box to find out what was happening. But just as he neared it the light went green, and he came racing back the quarter-mile or so to scramble in and wave his lamp breathlessly before we moved. This lamp was a beauty—there were only three left like it, he explained. It must have been over sixty years old, and had a shiny copper top which he burnished every day. The railway would not permit electric lamps he told me. They were thought to be too unreliable.

As an ex-airline man myself, I wondered if this could be right. We asked electricity to do more hazardous duties than that, I thought. The bond of mutual interest in transport loosened our tongues.

Ten thousand passengers go through, then one crops up to destroy one's faith in humanity. I recalled how, nearly twenty years ago, a certain film star held up a plane for twenty minutes while she powdered her nose. Then, when she was left behind, she raised Cain, through the chairman and beyond. A short while later I said to our traffic manager at lunch: 'Today I met the perfect passenger.' The poor chap, still smarting from this experience, replied 'Was he dead?'

My friend named a man, well-known for his public bonhomie, who was the line's un-favourite passenger, always insulting the unfortunate staff, however junior, for deficiencies for which they could not possibly be responsible. My experience was the complete answer, for as soon as the throng of passengers produced an individual case like mine, in even minor misfortune, everyone leant over backwards to help to the limit of their powers.

We stopped at Reading West for another change of guard, and at last, just on midnight, drew up in Reading. And there, on the platform, was Kitty waiting for me. Taunton had phoned her, and there she was. I feared she might be cold and (for her) cross, after a wait of an hour and a half. But not at all—the entire station staff had rallied round, and kept up a running report on my progress. By some telepathic process, the driver of the freight train ahead of mine knew all about it, and came back from his engine to report to her that he had passed mine a short way back and I would soon arrive. We both said goodbye to all our new friends and drove home, getting to bed in the early hours of the morning.

With my Mosquito incident of more than twenty years ago still in the background of my thoughts, I followed the airline discipline of always reporting a possible defect, however minor, so that action can be taken to avoid a recurrence. On the next morning I went to the Station Manager at Paddington to tell my story. He warily got out a form, probably labelled 'Complaints', but I quickly told him that, on the contrary I was truly grateful for all that had been done for me. Still on reflection, since two ladies had had the same experience the week before, might it be that the sign on Platforms 2 and 3 was displayed in such a way that a passenger in a hurry could be misled? If so, they could well have the milk-train from Taunton inconvenienced weekly. He gratefully took the point, and promised to check. So I fear I may have been the last to have such a pleasurable evening.

4

∽∽∽

The Powers that be

Our undercrowded air

In 1901, the motorcar started to appear on the roads of Britain, and there was a public outcry about the dangers of this new mode of locomotion. The alarm was so great that a law was passed requiring each automobile to be preceded by a man on foot bearing a red flag. In those days the USA was technologically more backward than us, and in 1908 the traffic regulations in Texas included:

1 On discovering an approaching team of horses, the motorist must stop off the side of the road and cover his machine with a tarpaulin painted to correspond with the scenery.

2 In case a horse will not pass an automobile, notwithstanding the scenic tarpaulin, the automobilist will take his machine apart as rapidly as possible and hide the parts in the grass.

3 Automobilists on a country road at night must send up a red rocket every mile and wait ten minutes for the road to clear—then proceed carefully, blowing their horns and shooting Roman candles.

Shades of Concorde 1972!

It was not long however before such laws were repealed, and today everyone laughs at what in retrospect appear ludicrous precautions. But were they?

Supposing some prophet in the first decade of our century had been able to convince the people of the truth—that if this monster was allowed to develop, unchecked, within half a century it would claim over 6,000 deaths and a quarter of a million people injured every year in our country alone—would the pedestrian red flag have remained in being? And would we all have been better off thereby? I think most people today would say no, because we have benefited by an unforeseen growth in the richness and texture of life.

But supposing the first growth of motoring had come on the professional side, with bus and lorry drivers virtually monopolising the roads, and private cars so expensive that only the rich enthusiast could afford them? Then it is certain that these professionals would have organised themselves to put the case for safety—'leave this difficult business of driving automobiles to us and save thousands of lives and hundreds of thousands of injuries a year.' The Ministry of Transport would step in and impose ever higher safety requirements, medical checks and what-have-you before anyone would be allowed to drive a car. Tens of thousands of technical and bureaucratic experts would form a vested interest which would spend hundreds of millions of pounds in a structure of controls and restrictions to preserve the safety of the roads, and would easily convince the public that these safeguards were necessary, and that anyone fit enough and brave enough and clever enough to drive should be highly regarded and even more highly paid.

Now let me be quite clear about this: *the professionals would have been entirely right*—within their structure and terms of reference, which would place the safety of their passengers ahead of everything, including the public good. They are trained and hired to get their passengers and merchandise to their destination undamaged, and it would not be for them to worry about any impoverishment of the economy through the absence of a car industry, the texture of living, or any weakening of the national fibre which would arise from the exclusion from the roads of the private motorist.

Jump the whole case forward half a century, and substitute for road and car the air and aircraft, and this is precisely what has happened, except in the United States where, by the fortunes of history, private flying grew too rapidly to be nipped before it was fully rooted, and could fight for itself.

I am not pretending that flying is as easy as motoring, because the air is more complicated than the land, and less natural to man's navigation. But it is not as difficult or dangerous as it is made out to be, whilst the hazards of the road are widely underestimated. The technical disciplines required of car drivers are lamentably inadequate, those of the air-pilot disastrously excessive and ever-increasing.

This book explains that British gliding is less constricted than most, and even in powered sporting flying there are more red-taped-up countries than ours. For instance, the opening words of the Dutch equivalent of our Air Navigation Act—followed by an ever growing myriad of restrictions are: 'AVIATION IS PROHIBITED EXCEPT ...'!! This is probably the largest *carte blanche* ever given a bureaucracy.

Of all the myths about flying implanted in the public mind, that of our 'overcrowded air' is the most unfounded and the most destructive of our future prospects as an airfaring nation.

In 1901 and 1908, the risk of collision between automobilist and horse or pedestrian was very greatly over-estimated. In 1972, *once away from traffic nodal points such as the main airports*, public and official over-estimation of the aerial collision risk is probably of the same order.

Night after night during the last war there were a thousand aircraft flying blind over London, half hunting the other half, and 30,000 shells a night being pumped up indiscriminately into the lot. Nothing ever hit anything, until radar came along to help. In 1972, 40 aircraft in controlled airspace over the whole of the British Isles with up to 150 others outside at peak periods, are thought to overcrowd the air to the point of danger. Who are we to laugh at our grandparents?

Don't confuse me with the facts!

'Our overcrowded air.' How many people are absolutely convinced that, but for immense technical skill and a firm and ever-increasing control and restriction of air traffic, we would suffer almost daily aerial collisions?

A simple reference to the facts of the case might be thought convincing enough, but alas this is not so. The Conventional Wisdom, built up by decades of propaganda and the ardent advocacy of thousands of 'experts', overwhelms mere fact.

Perhaps the simplest way to convey the true situation is by reference to the following figure.

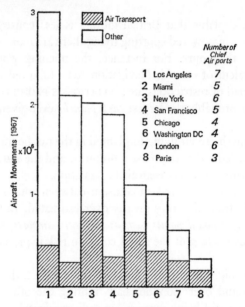

Figure 4   Chief centres of air traffic, 1967

It is obvious that the collision risk is proportionate to the overall density of air traffic. The figure shows that the total number of aircraft movements at the six chief airports of London are about one-quarter of those at the seven chief airports of Los Angeles. Yet the Air Traffic Control restrictions round London are far more severe than those round Los Angeles; and round, say, Manchester (with virtually negligible air traffic) the restricted zone is far larger than round London.

All restrictions must, necessarily, reduce traffic, and particularly the sort of traffic which cannot afford the (extremely expensive) equipment which is required for the purposes of control.

To the glider pilot, a complete overall system of control spells the end of his sport. So this is the crucial field for us, and the one on which we have had to wage the longest, hardest, most technically demanding, and never-ending battle of all. It is easy of course, to depict us as a body of irresponsible fanatics, prepared to hazard the lives of hundreds of innocent fare-paying passengers in the pursuit of our useless sport. And our case, in a materialistic world, is a difficult one: that we are exemplary of a set of values which is literally priceless; that life will only remain worth living if the kind of thing we do remains available to human beings; and that our flying can be shown to present no unacceptable hazard to anyone else.

Since the beginning of man, his most atavistic and belligerent feelings have been raised by quarrels over land. This is a basic part of his animal nature. There is an historic experiment, in which two sticklebacks are placed, with their nests, at the opposite ends of a tank. From time to time, they swim to the half-way point, make cross faces at each other, and then retire to their nests. Now, day by day, the nests are inched nearer together. The displays become more belligerent, until at a critical distance, when they meet, the two fish, instead of mere display, start tearing each other to pieces. If, before one is dead, the nests are moved further apart again, the war is over.

Most of man's wars root back to this basic animal need for space, and the invention of flying has produced exactly the same instinctive reactions in the third dimension. So when we are fighting and snarling at each other for airspace, let us take a long breath and try to tackle our problems with our intellects, not our animal natures.

Our difficulties in Britain have been compounded by the fact that we had to start the whole gliding movement again virtually from scratch after the war, and this was even more the case with other branches of sporting flying. So from 1946 onwards, for as long as fifteen years, the commercial and military branches were busily engaged in planning and erecting a system of control which, as it began to come into effect, had clearly never taken our needs into account—and to do them justice, I don't believe this had even occurred to them.

At long last however, their control zones and airways began to come into existence, and at the last moment we realised what was happening—by which time a radar network costing some £100 million was in the pipeline.

The situation in the United States was quite different, because the war did not ground their general aviation, so there the system was from the beginning planned with their needs in mind.

The result is quite frightening. In 1969 there were in the USA 720,000 active pilots of whom airline pilots numbered 35,000. There were 131,000 General Aviation Aircraft against 3,000 Airline aircraft. At least five airports handled around 500,000 General Aviation movements a year. General Aviation aircraft are welcomed at all airports and no priority is given to airliners using them.

In the UK, even taking into account the proportionate size and wealth of our two countries, our relative figures are derisory. We have less than 2000 General Aviation aircraft and the controls are such that few people can afford the time or money to own a personal aeroplane. Yet with the coming of the European Economic Community the importance of rapid personal travel throughout Europe, providing the restrictive regulations are the minimum necessary for acceptable safety, is probably even greater than in the USA.

It was not until as late as 1960 that our nests were prodded into fighting distance of each other, and I am bound to say that I for one started off with the usual atavistic reaction—perhaps magnified by the disparity between our tiny movement and the vast vested interests which were threatening our continued existence.

Fortunately indeed our problem engaged the interest of Nick Goodhart (now Rear Admiral H. C. N. Goodhart), a glider pilot with one of the most brilliant minds I have known, and with him to keep me on the rails we eventually, by 1967, produced a change of heart in the authorities which has greatly altered for the better our chances of survival. But the final clash was indeed dramatic involving two Ministers, the Chief of the Air Staff, the Director of Air Traffic Control Services, and the entire hierarchy of commercial aviation.

The first ray of hope came in 1963, when Nick Goodhart produced his historic paper 'The Probability of Collision between a Commercial Aircraft and a Glider', in which he showed for the first time that probability theory could be used to predict the mathematical possibility of collision between a glider and a commercial aircraft, because the glider is subject to random motion, and this being the case it is not necessary for the second party also to have random motion. This made it possible to calculate the collision risk and control it in the same way as are controlled all the purely mechanical hazards of flying—by the unemotional application of mathematics.

One warning at this point. We have been subject to much criticism all along the line, by people who should be better informed, by a failure to realise that our statements that the air was far from 'overcrowded' have applied to the extremely small collision risk, whereas this has been mixed up with the *noise* objections. Of course, people living round London Airport or in the south-east of England can rightly object that the air is overcrowded, because the noise created by the numbers of aircraft flying over their heads is intolerable—this is a subjective complaint, and a very real one, but outside the scope of our argument. In any case, gliders do not make any noise, so it is dishonest to put a case for their exclusion from the air by confusing noise objections with collision risks.

Safety factors and logic

In 1960 two airliners collided in controlled airspace over the city of New York, with great loss of life. The accident was, of course, basically due to defective operation of control, either in the air or from the ground. The Master of the top British professional body, the Guild of Air Pilots & Navigators, wrote an impassioned letter to *The Times* saying that such an accident must soon occur over London, *unless the area of controlled airspace around that city was immediately increased.*

I replied protesting, and a considerable correspondence ensued.

As described in Chapter 5, eight years later the British Airline Pilots Association used exactly the same irrationality on which to base a case for a larger control zone round Luton Airport.

In 1965 a four-engined aircraft approaching to land at Manchester Airport crashed and all on board were killed: the cause appeared to be engine failure. In its report on this accident, one of our most respectable and factual newspapers headlined its article 'The need for greater safety in the crowded sky'. I wrote pointing out that the accident almost certainly had no relevance to our allegedly overcrowded air, and was crossly rebuffed. The accident was eventually found to be due to failure of all four engines due to mishandling of the fuel cocks. When I next met the aviation correspondent of the newspaper concerned at a rather grand do some years later he cut me dead.

In 1971 a Japanese airliner pursuing its normal path at 28,000 ft was struck by a training aircraft of the Japanese Air Force, all on board being killed. In far away Denmark the then Minister of Aviation summoned his ATC staff and instructed them to produce a system which would ensure that such a disaster would never occur in Danish airspace.

In the autumn of that year two Danish gliding friends came on an urgent trip to see if I could advise them. Their authorities had produced a plan involving ceilings of 300 metres and 600 metres over a large part of their country for all free-flying aircraft. This would virtually wipe out all Danish gliding, and enormously increase the collision risk for all light aircraft flying in such a narrow band of air. The one thing it would not do would be further to reduce the already infinitesimal risk of a Danish repetition of the Japanese collision.

I could write a whole chapter full of such irrationalities, but I hope I have made my point. Whereas in all other fields the inherently dangerous practice of flying has been made as safe as possible within the bounds of economics and human knowledge by the strict and impartial application of logic, analysis, mathematics, and technical knowledge and skill, in this one field of the risk of collision the emotive content is so great that even professionals allow their subjective feelings to overrule the application of similar methods.

Since 1959 the whole effort of the British Gliding Association has been devoted to an attempt to overcome this conventional wisdom, and to put forward the case for the logical approach in spite of often fierce and angry opposition from many quarters, and I believe we have had a considerable measure of success.

In its February 1964 issue, our magazine *Sailplane & Gliding* wrote:

'Since the two articles published by Philip Wills and Nicholas Goodhart in our February 1963 issue on the campaign to introduce logic into Air Traffic Control, a great deal more work has been done to develop this approach. . . . And it is only fair to say that our Ministry has in fact taken great interest in (and even action on) the logical cases presented.

'This is of such primary and over-riding importance that we must shout from the roof-tops that our own Ministry of Aviation leads the world in this field, and that we, the mouse-like BGA started the ball rolling.'

The ball has had its fits and starts ever since, but in 1972 we still have a nil collision record for airliners over the UK, and still have a more reasonable degree of freedom in our airspace than almost any other of the advanced countries.

Flying cannot be completely safe. As I have written earlier, the solution which has been reached is to impose Safety Factors. A Safety Factor is a compromise between the unattainable complete safety, technical possibilities, and social and economic requirements. The first stages are to locate, analyse and quantify each area of potential risk. In this we have been immensely helped by the steady, detailed and unemotional work of the Air Miss Working Group, which is described in more detail in Appendix IV.

Nick Goodhart's paper, which follows, was as far as I know the first attempt to quantify the collision hazard, and its conclusion will, I expect, surprise many people. As soon as we know the size of a danger, we can begin to see what degree of control is necessary to keep it within acceptable limits. In sum all we are asking for is the same analytical approach to the Collision Risk as is the practice in other aspects of aviation—the application of a measuring rod to the problem.

Current risks of a fatal airliner accident from all causes are of the order of 1 in 300,000 journeys, within which figure the risk of fatal collision is an infinitesimal part. Efforts are of course constantly made to improve this record, but not at the cost of seriously contracting the whole scope of aviation. For instance, no one overtly states that all forms of aviation except military and commercial aviation should cease, although if this were done obviously risks would be reduced, if only slightly. No one requires that all four-engined aircraft should at all times be able to reach an airfield in the event of three engines failing, because the cost of such increased safety would be prohibitive.

When we consider the conflict arising from this cause between public safety and private flying, we must distinguish between the degree of risk the public *must* accept to achieve the benefits of aerial transport at an acceptable cost and the additional risk they should be subjected to in order to achieve the much more diffuse national and social benefits arising from, say, private flying and gliding. This is a difficult equation, and one that is political more than technical.

If, for instance, it were agreed that gliding was nationally valuable to the extent of taking an actuarial risk of one collision in 250 years, restrictions acceptable to all could be based on this formula, and an immense advance would have taken place in this at present most unsatisfactory field.

The outcome of such an investigation would undoubtedly in the main confirm our existing UK system of Control Zones, TMA's and Airways. Various nonsenses would be abandoned, and the increased respect for what was left would lead to increased safety. In other countries, less fortunate, large volumes of air at present controlled without a vestige of reason would be freed, with immense advantage to all. In some areas (but not in the UK I am sure) it might even be found that existing controls were inadequate. Logic and reason would take over from the conventional wisdom. We should no longer have places like Manchester and Jersey more restricted than New York and Chicago. May I live to see the day.

THE PROBABILITY OF COLLISION BETWEEN A COMMERCIAL AIRCRAFT AND A GLIDER

by Nicholas Goodhart

In general, it is difficult to estimate the probability of collision between powered aircraft since they tend to confine themselves to specific heights and routes and thus their motion is very far from random. Probability theory could only be used if the degree of concentration in particular areas could be defined.

In the case of gliders on cross-country flights, however, it is not far from the truth to consider their motion as being truly random both as regards route and height, though within certain limits.

In order to use simple probability theory to predict the possibility of collision between aircraft, it is not necessary that both the parties to the collision shall have random motion. Provided one does, then the degree to which the other is canalised or concentrated at particular points is immaterial.

In the case of glider versus commercial aircraft, simple probability theory can therefore be used to predict the collision risk, provided the limits can be specified within which the glider motion is reasonably random.

It would not, for example, be fair to assume that glider flying is spread over the whole UK, when in fact it is largely concentrated in Southern England, as this is where the major part of commercial flying is also concentrated.

The area in which glider flying may be considered to be substantially random is shown in the Figure below. South-East England has been excluded as an area in which a relatively large proportion of commercial traffic exists and in which some regulation of glider traffic is appropriate. The size of the area in the figure is about 25,000 square miles.

Area of random glider flying in the U.K.

The other limit to the volume in which gliders fly randomly is height. Though very occasionally they may be found at heights up to 30,000 ft in this country, it is reasonable to assume that in general they move randomly in the lowest 12,000 ft of the atmosphere.

The gliders can therefore be assumed to move randomly in a box of base 25,000 square miles and height 12,000 ft.

Now consider a single airliner flying in this box at the same time as a single glider. For a collision to take place it is necessary, at any given instant, for a part of the glider to occupy the same point in space as a part of the airliner.

The two aircraft may collide in any relative attitude, but the worst case is when the glider is banked and crossing in front of the airliner at right angles. It is proposed to take this case, but as a balancing factor it is proposed to eliminate the tails of both aircraft. They can then be considered as flying bars of length equal to wing span.

In order to give numbers to the problem, the glider is assumed to be of 60 ft span in a 45° bank and substantially stationary. The airliner is assumed to have a span of 140 ft and to be flying level at 400 ft/sec.

The glider projects a span of 42 ft to the airliner; thus a collision takes place if the glider is within 21 ft above or below the airliner and anywhere along its 140 ft span. The 'collision cross-section' is therefore 42 ft × 140 ft = 5,900 sq ft.

In one second the airliner sweeps out a volume of 400 × 5,900 cubic feet = $2\cdot36 \times 10^6$ cubic feet.

Thus in any particular second the probability of the glider being in the volume swept out by the airliner is

$$\frac{2\cdot35 \times 10^6}{8\cdot35 \times 10^{15}}$$

Converting from per second to per hour of airliner flight, we get

$$\frac{2\cdot35 \times 10^6 \times 3,600}{8\cdot35 \times 10^{15}} = 1 \times 10^{-6} \text{ per hour of airliner flight.}$$

Application to the present situation

Having obtained the basic probability of one glider versus one airliner, it is now necessary to consider the application of this figure to air traffic over UK.

The latest available statistics (1961) indicate that about 3,000 hours of glider cross-country flying was done in the year. There are 8,760 hours in a year, thus the average glider population over that year in the whole volume of airspace over the UK were

$$\frac{3,000}{8,760} = 0.35 \text{ gliders.}$$

Airliners over UK are not confined to the box, thus on average each spends only a limited percentage of its flight-over-UK time in the box. Examination of the latest available statistics indicates that approximately 15% of airliners airborne over UK are on average in the box at any one instant.

Thus the probability of collision between an airliner and a glider over UK is

$$1 \times 10^{-6} \times 0.35 \times 0.15 = 5.3 \times 10^{-8} \text{ per hour of airliner flight.}$$

Or, to put it another way, the probability is one collision for every 19,000,000 hours (2,200 years) of airliner flight.

And all this is based on the assumption that all the flying takes place in solid IMC (flight in cloud) or alternatively that both pilots are blind.

The real risk

At this point it is difficult to go further since, in the absence of any statistics other than the present perfect record, no figures can be assigned to the effectiveness of 'see and be seen' as between gliders and airliners. That it is effective in VMC (flight in clear air) there is no doubt; but whether it eliminates 9 out of 10, or 99 out of 100, or 999 out of 1,000 incipient collisions is hard to say. Taking a really pessimistic view let us assume a figure of 9 out of 10.

Experience indicates that glider flying is largely done in VMC and again in the absence of exact figures a reasonably pessimistic assumption is that one-tenth of glider cross-country flying is in IMC.

Thus 10% of incipient collisions will be in IMC and will actually take place, but the other 90% are in VMC and 90% of these are avoided by 'see and be seen'. Therefore only 10% plus 9% of collisions take place and the real risk becomes

$$5 \cdot 3 \times 10^8 \times 0 \cdot 19 = 1 \times 10^8 \text{ per hour of airliner flight.}$$

This is one collision per 11,000 years of airliner flight.

Since on average there are about 30 airliners simultaneously airborne over the U.K., airliner hours are being scored up at the rate of 30 per hour. Thus while any one airliner could expect to average one glider collision per 11,000 years of continuous flight, there would be on average one collision over U.K. every 370 years. To put this in perspective, *if there was no controlled airspace anywhere except the south-east of England*, if the last collision had been in Queen Elizabeth I's reign we would be keeping up to the average if the next one was about now, provided of course commercial and glider flying had been at the present level during the intervening period.

This paper was submitted to the Civil Aircraft Control Advisory Council, a notable and, as far as I know, a unique body set up to ensure good channels of communication between pilots and the authorities. Membership includes on the one hand Ministerial ATC officials, and on the other representatives of each civil user of the air—Air Corporations, commercial, sporting and club flying and gliding. At their meetings all conflicting interests are discussed, and the necessary compromise reached, after each party has been brought to realise the problems of the others.

In March 1965 CACAC was presented by the ministerial representatives with the following paper. In how many countries would the responsible officials accept from a sporting body so apparently revolutionary a concept?

Glider crossing of airways: collision risk

1 Arising from previous discussions in CACAC on a statistical study of collision risk, a specific point emerged regarding the risk figure involving gliders, principally in airways. A separate study was therefore undertaken on this based on a method of estimating proposed by Captain Goodhart of the BGA.

2 Captain Goodhart provided estimates of the density and height distribution of cross-country gliders and figures for the relevant airways traffic were obtained by the Ministry.

3 In order to give a realistic picture of the airspace most concerned with the problem, the study was limited to the overland area south of 53°N. Allowance was made for correlation of seasonal, weekly and daily variations of traffic densities. No allowance was made for the possibility of collision avoidance by visual observation nor for the fact that gliders penetrate the airways in VMC only.

4 The result of the study gives the estimated risk of collision in airways involving gliders to be 1 in 250 years.

5 In considering the implications of this report the Ministry take the view that there is no reason to alter the present system whereby gliders can cross airways in VMC.

Lyneham: the crunch

All right, I admit it. I too was a stickleback. But every now and then Nick brought me back to earth, and we plodded away at the reasoning approach.

The crisis came in 1967, over Lyneham.

Lyneham is an RAF airfield in the middle of southern England. It was a centre of RAF Air Transport Command, and as such had a light flow of passenger-carrying traffic. The retiring AOC decided he must have a Control Zone, and was not prepared to listen to any argument.

We extracted the figures. Over week-ends—when the bulk of glider flying takes place—there was less than one take-off and landing of passenger-carrying aircraft each day. If gliders were to be excluded from 300 square miles around an airfield up to 3,000 ft in fine weather with such a light traffic-density, then we could not in future have any logical argument against our exclusion from similar areas around all airfields in the country with similar traffic densities; this would be the end of us.

We had tried everything else; there was nothing left other than a complete confrontation, for there was nothing to lose.

Nick produced a map of all controlled airspace at that time in the pipeline: it presented a catastrophic picture. It was abundantly clear that the military and civil planners had failed to co-ordinate their plans.

Our Vice-President, Air Chief Marshal Sir Theodore McEvoy came to our help and sent the Chief of the Air Staff a copy of our map, pointing out its fatal implications to us, and received from him a helpful reply showing that he took our point.

We attended a giant meeting, with the Minister in the Chair, and all the Departmental Heads present. To avoid any charge of mere impertinence, I had to start by outlining my qualifications for the somewhat bold line I proposed to take, amongst them that I had chaired both the Accidents Committee in ATA and the Air Safety Committee in BEA and had been in charge of the pilots of both organisations, so I had had experience of both sides of this problem. I then told the Minister that we had had many meetings with the National Air Traffic Control Services, asking them to state a policy on which to base the necessity for control in any particular areas, which had been brought to a head by the plan to exclude glider traffic from a large area round Lyneham, where the traffic was insignificant. The only effect had been a paper headed 'The application of ATC to gliding' containing the significant sentence '[ATC] measures should not be more prohibitive than they need be to any form of aviation *which can show a need to exist*' (my italics).

I questioned the right of NATCS to judge whether any sector of British aviation was to be deemed worthy of existence, and said that I considered that such decisions, if indeed they had to be taken, should be made by our elected political leaders, and I should expect at not less than Cabinet level, and not by a group of technical experts in a Government Department.

Nick Goodhart then produced his map (p. 89), which was greeted with silent surprise. Over 50% of the traffic over our islands was to be excluded from all the areas marked. The resultant congestion in the narrow passages between the controlled areas (i.e., the N–S passage in the lane over the Thames just west of the London Control Area) must introduce really serious collision hazards to the traffic confined to it, and in fact for uncontrolled traffic the proposed new zones almost cut off the north of our country from the south.

By this time there was an aghast silence. Then the Minister asked DNATCS to reply, and after further discussion he said in effect that Lyneham must go on, but he certainly accepted that gliders

Goodhart's map of prospective air traffic control plans in 1967

'had a need to exist' and he undertook to look again at all the future proposals under consideration. He then left for another appointment, and the senior Civil Servant present took the Chair. We had an uneasy feeling that we had lost. We came to Any Other Business. I tried one last desperate shot.

'Please, Chairman, may I ask whether the Air Traffic Control Services accept responsibility for the collision risk outside controlled airspace—in the constantly decreasing Free Airspace to which we are confined?' DNATCS had had enough. He bit it—he said curtly 'No!'

It was Nick who saved the day, and who uttered the words which

changed the whole future of British gliding and of much else beside.
'*Then who does?*' said Nick.

I have never heard so long a silence at any meeting. Have you
ever, dear reader, walked through the Rain Forest towards the
frightful chasm into which the Zambesi throws itself over the
Victoria Falls? If so, you will have heard a susurration of the air
grow to a whisper, the whisper to a mutter, to a grumble, to a hum, a
shout, an overwhelming roar of falling waters. Behind this silence I
thought I heard something of the same sort—but it was the roar of
pennies dropping.

Why it should have happened at this particular point of time I
have no idea. We had said and written and argued this very point
over the past years always to come up against a blank inability to
comprehend. But suddenly a moment had been reached when those
who mattered were ready to take it in. If you reserve large chunks
of air to one sort of traffic, and then make those chunks even larger,
it surely doesn't take much thought to see you are constantly reducing the volume of air used by the rest, so increasingly crowding
them in what is left, and increasing their collision risk. The authority
concerned with the reserved airspace cannot possibly evade responsibility for what they are doing to the rest. But for twenty years
they had not spotted it. They did now.

The silence ended, our Chairman said, in a heavy voice: 'I see
what you mean.'

The meeting ended, and we left the room. But most of those present stayed behind, chatting together in urgent tones.

The next day we were told that we had made a very great impression, and that all plans were suspended pending a reconsidera-
tion of the problem *as a whole*.

We lost over Lyneham—the thing was too far down the river to
stop it. Its existence in fact seriously diminished the freedom of
our sport, and particularly adversely affected all competition flying,
since all tasks had to be set round a zone straddling the centre of
southern England, and there is still no shadow of doubt in our
minds that it was an entirely unnecessary obstruction, and a lament-
able example of pressure from vested interests overwhelming a
minority in the face of a reasonable assessment of the facts.

Another very serious aspect of the Lyneham case brings in the

Viking proving flight, Lisbon, 1947

Lorne Welch at the 1948 World Championships in Samaden

Sutton Bank, 1937

Kit Nicholson and Gull IV, 1948

very roots of our democratic freedoms. In a democracy, the function of the armed Services is to preserve for its citizens the sort of society in which they wish to live. To do this, they must not depreciate more than is absolutely essential the quality of life available to those citizens. They must not debar the ordinary man from more territory than is necessary for their function, either on land or sea, *or in the air*.

In the Lyneham affair, the Royal Air Force succeeded in excluding us from flying over an area exceeding 300 square miles without attempting to justify this even on safety grounds, for the simple reason that it was impossible to do so. If our armed forces are not permitted to take such negligible risks on our behalf in peace time we had better do something about it.

There have, to date, been no more Lynehams. We must face it— there may be growing restrictions on our sport, but they will, I hope be based on a proper balance of the risks to everyone involved—and this we accept, for we have no wish to hazard ourselves or anyone else.

There is perhaps one last point to make. One major reason why it is so difficult to make the case clear in this abstruse field is that the ordinary passenger, fighting his way through the milling crowds at Heathrow, must take it for granted that the surrounding air, like the terminal building, is seething with moving objects. But the crucial point here is that it all depends on the size of the aircraft.

If 10,000 people a day arrived at Heathrow all in two-seater aeroplanes, the air would indeed be overcrowded. But if they come in twenty Jumbo Jets, the collision risk would be negligible, though the crowds in the terminal would be spasmodically insufferable.

The tendency over the history of civil aviation has been for aircraft to get steadily bigger, so the increase in aircraft movements since the war has been of the order of 10% per annum, whilst that of passengers handled has been about twice as large. The very latest evidence indicates that the numerical size of the civil air fleets of the western world has peaked at around 7,000 aircraft, and for some years ahead will increase, not in number, but in average size.

Airworthiness

One of the most frustrating and expensive aspects of running a powered aircraft is that its owner is automatically treated as if he were a mechanical moron, and unless he sits a lot of exams to obtain official qualifications, he is not allowed to touch his aircraft in any mechanical sense, to give it its Daily Inspection, or even to clean its sparking plugs—every little thing has to be carried out by a Licensed Ground Engineer, at great expense.

The BGA has however managed to retain a very great degree of freedom in this field, has been allowed to lay down its own standards and procedures, and as elsewhere has achieved this by a long history of responsibility, self-discipline and technical integrity, and by close co-operation between itself and the Air Registration Board.

A great deal of the credit for all this goes to Sir Robert Harding-ham, who for many years was Chief Executive, and of course from our side to the distinguished and competent men who have chaired the BGA Technical Committee—since 1951 this has been Frank Irving, Warden of Imperial College—and the colleagues who with him take the burden.

The ARB is one of those unique British institutions that obviously shouldn't work, but in fact is more effective than any equivalent in any other country I know of. Although it has been closely associated with the relevant Ministry, it has had a large degree of autonomy, and the Board itself consists of representatives of the various segments of British Aviation, including one member representing light and sporting aviation.

The structure of the ARB is such that it has never, to my knowledge, been attacked by the distressing bureaucratic disease of Parkinsonism. Rather than take over all possible work, irrespective of cost, by simply indenting for more staff, it has always preserved the philosophy of delegating all possible responsibilities to those on the spot, in factories or maintenance shops or on the field itself.

In the field of gliders, it had to produce a set of British Airworthiness Requirements, and it had to make available to those who wanted it an official Certificate of Airworthiness, for otherwise many countries would not accept exports of our gliders. But to the majority the BGA issues its own C's of A which are accepted not only in this country, but in some others, and the ARB encourages this. It met the first need by asking the BGA just after the war, to produce draft requirements. It then accepted these almost as they stood and not only issued them officially, but *acknowledged their source*. The printed foreword in Section E, British Airworthiness Requirement for Gliders, reads as follows:

'Acknowledgment. The Air Registration Board has pleasure in acknowledging its indebtedness to the British Gliding Association for the closely co-ordinated effort which made possible the publications of this Section E of the British Civil Airworthiness Requirements.

The Association undertook the main work of preparation of the amendments which are included in this second issue of Section E through its Design Requirements Sub-Committee which represented the various interests which glider requirements might affect.'

I know of no other country where such a relationship between an official and an amateur body could be built up, and I know no other country in which it could be consciously realised that such a relationship was a major contribution to safety. Of British glider pilots it has been written that their girl-friends complain that they have only two ideas in their minds, their wives that they have only one. With this kind of trust placed on us, we are apt to look after our gliders as carefully as we do our wives and children.

Perhaps the sternest test came in late 1951, when the Board's test pilot had certain criticisms of the handling qualities of the prototype Slingsby Sky, with which the BGA Test Pilots group disagreed. To modify the aircraft in an attempt to meet this criticism in full would have ruined its performance, and the 1952 World Championships were looming, in which we were to be equipped with the Sky.

During its whole life, the ARB has been working at full pressure on matters of prime importance, such as the certification of the Viscount, the Comet, the 707, and nowadays, no doubt, the Concorde. Here was a case of a spot of trouble in an insignificant corner of Bob Hardingham's bailiwick yet the head man himself found time to come, with his colleagues, to an after-hours meeting in Londonderry House to help sort it out promptly.

With Frank Irving, Sir Arnold Hall, the preceding Chairman of the BGA Technical Committee, and the rest of us, we fixed it all in one meeting, agreed a few minor modifications, and the Sky went on to win the 1952 World Championship and put British sail-planes in the lead for a decade. In other countries, or with most other men, whilst we should eventually probably have achieved the same final technical answer, the normal delays of bureaucracy would have made us miss the critical time-scale, and British gliding must have been permanently affected.

The BGA standards for the granting of a C of A are of course the same as those of the ARB, but it can act more quickly and of course economically than the larger body. But there is one situation in which it can find itself in an invidious position.

In some countries, requirements may in some detail be lower than ours, and a British pilot can import a foreign aircraft with its foreign C of A, and then accuse the BGA of nationalism in refusing auto-matically to issue a BGA certificate, since there may be plenty of evidence that the aircraft is perfectly safe. But if the BGA does accept this lower standard, then British manufacturers have a perfectly sound case for complaint unless the standards required of them are also lowered. In such a case the BGA may press the ARB to take over the responsibility; however, over the years British pilots have come to see the problem, and the ARB does its best to keep out of the picture.

On the question of modification, repairs and maintenance, owners can do what they wish, but the BGA sets clear limits beyond which any work done must, after it has been completed, be checked by a qualified BGA inspector before the C of A is re-validated.

Through all this, however, our basic philosophy runs straight and clear. There is nothing in British law, or BGA regulations, to pre-vent a man designing and building his own glider, flying it from his own field, and breaking his own neck, but he may not do it from the site of any member club.

It has happened only once to my knowledge, over the past forty years.

Because the Air Registration Board has been controlled by people engaged themselves in the various branches of civil flying, and its structure is therefore rather similar to that of the BGA, both bodies have over the years produced a similar philosophy as regards safety.

The ARB philosophy was enunciated by their present Chief

Executive, Walter Tye, in the 26th Commonwealth Lecture delivered by him to the Royal Aeronautical Society in November, 1970.

'It has become technically possible, in some airworthiness areas, to relate the particular requirement to probability of occurrence of accidents. Thus we can sometimes predict that a requirement of such and such a level will be likely to result in an accident once in one million occasions, but that a requirement which is X% more stringent will result in an accident on one in ten million occasions.

As soon as one is able to make this kind of prediction, it becomes necessary to face the responsibility for deciding the "acceptable" level of frequency of accidents. No longer is it possible to take refuge in the feeling that the risk was unpredictable.

There was, and probably still is, a dislike of stating that an accident rate or probability is "acceptable". The word itself is unfortunate. However, it is evident that no form of transport is wholly free from risk. It is also evident that to seek to eliminate all risks would give rise to such prohibitive costs as to rule out that form of transport. *It is possible to achieve very low orders of risk, but not zero risk* [my italics].

The fact that the public choose to use a form of transport for the benefits it gives despite the residual risk, means that some level of risk is "acceptable".

Thus in one sense the fact that we are increasingly able to estimate the probability of accident, has changed nothing. We have always had as a subconscious aim the need to provide an acceptable result. But technically this ability to predict is important, as it concentrates attention on the real objectives, and in this sense it is probably the most significant change in airworthiness thinking in the past two decades.

At what level the acceptable risk should be set is a matter for endless debate. The question can be approached on a comparative basis, for example, by comparison with other forms of transport. But this leads to difficulties with the yardstick—the mile, the hour, or the journey. Another approach is to consider the economics of safety. The total cost associated with a given level of risk can be viewed as having two elements, the cost of the provisions made to secure safety, and the cost of the accidents which nevertheless occur. If a level of safety much beyond the state-of-the-art is sought the cost of providing safety increases rapidly, but the saving from fewer accidents is small. Conversely if safety is allowed to slip, the cost of accidents swoops up, without commensurate saving in cost of the safety provisions. Hence there is an economic optimum and the safety limit sought cannot differ greatly from the level corresponding to this optimum. The accompanying graph illustrates the point. It is fortunate that as the state-of-the-art of design, construction and operation advances, this economic optimum moves in the direction of increasing levels of safety.'

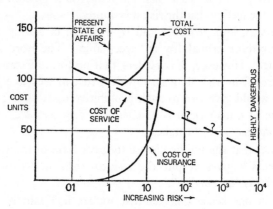

Figure 5   Cost versus risk

It is interesting to compare this quotation with that from the Policy Document of the U.S. Federal Aviation Agency on p. 58. The similarities are remarkable. The difference however is that the FAA is an all-embracing body carrying authority throughout the entire field of US aviation, whilst the ARB is a small body with a most unique constitution, controlling only the single field of airworthiness in the UK.

The UK is about to set up an all-embracing authority similar to the FAA which is going to engulf the ARB and it is open to question whether or not the ARB philosophy will permeate its devourer or the reverse.

5

∾∾∾

Land Ho!

Sutton Bank and Lasham

The future of British gliding depends on two things, and two things only, land and air. There will always be more than enough people who want to do it, and to pay enough to do it—since to anyone keen enough to pay by work rather than money, the cost is quite small.

The rate of expansion (or contraction) of gliding therefore hinges on, firstly, the acquisition of suitable sites, and secondly, on sufficient freedom of the air to permit gliders to fly.

In an overcrowded country such as ours, every new site is a battle with all the conflicting claims on the land, and every single club with security of tenure (and there are horrifyingly few of these) could write a chapter on the struggles it went through to achieve it. I was closely associated with only two—Sutton Bank and Lasham.

We started negotiating with the Ecclesiastical Commissioners for a 21-year lease of Sutton Bank in Yorkshire in 1933—a committee consisting of Fred Slingsby, Norman Sharpe and myself was set up to acquire and develop the site, but for many months I ran up against a brick wall—the Commissioners could not see their way to grant a lease to a sporting organisation which was going to use their property to let its members enjoy themselves on the Sabbath! We could have a lease providing we undertook not to fly on Sundays. I tried everything I could think of. I even (quite truthfully) told them that I personally felt a great deal nearer to God surveying the extraordinary beauties of Sutton Bank from my sailplane than ever I did in the most inspired cathedral.

All was of no avail until, some 18 months older, I offered a formula: on Sundays we would fly, not for sport, but for education and instruction. The Ecclesiastical brow cleared, the lease was signed. Fifteen years later the property was purchased outright.

I know no more beautiful site in Britain, and few in the world. I am certain it has brought a realisation of the handiwork of God to many people who, not being churchgoers, would otherwise have been unenlightened.

The battle of Sutton Bank, however, was a mere skirmish compared with the battle for Lasham, which included the complications involved in 'Crichel Down'.

'Crichel Down' decreed that, whenever dispossessing itself of an airfield, the State must offer it back to the original pre-war landowners. Since these usually consisted of three or more separate farmers, it was almost impossible for a potential gliding club to negotiate successfully with all parties concerned: only one had to refuse, to cut up the land in such a way as to render it unsuitable.

If the original owners were not interested, then the land would be put up for auction, but divided in such a way that no club could bid for one lot unless it knew it could acquire part or all of the others. The outcome was that, whilst at the end of the war the country was peppered with hundreds of airfields, with runways, hangars and buildings all available, on which a thriving private flying and gliding movement could have been founded with minimal expense, almost all of these were cut up, the runways left to break up, the hangars and buildings to rust and fall down.

The Surrey Gliding Club, after the war, started up again on Redhill airfield, but in 1950 was forced to leave because of the buildup of neighbouring Gatwick as the second London airport. A long and widespread search led to Lasham, where the Club was given a lease on a monthly tenancy only. The tenancy included a ramshackle hut, which was turned into a club-house, and a vast and rapidly rusting hangar.

As the years went by, more and more people and clubs came to Lasham, and it became the largest gliding centre in Britain, and possibly in the world, with upward of 900 members. Whilst, however, we could afford to keep the clubhouse in repair, on a mere monthly tenancy we could not afford to spend any money on the hangar, and the Air Ministry steadfastly refused to do so either. So the time arrived when every gale brought jagged bits of rusty corrugated iron crashing down inside the hangar, and rain blowing in at all angles, and the gliders driven into smaller and smaller corners.

Meantime, it became quite clear that, unless we could remain at Lasham, and obtain sufficient security of tenure to let us put some real money into it, all the Clubs there would simply vanish, as there was nowhere else to go within reach of London. So Ministers, MPs, VIPs of all shapes and sizes, were asked to Lasham, the Press and television wooed, and over the years the sheer size of the operation began to impress itself on the world at large. For two or three years we were able to say that the number of movements at Lasham exceeded those at London Airport itself. Meantime a special committee was set up to negotiate with the Ministry of Civil Aviation and Air Ministry. In 1960 we got so far as an offer to buy the site for £70,000, but this sum proved beyond our ingenuity to raise. But we got a lot of Parliamentary and Ministerial support, and early in 1961 an idea came through that the Ministry of Civil Aviation should itself purchase the site from the Air Ministry and then grant us a 21-year lease.

By the middle of this year, with the helpful assistance of the then Minister, Geoffrey Rippon, this proposal had reached a stage where we had been assured all would go through and that we should get ahead with our plans. We had raised several thousand pounds from our members and sympathisers to enable us to start the recladding of the hangar, and started planning for further urgent developments, such as a new club-house.

Then disaster struck. By one of those changes of Minister which makes such negotiations absolutely despairing, the opposition to our acquisition of the site was inspired to renew its attack, and the new Minister, Basil de Ferranti, was obliged to hold everything up whilst he got briefed from the beginning all over again.

The root cause of our fresh trouble was paradoxical in the extreme: it was that de Ferranti was technically the best equipped Minister ever to be appointed to this particular post. Not only was (and is) he an extremely able businessman, but also he was an extremely competent private pilot. The misfortune lay in the fact that his business manufactured, amongst other things, the most advanced electronic equipment for Air Traffic Control, and this being the case he had been living for the past ten years and more in the centre of the mythology, which had now become the conventional wisdom, justifying the vast capital sums which had been voted to create a network of Air Traffic Control Centres far more elaborate than anything to be found in the USA, where the traffic is many times more dense than ours in the UK.

The total scheme cost over £100 million, and this was the weight of the system that was now summoned to the aid of those who had other plans for Lasham. Everyone inside the scheme, of course, believed in its necessity with a passionate intensity. Only the very few outside it, who both understood it technically and also had the overall view, could possibly envisage its wider implications. I had been here before, since fifteen years earlier in BEA I had had a hard struggle to keep the Viscount an economical aircraft, against the pressures of a specialist Ministerial Department which, being interested only in fire precautions, had tried to insist on it carrying an impossible weight of anti-fire devices, instead of any passengers. Specialists unchecked can play hell with real life.

de Ferranti opened our first meeting on the subject of Lasham with the ominous words: 'If I had been in this from the beginning, it would certainly not have got so far. You must know as well as I do that in a few years' time the density of air traffic over southern England will be far too great to allow gliders to fly around at all.'

After a few seconds stupefied silence, I said 'Chairman, if you really believe that, and act accordingly, you are dooming not only gliding, but the whole of British aviation, to a third-class world status. If the use of the air is going to be limited to what the Air Traffic Control authorities say they can handle, rather than the other way round, then there is no hope for us.'

The weeks rolled by, and a terrific ATC case was built up, Lasham being so near London, and all that; not that it had got any nearer in the previous ten years, but now this was seen to be our Achilles heel with the new Minister, the old arguments were revived.

However, our case was now so strong that at last it was reluctantly accepted, and a lease was drawn up, ready for signature. Whereupon de Ferranti was succeeded by Julian Amery.

It was now February 1962. In August 1961 Heads of Agreement had been signed. Although the lease was still not signed, since June the previous year we had been paying rent, had been collecting rent from sub-tenants, and granting them sub-leases. We had re-clad our hangar at a cost of £7,000. Once more, a new Minister came in, and had to be briefed again from scratch.

Our brief to Mr Amery was pretty strong, in a desperate kind of way. It ended thus:

'If a section of a ministry cannot be relied on to carry out an instruction of its Minister (issued after exhaustive investigations of the relative factors), but instead attempts by procrastination to get a reversal from a subsequent Minister, a truly desperate situation arises. For what protection is left the citizen against domination by the executive?'

This, then, was the situation when we were summoned to the meeting to end all meetings, at the Ministry of Aviation, Julian Amery in the Chair, the date 15 November 1962. At the head of the table, the Minister, flanked by around 20 advisers. Our party, David-like, consisted of myself, David Carrow, Nick Goodhart (our ATC expert), Wally Kahn, and two stout Parliamentary allies, Freddie Gough and Joan Quennell, Members of Parliament; the former was Chairman of the Royal Aero Club, whilst the latter represented the constituency in which Lasham is geographically situated.

Miss Quennell opened by stating the Society's case for immediate signature of the Lease and said that this must be finalised before the Special Council Meeting of the Lasham Gliding Society called in nine days time to finalise the contract for a new club-house.

The Minister replied, recording the moral and legal obligations of the Ministry towards the Society. He had been advised however against immediate signature, pending clarification of the possible ATC problem arising. He was therefore setting up a working party to thrash out this problem once again. He did not see however how this could finish its work in nine days.

The proposed size and function of the Working Party, which would *inter alia* take evidence from the BGA and then report to the Minister, was then outlined.

I then asked the Minister to understand that the members of the Society at the meeting were under duress. Acting on the advice of a previous Minister, given when the lease was commenced in June 1961, they had raised from fellow members and sympathisers large sums of money, for which they were trustees, for the purpose of building the proposed Centre. This money could not be repaid now, since some of it was already spent, and much of it was in the form of 7-year covenants. The dreadful Ministerial weapon of procrastination had driven them imperceptibly over the edge of what was proper in their role of trusteeship, and their own integrity was now at stake.

The final stroke was the recent resignation of Mr Basil de Ferranti, who had had the negotiations in hand, hence their request for this final meeting with the Minister. The Working Party now proposed should have been set up a long time ago.

Mr Carrow said we welcomed the Working Party, but asked that the lease be signed now. The Minister repeated that he was advised that if this was done, difficulties might arise later.

Mr Kahn said the position was intolerable. Every difficulty had been discussed and finally resolved, and a meeting held at which it was agreed that there was no further problem. He had canvassed for money from other members, industry, MPs, even the Royal Family, on the basis of the Ministry's agreement to a lease. It was impossible now to go back.

Col Gough asked for a clear answer as to why the proposed Working Party had not been appointed previously. The Minister in his reply, did not cover this question.

Mr Kahn and Mr Carrow reaffirmed the requirement that the lease should be signed today. The Minister repeated that he was advised not to do so, and insisted that the Working Party be set up first.

Col Gough said the story was one of muddle and incompetence over a long period. The Government had agreed the lease and should sign now. He felt that unless this was done his support of the Government would be seriously strained and he would find it necessary to ask a question in Parliament. He felt the honour of the Government was at stake.

The Minister said that since he was advised that he should not sign the lease now he could not change his position without consulting his Department and the Treasury.

Mr Kahn and Mr Carrow reaffirmed the need for signature now.

The Minister, reviewing the situation, said (1) he had made a proposal (2) this was not acceptable to the Society which (3) was facing a crucial meeting in nine days time. He would therefore ask for these nine days to reach the point of signature.

Mr Kahn and Mr Carrow repeated the need for signature now.

Col Gough asked why the lease should not be signed at once. The Government had accepted the obligation to do so.

The Minister repeated the substance of his advice.

Col Gough repeated his views.

At this point the Minister asked for an adjournment for further discussion with his officers.

Twenty minutes later the official party returned, and the meeting was resumed.

The Minister said there were two issues: (1) The ATC Committee: the BGA had asked for representation, but the Committee would first have to sort out certain internal differences, and he would wish that only after this had been done would discussions take place with the BGA. (2) With regard to the lease, the Government recognised their obligation, but did not want to sign the lease until the ATC problem had been sorted out. However he was now prepared to have the lease signed at once, but would first send a letter warning the Society that there might be later restrictions in ATC.

Col Gough thanked the Minister and pointed out that the Contract was already in existence and therefore the onus still remained with the Government, in that they had granted the lease and thus accepted that the ATC problem was soluble. What had happened since then would not be affected by their signature.

I also pointed out that the signature of the lease satisfactorily acknowledged the Ministry's legal obligation; their continuing moral obligation remained unaffected.

It was agreed that the lease should be signed forthwith. The BGA entered a strong plea that their representative should be accepted on the Committee full-time. The Minister agreed to note this when the Membership was being decided.

Miss Quennell thanked the Minister for giving so much of his time to this difficult matter and expressed the gratitude of the delegation at its satisfactory outcome.

There is little more to record. My subsequent letter to Freddie Gough may be of interest:

Col C. F. H. Gough, MC, TD, MP
22, Sackville Street,
London, W1.   15 November 1962

We left the Ministry in a daze, and went and had lunch together which was pretty uproarious except for two bits of trouble. The first was that we had not asked you and Joan Quennell to join us and the second was who was going to write you letters expressing our feelings for what you have done. I won the second argument so here goes.

To put it in a nutshell, what happened this morning would have restored anyone's beliefs in the virtues of our particularly weird brand of Parliamentary democracy. Because you and Joan Quennell were prepared to give us so much of your time and press our case with such fortitude we are now at last on the right side of the bedclothes with our 900 members, and with all the friends and colleagues from whom we have raised money for the development of Lasham. We have also seen that, when it comes to the crunch, the Government's word is as good as its bond.

The difficulty about writing a thankyou letter is that most of them are merely polite necessities, so when you come to write one that comes really from the heart it is difficult to make it sound genuine. Whatever it reads like, please put this one in the latter category.

We received the signed lease four days later, on 19 November 1962. It was the end of twelve years hard fighting. I feared we might have upset a lot of important people, and put our spies to work. But no—the Minister (who had just come from the Colonial Ministry) was reported to have said, just after we had gone: 'Gentlemen, I have not met such a tough lot since my negotiations with Archbishop Makarios. I respect them.' In fact, I learnt an important lesson from all this: in spite of their great powers, if you fight clean, and win (which is seldom) our senior civil servants bear no malice. It's as good a reason as any other for not emigrating. My Christmas report on the year in *Sailplane & Gliding* included: 'Lasham is really ours. We can hardly believe it. The *accoucheurs*, exhausted by their long struggles, lie panting in heaps around the perimeter. The child gives a long, hungry and querulous cry. It will not be its last. But it is there.'

It is still there, ten years later. Everyone has come to terms with it: the committee set up to examine the ATC problem reported favourably: the difficulties foreseen have vanished. There is still enough air for everyone: long may it remain so.

The Battle of Dunstable

To give an idea of the amount of work involved in the constant fight for air, it may be interesting and instructive to look in some detail at one single case in which pressures were built up for the restriction of a particular volume of airspace vital to the survival of one of our largest and oldest gliding clubs—the London Club at Dunstable.

The London Club first settled at their existing site on Dunstable Downs in 1931. Many years later a small municipal airfield was established at Luton about 7 miles from Dunstable, and by the end of the 1960s, its proximity to London, and the approaching saturation of the main London airports, brought to Luton an increasing volume of traffic, particularly summer holiday traffic by charter airlines.

In common with all other operating airfields, Luton was surrounded by an 'Airfield Control Zone', 2,000 ft high and extending 3,000 yards beyond its boundaries, into which only aircraft taking off or landing at the airfield were allowed to penetrate.

By world standards, the number of 'airliners' using the airport was still very small, but inevitably pressure started building up for an extended zone into which no one would be allowed to fly except when in radio contact with Luton, and with the permission and under the direction of Luton Air Traffic Control. Such a restricted zone, unless very carefully tailored, must spell the end of the London Gliding Club.

The pressures started on a small scale, with a number of minor paragraphs in newspapers and on the radio reporting that the professional pilots flying from Luton were experiencing 'near misses' with light aircraft, and mentioning the large number of gliders flying from nearby Dunstable. Then *The Times* published an article from their air correspondent on 23 June 1969.

Since Nick Goodhart's reply, refuting these stories, was not published, we decided that the only way to bring the facts out into the open was through our principal aviation weekly *Flight*, so I wrote them a letter which appeared in their issue dated 17 July.

Luton's Airspace: The BGA View

Sir, Through the courtesy of your columns I should like to draw the attention of the flying community to a campaign being waged by the British Airline Pilots Association which, if successful, could among other things result in the destruction of the London Gliding Club, which has operated from Dunstable for 38 years, and currently has over 500 members.

The campaign is for the introduction of a special-rules zone round Luton.

An article, obviously inspired by BALPA, appeared in *The Times* for 23 June under the heading 'Luton to Ban No-radio Light Aircraft.' It reported as a fact that a Government decision would be made shortly to ban light aircraft without radio from flying near Luton, and that this would mark victory for the campaign originated by BALPA. It then instanced alleged cases of 'near misses' in the area; but one does not, of course, know how many of these would stand up to proper analysis. All one does know is that, of the nine air misses properly reported and analysed over the past three years, eight proved to involve no risk and one to be due to pilot error.

The British Gliding Association's reply, which was not published, was as follows:

'Sir, In a report by your air correspondent (*The Times*, 23 June) it is suggested that the Government is shortly to make a decision to ban no-radio aircraft from the airspace adjacent to Luton airport and that this decision derives from some near misses between commercial airlines and small aircraft.

In reality the position is very different; there are no reported near misses relevant to the problem (though there are a small number of sightings) and, while it is true to say that the Board of Trade is reviewing the situation in this area, it has certainly not said that a decision to establish a special-rules zone is to be made shortly.

St Francis of Assisi would have been sur-prised . . .

Pronzati, Adele and Georgio Orsi, and the Skylark 3

Italian eagle and British Dart share a thermal in the Apennines

Before such a zone is established, it is necessary to determine whether there is excessive risk of collision and the exact shape of zone which will adequately meet the many requirements for the use of airspace in this area. This cannot but be a lengthy process.

We in gliding are as committed as the airline pilots to ensuring an acceptable level of safety from collision for commercial air traffic (and for ourselves) but we are quite certain that this aim is best achieved by working steadily and objectively with the Board of Trade rather than by emotive and unsubstantiated stories about air misses.—Yours faithfully, H. N. C. Goodhart, Chairman, Airspace Committee, British Gliding Association.'

There have been similar instances over the past weeks in other newspapers and on the radio.

I want to point out to all concerned the impropriety of this sequence of affairs. BALPA has access to the organs of the Press and radio, the BGA not to the same extent. BALPA feeds the Press with uncorroborated scare stories of 'near misses'. They know as well as we do that, if these incidents did indeed occur, it was the duty of the pilots concerned to report them officially. Each would then have been investigated; and, if indeed any actual danger occurred, remedial action to prevent recurrence would then have been taken.

Instead of this, BALPA appear to be using the high status accorded the profession of those they represent to disseminate scare stories directly to the Press. I am quite certain very few of their members would approve. Might I ask them to register their protest to their representatives, who are after all elected by them to carry out their wishes?

The assessment of the necessity or otherwise of a special-rules zone for Luton is a matter of extreme technical complexity, to be decided by competent professionals, not by an appeal to inevitably uninformed public opinion.

PHILIP WILLS

London SW1.   *President, British Gliding Association*

This letter produced two results: firstly *The Times* opened its columns to us, and the BGA was from then on given the necessary space to present their case; secondly, the pilots' union, the British Airline Pilots' Association, came out from behind their bush with a vengeance. In *Flight*'s issue of 31 July they wrote:

Luton's Airspace: The BALPA View

Sir, Mr Wills's letter 'Luton Airspace: The BGA View' (*Flight*, July 17) does no credit to him or to the British Gliding Association.

His allegation that BALPA has used 'uncorroborated scare stories' in a campaign which will result in the destruction of the London Gliding Club would be laughable were it not tied to his office of president of the BGA. Mr Wills should check his facts before publicly airing his opinions on such an important issue.

BALPA has an active Technical Section whose sole function is to study technical matters affecting aviation; safety is one of these. Under advice from this section the Association for some time has been seeking stricter control over Luton, Stansted, Elstree, Radlett and other areas.

In June of last year BALPA wrote to the Board of Trade expressing concern about Luton airspace. The Board replied that it was aware of the situation and was examining means of improvement. In the spring of this year a draft Notam from the BoT informed us that a Special Rules Zone would be introduced on June 26.

Our view was that this was both inadequate and too late, but nevertheless a step in the right direction.

Subsequently, a meeting of the Civil Aircraft Control Advisory Committee on June 17 decided that the implementation of the Special Rules Zone should be postponed.

It may be contended that pressures from private flying clubs (including the London Gliding Club) present at the meeting were not unconnected with this decision.

At no stage did the Association attempt to make this a public issue. The matter came to public attention when thousands of spectators at the recent Vauxhall Motors open day saw a Britannia aircraft, landing at Luton, narrowly miss two Army parachutists in a display.

While Mr Wills's suggestion that *The Times* prints articles 'inspired by BALPA', and that the Association has some special influence with the National Press, is rather flattering, I can assure him that we did not arrange a near miss in front of half the population of Luton, and did not dissuade *The Times* from printing his letter.

BALPA is campaigning for air safety and does not bear any ill-will towards the London Gliding Club or anyone else; in fact, many of our members enjoy the sport. However, the BGA's president seems no longer to be interested in sportsmanship and appears to be more concerned with gamesmanship.

He is not a BALPA member and therefore it is impertinent of him to suggest that we are acting against the interests and wishes of our members. Our actions are the direct result of representations from over 200 of our pilots who operate out of Luton. He suggested that our members protest to us about the action that we have taken; there has not been one single response to his suggestion.

The problems of air traffic control in this area can be solved by competent professionals, as he states in his letter. I suggest he leaves it to them.

Hayes, Mddx
A. F. SHERMAN
General Secretary
the British Air Line Pilots' Association

Me : (to Mr Average Intelligent Man) Well, what do you think of it?
AIM : Well, I'm very sorry for you chaps, and I can see how rotten it is for you all, but obviously people mustn't be allowed to parachute around in front of aeroplanes landing full of fare-paying passengers.

Me : Of course, I must agree. Look at my next letter to *Flight*—

Luton's Airspace, BALPA and BGA

Sir, BALPA's reply to my letter (*Flight*, July 31) puts into very sharp focus the undesirability of what they are doing. They say they have not made this a public issue. In this week's Press there appears a report that they are considering increasing their pressure by instructing Luton pilots to ignore certain noise-abatement regulations. Did they, or did they not, leak this astounding suggestion to the Press?

BALPA now go on record that they are basing a case for a Special Rules Zone round Luton partly on a parachute display which they omit to say took place *inside the Luton Airport Traffic Zone*. The public, not knowing about this already existing zone, cannot be expected to spot the *non sequitur*, and may be consequently alarmed.

It is difficult to see how BALPA could make this elementary howler; but this sort of thing happens, even to competent professionals, when they attack a problem from the wrong end, with an intuitive certainty that they know the answer. So all the facts get rationalised, or even stood on their heads, in order to confirm it. May I plead that we do not get hot under our collars about this whole subject? I am not indulging in gamesmanship or sportsmanship, but propounding something of fundamental importance to our country.

I happen to have a good deal of experience of both sides of this problem, and we all have the identical aim—a high standard of safety.

The method of clamping on restrictions as soon as someone thinks there might be a danger, achieves such a standard; but in the process it must end by knocking more than half the aircraft now using it out of our sky—thus producing a Little Britain. Our proposals mean a bit more work—properly reporting and analysing the facts, and if they show one to be necessary, producing a system of control involving the minimum restrictions necessary to achieve the required standard of safety. This method achieves the same aim but allows everyone who wishes to do so to continue to use the air—a Great Britain.

There are today about 7,000 commercial aircraft in the world, and 170,000 others. Only about 1,000 of these others are in the UK, largely because, until quite recently, what could be called the BALPA approach prevailed. Do BALPA really think safety demands control round Luton in some ways more restrictive than those around the New York airports?

London SW1   P. A. WILLS

President, British Gliding Association

In the same issue of *Flight* appeared the following letter, indicating that the message was beginning to get over, at least amongst flying folk.

Luton's Airspace

Sir, The extraordinary personal attack made by Mr A. F. Sherman on the president of the BGA (Letters July 31) leaves unanswered the one vital question: 'What specific evidence is there to indicate the need for further restrictions on Luton's airspace?'

Personal attacks are no contribution. Some facts and figures would be.

Winchcombe, Glos   R. MARSHALL

Meantime, what was happening after the unexampled threat that BALPA would encourage their members to break the law regarding minimisation of noise?

The immediate result had been that Press and public had got it firmly in their minds that, from now on, Luton pilots would ignore all noise abatement regulations.

The Times published a Leading Article on 12 August:

Safety Around Airports

Safety in the air arouses strong emotions, and it is difficult to separate emotion completely from what has been happening in the air space around Luton airport. According to the British Air Line Pilots' Association, their members flying from the airport have been involved in several near misses with light aircraft. Any such incidents are strongly denied by the light flyers and gliding enthusiasts whose view has been supported by the Board of Trade, the responsible government authority in air traffic control and airport matters.

While they assert that there is no danger, the Board of Trade do want, however, to introduce a control zone for Luton into which no aircraft would be allowed to fly before receiving radio permission. Both light flying and gliding fraternities have violently objected to this proposal. The result is that lengthy discussions have been started and the zone will not be in operation before the end of the year.

Whatever the emotional content in the dispute, the proper way would have been to have reversed this procedure, to have introduced the control zone at the start of the busy summer air traffic season, and to have amended it as shown to be necessary by the subsequent talks. When the lives of hundreds of people both in the air and on the ground are possibly at risk the tortuous procedures of democracy must surely take second place to safety regulations.

The predicament at Luton raises far wider issues. National airport planning and the place that light aviation is to find in Britain's overcrowded skies are shown to be in need of urgent consideration. Should Luton, placed as it is in the middle of a whole complex of airfields—executive and sporting, manufacturers' and Royal Air Force—have been allowed by the Government to develop so much that it begins to rival Gatwick and Stansted in the numbers of passengers passing through? The Roskill commission, now considering the siting of the third London airport, will be doing the country a service if they include this question within their deliberations.

What is to happen to light flying in Britain as the jumbo jets and the supersonic airliners join the thickening stream of jets? As a sport it receives scant consideration from the authorities at present, and there is a danger that if the Luton case is repeated in the future the country will become hedged by control zones with light aircraft so constrained that the sport will become worthless. What is happening at Luton should provide the Government with an ideal opportunity for a full-scale inquiry into the uses of Britain's air space so that both heavy and light aviation can live together happily—and in safety.

On this occasion, Nick Goodhart's reply was published on the 15th, but a letter, published immediately after his, appeared to set us back again.

Safety Around Airports

Sir, In a leader (August 12) you bring out most clearly the difficulties facing the Board of Trade in solving the conflict in the Luton area between commercial aviation and the light aviation (including gliding) interests. However, your suggestion that the proper way to deal with the problem would have been to introduce a zone regardless of the need for it and then start discussions, verges on the shoot-first-and-ask-questions-afterwards philosophy. It would be just as reasonable to stop all vehicles other than lorries and coaches using the M1 on the grounds that private cars might contribute to a crash.

What is needed is, as you so rightly suggest, a full inquiry into the uses of Britain's airspace. Fortunately the National Air Traffic Control Service (a division of the Board of Trade) is and has been doing just this for some years and, while we in gliding have not always agreed that the controls it has introduced are the least restrictive necessary, we do believe that the required level of safety can best be maintained if all airspace users cooperate reasonably and unemotionally with the NATCS to reach acceptable solutions.

As an example of the difficulties facing NATCS it is of interest to note that more than half the aircraft over the United Kingdom do not operate within the air traffic control system, thus any expansion of controlled airspace for the benefit of those within it has an opposite effect in reducing airspace and thus increasing collision risk for those outside it.

It is also perhaps relevant to note that in 20 years of air traffic control in this country there has not been an air collision involving a commercial aircraft. Statistically, collision with the ground is the more important safety issue, not collision in the air.

Yours faithfully,

H. C. N. Goodhart,
Chairman Airspace Committee,
British Gliding Association

No Longer Peaceful

Sir, I have neither experience nor knowledge of aeronautics but surely it needs little of either to appreciate the danger in the situation at Luton Airport today. The British Airline Pilots' Association, we are told, has notified its members that when taking off from Luton they should ignore any noise regulations and apply full throttle, the better to gain height more quickly and thus avoid a fatal collision with one of the many private aircraft or gliders weaving and circling in the immediate area.

As the owner of a property lying squarely in the line of approach (or take-off, depending on wind) to one of the main runways at Luton, readers will appreciate what this means to my household in terms of noise. All too frequently is the peace of the summer weekend disturbed by successions of BAC 1-11s or Boeing 737s taking off with their loads of package tourists with rocket-like blast.

Notwithstanding this ear-splitting inconvenience I have every sympathy with the attitude of BALPA, having seen for myself the antics of some of the private flyers.

On one notable Sunday several weeks ago, when activity in and out of Luton Airport was no less heavy than usual, I watched as a succession of gliders were towed by Tiger Moths into the immediate approaches to Luton where they were promptly released, presumably to work their way back to the gliding centre on Dunstable Downs.

On another occasion, hearing a small aircraft engine under obvious stress, I ran into the garden in time to see a single-engined craft lazily performing aerobatics directly in the take-off path from Luton and at a height which at best would have created a close quarter situation or at worst a fatal disaster had there been a commercial aircraft gaining height at that moment. Moreover, as though to add to his seeming unawareness the pilot, having completed one loop, proceeded to repeat the performance twice more.

While certainly not wishing to curtail the enjoyment of the weekend pilot, it might be brought home very forcibly to him that no longer is Luton the relatively peaceful airport of yesterday. The age of the package tour is here to stay and Luton, for better or worse, is one of its chosen centres.

It is sincerely to be hoped that effective action is already being taken by the appropriate authority to rectify the situation; otherwise one would become tempted to encourage BALPA to ban the use of Luton altogether, or even to discourage the unsuspecting passenger from allowing himself to be whisked into the sky under such potentially dangerous conditions.

Yours faithfully,

MALCOLM FIMISTER
Blake Hall, Kensworth,
Nr. Dunstable, Bedfordshire

We took urgent steps to contact the Chairman of the London Gliding Club, who was away on holiday. Roger Barrett, the Vice Chairman, sent a reply published on 20 August.

Safety in the Air

Sir, Your leader on August 12 may have given the impression that glider pilots are less concerned about safety in the air than BALPA or, indeed, the Board of Trade. I should like to reassure you that this is not the case. The gliders we fly are mostly made of plywood and fabric and have a wing span of only about 50 feet, so we have every reason to support regulations that can be shown to reduce the chances of an air collision.

However, the present proposals for a control area around Luton are, in our view, unnecessarily restrictive; gliders would thereby be prevented from flying in large areas of airspace at times when aircraft from Luton would be using approach and take-off routes that would keep them several miles from any gliding activity. The British Gliding Association has therefore suggested modifications to the shape of the control area which, while in no way increasing the risk of collision, would still allow gliders to fly from Dunstable, as they have done for nearly 40 years.

Mr Fimister writes (August 14) that recently he watched Tiger Moths tow gliders into the immediate approaches to Luton Airport. He is undoubtedly correct in saying that he saw gliders in the airspace between Dunstable Downs and Luton. However, there already exists an aerodrome traffic zone around Luton airport, 3000 yards from its boundary and 2000 ft high, and no gliders or tug aircraft are permitted to enter this. In addition, pilots flying Tiger Moths from this Club are carefully briefed to avoid dropping gliders in areas outside this zone that could cause any embarrassment to aircraft flying into or out of Luton. Mr Fimister will be relieved to know that only yesterday the Senior Air Traffic Control Officer at Luton airport confirmed that he has never had any reason to complain about Tiger Moths towing gliders from this Club.

Both the Luton airport authorities and the Board of Trade have stated that the airspace around Luton is not dangerous. We believe this to be true and we are sure that a solution to the problem of conflicting interests over Luton airspace can be found that is acceptable to all parties concerned if the matter is considered rationally and not emotionally.

Yours faithfully,

ROGER Q. BARRETT,
Vice-Chairman, London Gliding Club,
Dunstable Downs, Bedfordshire

This resulted in a very friendly personal reply from Mr Fimister, and insofar as *The Times* was concerned, the thing seemed to have been buttoned up as well as possible.

But on 15 August, the subject was reopened by the *Evening News* in an article which read:

SCREAMING JET TERROR OF HOSPITAL BOY

A small boy, screaming with fright, almost fell from his hospital bed when a jet aircraft roared overhead.

The jet, from Luton airport, thundered over a children's ward just as the boy was coming round from an anaesthetic after a tonsils operation.

The incident illustrates the problem of aircraft noise at Luton and Dunstable Hospital Children's Annexe, say hospital chiefs.

The annexe, at London Road, Luton, is in line with the main runway and under the flight path of massive jets.

Noise has increased recently because many pilots are ignoring anti-noise procedures, and flying over the town at full throttle.

The pilot's union, the British Airline Pilots' Association, advised its 250 members using Luton Airport to ignore the rules, in the interests of safety.

Pilots claim that unrestricted light aircraft and gliders make Luton Airport dangerous, but noise abatement procedures force pilots to fly head down, with eyes on instruments instead of watching for hazards.

An MP, magistrates, town councillors and anti-noise campaigners have protested about the increased din.

After this, the ordinary reader must inevitably conclude that the glider traffic was forcing Luton pilots to fly low over the hospital, though in fact, no Luton pilot ever found it necessary to alter his normal take-off flight path during the whole of this or any other period. Yet every time anyone in the area was disturbed by aircraft noise, the tendency would be to blame the glider pilots.

Whilst all this was going on, we had of course other organs of the Press and radio to deal with, and whilst most were friendly, the general feeling was 'Bad luck on you chaps, but . . . progress you know, and all that.'

The *Daily Telegraph* was as sensible as usual, and published this on July 29th:

'AIR SAFETY BOX' PLAN THREATENS GLIDING

Representatives of glider and flying clubs are afraid that the creation of large 'air safety boxes' over Britain's minor airports would seriously endanger their sport. Only aircraft and gliders equipped with expensive radio equipment would be able to fly into the zones.

The situation arises from complaints by airline pilots using Luton, Bedfordshire, airport that there have been a number of 'near misses' between airliners and light aircraft in the airport area.

The pilots have recommended through the British Airline Pilots' Association the creation of a 'safety air box' around Luton of 11 miles by five.

If the 'box' were introduced it would seriously hamper Britain's largest gliding club at Dunstable. It uses the thermal currents from the Chilterns for its flights.

Light aircraft and gliders all carry three-channel radio, which costs about £120, giving them adequate communication in ordinary flying circumstances. To fly in the 'safety boxes' would mean having 360-channel radio, which would make gliding and weekend flying prohibitive for all but the richest people.

'We are as conscious of air safety as airline pilots,' an official of the British Gliding Association said yesterday, 'and if we accepted there were the dangers suggested by airline pilots we would immediately accept the proposed safety air zone.'

He added: 'But we feel the airline pilots should produce facts and figures to back up their claim that light aircraft are a danger.

'We are afraid that if a too-large safety zone is created at Luton the principle would be extended to all minor airports, which would virtually mean the end of gliding and weekend flying in this country.'

The Board of Trade who say that the flying situation at Luton is not at the moment dangerous, is to make a census in August of aircraft flying through the eleven by five mile safety box. It has also asked the British Airline Pilots' Association, gliding and flying clubs for technical evidence on flying conditions.

Flying clubs are asking the Board of Trade and Air Traffic Control Service to obtain evidence on the question of safety zones from America, which copes with a far greater volume of sporting and light aircraft than Britain's estimated 1000.

The British Airline Pilots' Association regard the danger factor in the Luton area so seriously that it is to discuss abandoning noise abatement procedures at Luton airport next month.

The use of full power would both enable pilots to climb to an altitude above that used by light aircraft more quickly and enable pilots, not having to watch instrument panels, to maintain better all-round observation.

An article in the 14 August issue of the *New Scientist* will form a tailpiece:

BATTERING RAM AT LUTON

When trade unions take industrial action to secure reasonable conditions for their members, the public usually bears the bulk of the inconvenience. That is the situation at Luton, where commercial pilots using the airport have just been given the support of their union in ignoring the regulations which, to reduce noise levels, govern take-off and climb. What makes this wrangle unusual is that the pilots have no grievance against their employers or against the Board of Trade's take-off rules. Their objection is to the failure so far of that government department to regiment those private flyers and glider pilots who take their lessons and their pleasure within a few miles of the airport. The gliding club has been on Dunstable Downs for more than 40 years: most of the flying clubs and schools were operating before Luton airport became commercially busy. But this gives them no inviolable right to free use of the air space when the cry of 'safety' is raised as it is in this instance.

Given freedom to use full power at take-off and on the climb, the airline pilots can get above the height of the amateurs before they arrive in their vicinity. That is what they are doing at present, to the distress of people on the ground, who have to endure the extra noise. They are, presumably, ready to revert to the muffled procedure if the Board of Trade sets up a 'special rules zone' around the airport. Within this zone all aircraft, whether commercial or private, would be subject to the air traffic controller. That would mean they would have to be equipped with radio. Furthermore, they would have to be capable of moving in accordance with instructions from control.

Both points make a difficult prospect for the glider pilots. They have had to cope hitherto with the threat of exclusive regulations in the neighbourhood of the air lanes which now run up and down and across the country, and have argued that the liners have little or no use for air space below 3000 ft. In the present argument, they are as desirous as the commercial pilots to ensure safety and the Board of Trade has held its hand while a full investigation of the risks and the possible plans for avoiding them is completed. Luton is little concerned with regular air services. Its business is mainly charter flights for packaged tours and is highly seasonal in character. Nevertheless, the town council which owns the airport and the operators who use it are anxious to dispel any suggestion of abnormal hazards lest the flow of traffic should suffer.

No support from these sources can be expected by the gliding club (the biggest in the country) and the aeroplane clubs. The town council and the Board of Trade are more likely to come under pressure from the public to let the commercial pilots have their way: and another example of the technique among the trade unions of using the public as a battering ram is in the making.

What consolation, if any, can we get from all of this? By the standards of the USA, the amount of traffic using Luton is, and always will be, derisory. Within 15 miles of Miami is an international airport handling more traffic than Heathrow, and 3 airfields handling over 400,000 movements of light aircraft a year, and no similar zones are dreamt of. Until we get our sense of proportion right on this subject of collision risk, we cannot hope to achieve our rightful place in the air.

But this was the very first occasion when we got some support from our Ministry for our case, and it must have required some political courage to stand up against the big boys. At least the Ministry insisted on time to get the facts of the case into focus, and the Press and public showed a dawning awareness that we have some right to continue to exist.

The end of it all was that six months later we got a zone imposed tailored in such a way as to enable the London Gliding Club to continue in existence.

But from this single instance it will be seen that the amount of spare-time work involved is almost insupportable and it is hard to see how we can keep it up.

Finally, during this time of stress and tension, I received a number of personal communications from individual members of BALPA saying how much they agreed with us, but that they dare not openly resist their Union's case.

6

∞

Fair Competition

BGA Council and marking systems

The Council of the British Gliding Association is a remarkable body. Each member, working of course in his or her spare time and for free, is a dedicated enthusiast. All are pilots, many extremely competent ones. Each shows the strange mixtures, common only in the gliding world, of fierce—even sometimes prickly—individualism and a strong sense of co-operation founded on a common cause.

Up to its reorganisation in 1969 the structure was such that, as the movement grew, so did the numerical size of Council. Thus by the end of my tenure of office as Chairman I had the increasingly intricate task of producing useful decisions over a large range of subjects, in say three hours, from a body consisting of over forty strong—and in some cases even pernicketty—individualists, including highly qualified experts in quite esoteric fields.

One curious outcome of this unusual human amalgam appeared to be that we always had one subject on which the entire Council would suddenly and irrationally lose its head. Not the same subject for the whole of my thirty-five years on Council, but as soon as one died down, another seemed to take its place. As an example, I will record the history of the competition marking system—the series of mathematical formulae applied to each flight of each pilot over the period of a competition, which decides the winning order at the end.

For a long time—at the time it seemed to be eternity, but it lasted possibly over two years—one of our monthly Council meetings would be proceeding smoothly and fairly efficiently, when up would come the subject of the marking system. Wearily the Chairman would don his oilskins and sou'wester, hoist the storm-flag, and tighten his safety-harness. Within five minutes pandemonium would reign.

Fists would crash on the table, eyes would bulge, lifelong friends would be at each other's throats. Out of the corner of his eye, the desperate Chairman would see the great head of Wally Kahn beginning to lower, whilst gravel began to spurt from under his sharp front hooves. With the inevitability of fate, down it would go, and off would gallop the roaring mass, horns at the ready, in a dead-straight line for the nearest, most expensive china-shop. As it went by, the Chairman would make a hopeless grab at the flying tail in a last-minute endeavour to deflect it by just the vital few degrees which might save the day. A few seconds later the crash of broken crockery would signify his utter failure.

Through all this hurly-burly, the Chairman should have been striding purposefully with soothing words, pointing out here an error in that v should surely be squared, not cubed, there that an integral function had been displaced, there again that surely the last speaker had slipped a cosine. But since the argument had long soared way out of sight over his head, he could do little more than utter occasional mollifying noises of the most general kind.

Gradually both the subject and its participants would become exhausted, and the meeting would mop its brows and pass on to the next item. Until, a month later, someone would have worked out the fallacies of the system finally agreed at the previous meeting, and up would come the whole darn thing again. . . .

After many months of this, there was only one quite clear conclusion to be drawn, and this was that there could not conceivably exist a marking system which was demonstrably fair and correct in all circumstances, so the depressing corollary of this was that the arguments could easily go on for ever. So it was extraordinary when one day I realised that over the past few meetings the monthly crescendo on the subject had actually been diminishing. At our next meeting I got a distinct illusion, as if a thermal bubble had broken away from the floor and was gradually ascending to the ceiling, carrying inside it the sound and fury of the argument. A few meetings later, all that could be heard was a distant hum as the last arc of the bubble disappeared through the roof—then all was calm.

Thinking it over afterwards, I came to a firm conclusion as to how this had happened. As the arguments and formulae had become more and more rarefied, one by one each member of Council had found they had soared out of his reach. One by one each individual, thinking he was the only dim-wit had therefore fallen silent. Eventually no one in the room understood the latest proposed system and peace reigned supreme. Since no one now understands the formulae, nowadays the marking system is done by a computer, of which the main advantage is that it cannot under any circumstances feel indignation.

That the latest system is no better or worse than any of its predecessors is shown by the fact that when occasionally someone applies all the marking systems used in the past to one particular competition, they all produce exactly the same winner. But it *is* better in one vital respect—it can only be worked out by an unemotional computer.

Fair marks

There are I suppose two basic motives which draw people into gliding. I might classify them as the Romantic and the Modern.

When I started—indeed when anyone started in the 1930s—it was undoubtedly the romantic appeal of real flight which captivated me, and which has remained my main pleasure through all the years. How can anyone resist the sheer fascination of being able to fly like a bird, the unexampled and manifold beauty of earth and air from the cockpit of a sailplane, the grace of the craft, the successful pitting of one's wits against the enormous powers latent in the atmosphere, the spice of danger, the comradeship of folk of like mind, the freedom and wonder of it all.

But as succeeding generations of pilots came in, the fact that it had been proved possible to fly without engines was inevitably taken for granted, and whilst Romantics kept on joining, an increasing number were attracted by the technical side—we are, after all, working on the edge of knowledge in our particular field, and the design of aircraft and instruments of increasing sensitivity and precision, the advance of micro-meteorological knowledge, and the mathematical calculations and theories of how best to get the maximum results out of a particular day's flying were and are indeed fascinating problems.

Now I am the last to deny the terrible and austere beauty of a major discovery of Science. Shakespeare in all his writings could not put together a statement so pregnant with meaning, so wondrous in its apparent simplicity, as did Einstein when he brought together into one net the apparently disconnected quantities of Mass, Energy and (of all things) the Speed of Light, and gave us the doom-laden statement: $E = Mc^2$, which transformed at one stroke the future of Man and his understanding of the Universe.

But this is beauty on too grand and harsh and impersonal a scale for most of us Romantics, and gradually the Romantics are being outnumbered by the Moderns, aided indeed by the direction of the development of society itself. An increasingly overcrowded world makes it more and more difficult to deal with a Romantic. He is apt to do the unexpected, which makes him difficult to organise. You can't put Keats on to a computer. A Great Britain composed of 52 million Romantics would be a bureaucratic impossibility—each would need a special Form for himself. There would not be enough magnetic tape to go round.

A gliding Romantic's favourite competition task is Free Distance, because it brings in a number of glorious uncertainties, such as where he is going to land, who he is going to meet when he gets down, when and how he is going to get back to base.

As commercial air traffic increases, so does the demand for more and more controlled airspace. The Free Distance task cannot be confined to a comparatively small area. Horrors! The result of the day may even involve an element of Luck! It might not be *fair*.

This dreadful word 'fair' is, I submit, at the root of many of our country's troubles. Strikes take place, not because men think they are underpaid, but because they think it isn't fair that other men elsewhere should be paid more. If ever Great Britain finally sinks beneath the waves, the last words coming from state-rooms, as the Union Jack at the masthead finally disappears, will be, in a whining roar, 'It isn't *fair*!'

God is the Great Actuary. Anyone believing the nonsense about sparrows is heading for intellectual contortionism or a cynical atheism. Tell it to the Brontosaurus, the Incas, Bushmen, Australian Aborigines, or Red Indians.

What we have to realise, in gliding as in life, is that the Universe is not constructed to be 'fair'. We can ameliorate its unfairness, but beyond a certain point this process becomes merely deadening. Our tax system has become so complex as to be incomprehensible, all in the pursuit of fairness, with a damping effect on human effort which is almost universally recognisable. And precisely the same fate, in our much smaller field, has overtaken our Competition Scoring system.

The Modern enthusiast has, by definition, a precise mind. Everything must be accurately measurable, and two plus two must be exactly four. What he fails to realise is that all the techniques, all the sciences, involved in our sport lead up to finding out something that is only very approximately quantifiable. He wants—we all want—to find out who amongst us is the Better Pilot—or more exactly, the better combination of pilot, instruments and team. And most of us want to know this in order to learn how to improve our skill, though some may need the more elementary proof of their superiority over the rest. This we attempt by all flying against each other in competitions, when on each day each pilot is set the same task, and everyone's achievement is measured against the most successful pilot on that day.

Now the measurement of performance on a free distance flight is superficially easy—you can persuade yourself that if Smith flies 100 miles and Jones only 50 miles, Smith should get twice the marks. But since the last war, for various good and some not-so-good reasons, distance flying has increasingly given way to speed flying over a set course. How does one fairly equate Smith, covering the course at 40 mph, against Jones who only achieves 20 mph?

The whole fallacy at the heart of this subject is the pretence that you can accurately measure something which is only very approximately measurable—pilot skill. A marking system presents one of the most remarkable of confidence tricks—it actually persuades highly intelligent people that it can do the impossible, and these people then act on this assumption.

At the end of the competitions, out of a total possible 7,000 marks, Smith may come 10th with 5,000 marks and Jones 9th with 5,005 marks. People really believe that Jones is 0·1 better a pilot than Smith—whose future gliding life may be substantially affected by this piece of nonsense.

As an example, on a race day the most skilled pilot may achieve the goal, but only after a long slow struggle, when another less skilled one lands short, rushes back for a second start, the weather unexpectedly improves, and he covers the course which has now become easy, more rapidly than his competitor. So the marking systems announces that he is the most skilled.

Now your Modern will say of such a day 'I had much rather we had not flown at all', whilst the Romantic will say 'Nonsense, it was a *lovely* day, full of beauty and interest. I am a better man as a result of it, I have learnt a little more, I came here primarily to *fly*. If a bit of bad luck crept in as far as I was concerned, it will cancel itself out next time.'

In my time I have had my fair share of bad luck.

In the 1948 World Championships the organisers gave us Peravia barographs. They installed the charts each day, set and sealed the instruments, and we put them in the gliders. On the only important height day, I achieved a clever climb to some 15,000 ft in cloud, but on landing, the chart had snarled itself up. I dropped at least 10 places.

At a later World Champs, I was all set to become World Champion for the second time. Unfortunately, on the last task someone who should have known much better at base overheard a radio message to Kitty that I had found a wave in a most unexpected place. He incautiously spread this good news around, my nearest runner-up heard it, took off after he had decided to give up for the day, and flew far enough just to beat me.

But I have also met more than compensating good luck. I can think of at least two flights from which nothing but luck brought me back alive—and one can't ask more from luck than that.

Placing systems

The alternative to a marking system is a placing system. This too has its defects, but is a good deal easier to understand. The furthest or fastest pilot gets 1 point, the second furthest or fastest 2 points, and so on. At the end, the pilot with *least* points is the winner.

For various reasons, it can't be quite as simple as that, but a lot of work on placing systems has been done (and published) by C. E. Wallington and others, and the result is still comprehensible to all, including the Press and public.

The objections are: (1) The system will not produce a highly
selective result—there will tend to be a number of '1st equals',
'2nd equals' and so on. But this simply acknowledges the fact—that
we cannot measure this particular quantum except rather coarsely.
Thus the result of a placing system would be 'fairer' than those of
any marking system.

(2) A placing system may not produce a 'pilots' rating list'. This
dreadful requirement arises from the fact that more pilots want to
participate in a Championship than can be handled at one time. So
some list of merit has to be produced—and it has to be felt to be
'fair'.

A placing system may result in a bundle of 1st, 2nd and 3rd
equals. So to sort this out, a committee of wise men should meet, to
bring in other considerations. Smith and Jones are 2nd equals. One
is to represent us at a World Championship.

Which is likely to give the best impression to the world as a
representative of his country? Which pilot is the better sportsman?*
Which does more good work for the gliding movement? Which is
likely to survive a Bad Luck day with fortitude and good humour,
and fly as well on the subsequent days? Which is likely to keep the
team together as a harmonious whole? Which has the more robust
constitution, likely best to cope with the odd times, food and
climate of Ruritania? Which is more likely to analyse and bring
back lessons and information which will enable us to improve our
standards in this country?

We have as nearly as possible measured their ability as pilots, and
found them equal. These other more subjective considerations
should now be taken into account.

(3) The third objection to a placing system is, in fact, that it is *too*
'fair'. After a single bad day, no stroke of genius or gambling shot at
an extremely difficult flight can enable a pilot to recover.

In a difficult day he may fly 300 miles against the next best flight
of only 100 miles—and will only score a single point more. So the

---

* I have heard a whole nation damned by the comments of the teams of 25 other
countries based on the behaviour of a single pilot flying for it. Because he was judged
a bad sportsman 'they' were all tarred with the same brush. I could write a whole
chapter on the misuse of the terrible word 'they'. It is a tool which ruthless politicians use to drive decent people to kill and maim each other in wars. Jones is a bastard.
Jones is an Englishman. Therefore all Englishmen are bastards. Kill them!

placing system favours the steady plodder. It knocks out good luck, but cannot eliminate bad luck, which it makes drearily irremediable.

But we Romantics must never give up. Maybe the increasingly overcrowded world must lead to more 'fairness' and less adventure. Maybe the 'grey-faced men who have traded life for experience and security for ambition' must increasingly take over the direction of our planet. But the colour of suicide is not Black, it is Grey. Let us battle on as long as we may, for one day, if we lose, I suspect the whole thing will blow up. Man does not live by fairness alone, and sometimes another word for that is—envy.

A really splendid bit of bad luck

Let me here interpolate one of the flights I shall always remember. A curious point about this day is that, if the mistake had not been made I might even have won the Championships, but my flight would have been infinitely less rewarding. A Modern would maintain that if there is to be an undue element of chance in the day, he would rather stay on the ground. A Romantic says, to experience such a flight as this is worth a hundred successful race days.

In 1966, I was invited to fly in the Italian National Championships flown from their National Centre at Rieti.

The sixth task set was a seemingly innocuous 101-km triangle over a well-beaten course: Rieti–Piedi Paterno–Poggia Azzuono–Rieti. It was probably set as a kind of semi-holiday after the ardours of Free Distance, which we had flown two days before and spent the whole of the next 24 hours in getting back from. I had myself flown over the various legs during the previous week in practice or in different tasks. The weather forecast was the usual—hot blue sun, thermals up to 9,000 ft by 14:00 hrs, a few Cu over mountain tops, surface wind light north-west, upper wind 20 kts at 10,000 ft. After Task 4 I had been in the lead; now I was a few points behind Giorgio Orsi in his SHK. This was the day.

Now let me try and set the scene—a nearly impossible task for those who have never seen the almost absurdly dramatic geography of the Italian Apennines. (See map, p. 130.)

Rieti is at the southerly point of a green, flattish circular valley, about 10 miles across, surrounded by mountains. The easterly wall starts with Monte Terminillo (a fashionable Roman ski-resort), 7,000 ft, and this range runs north, with spurs running out into the plain until you come to the precipitous gorge of the Val Neroni, running east and then north-east from Terni. The Val Neroni is nearly 3,000 ft deep, and at its bottom only a hundred-or-two yards wide. This area is more than fully occupied by a mountain stream, a road, a railway, and a few occasional tiny fields. For perhaps 15 miles it is one of the literally unlandable bits of the local countryside.

From the turning-point in the Val Neroni, the course runs south-west over the containing wall of the valley, into the Perugian plain at its southern-most edge, where Spoleto huddles round its medieval fortress and cathedral, under shadow of the mountains, to the south. Flying along this north-facing series of mountains, the course now crosses a narrow valley running south to Terni out of the south-west corner of the plain, over the south-west mountains to the second turning-point in the valley of the Tiber, then south-east over Terni (another large and unlandable area, occupied largely by power wires and steel works) over the final range of mountains and back into the Rieti bowl.

It sounds frightful—in standard August conditions it is a piece of cake.

But the organisers had an Idea. It was one that lost me whatever chance I had of winning, but I bear them no malice whatever, for it gave me, as I have said, one of the most exciting and instructive flights I have ever had. And I was later told that the poor chaps had only been given three days in which to run up the whole organisation, so they performed miracles in doing what they did.

Instead of using the previous turning-point, they had found a new one—a television reflector on top of one of the mountains hedging the Val Neroni. Now one of the rules was that each competitor must photograph the signal displayed at each turning-point, so it was jolly important to know exactly where this was to be displayed.

An aerial photograph was put up, and a lot of Italian went on, but from what I could understand, the photo did not seem to line up with the map. The photo seemed to mean that the point must be on one of the mountains on the east side of the valley, but the organisers insisted that actually it was the west. So, to make sure, after briefing

was over, I went up and got one of the chiefs to mark the actual
point on my map.

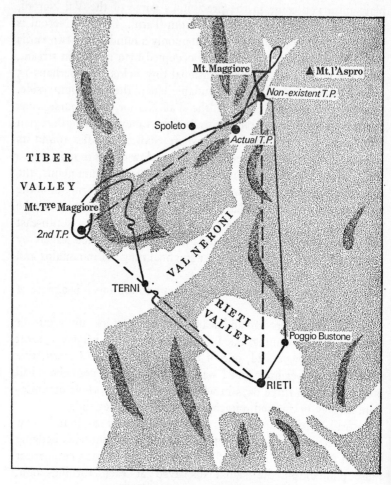

Rieti, Italy, and its environs to the north

Take-off was at 14:30, a thermal over Rieti took me to 3,000 ft, a
sniff at the mountain walls of Terminillo to 5,000 ft, and back to
dive across the start-line at 3,100 ft and 120 kts, north-east to
Poggio Bustoni, clinging to its mountain wall like a host of limpets,
straight into 5 kts up to 7,000 ft, an exhilarating dash along the first

leg, a sniff of 5 up over the mountains on Val Neroni opposite the turning-point, and straight as a dart over the valley to the dot on my map.

No television mast—no ground signal.

At this point, as I discovered much later, the field split up into various well-defined sections. There were those, mostly locals, who knew where the darned thing was anyway, and had not even listened to the briefing. Amongst these, Manzoni dashed round to claim an Italian record, only to find that the 101-km course had shrunk in the wash to 98 km. Hard cheese. There were others who had a general lie of the land in their heads and after around ten minutes' searching found it. There were some brave spirits who, after scratching around for anything up to half an hour, photographed the point they had been given and set off on the second leg—which then took them within sight of the blooming mast. And there was me.

I reasoned that the mast was likely to be on the highest point in the vicinity—4,700-ft Monte Maggiore, to the north. (It was actually 4 km. south on a much lower one.) I just had height to get there and see that it displayed no signals area, then fell away—on the east side, into the Val Neroni. The north-west wind coming over Maggiore then ensured I was swept down to a level making it impossible to get out. The problem of beating Giorgio's time round the course faded into insignificance—I *had* to get out, if it took the rest of the day.

The analysis didn't take very long. In the absence of a tunnel-boring machine I couldn't go east or west. There was no chance of getting lift in the valley, because any wind must blow along it and there were no spurs running out from its walls to obstruct its flow and make it rise. I couldn't fly south along it; that way was un-landable for at least 25 km. But I had some 2,500 ft in hand, and the map showed that if I flew about 8 km north, the valley split into two, and at that point any winds coming down the two forks must meet, and in their conflict, produce lift. The $64,000 question was whether there *were* any winds all that way below, but when I got there, there were, and they did. But it took an hour; I wasn't going to hurry things, particularly as, in the fork, I had spotted a FIELD! (It would have been an interesting retrieve for Kitty. Motoring up the Val Neroni, looking for a glider, would have given her the jim-jams.)

Anyway, an hour later the onlooker at Spoleto would have seen me lift over the skyline again, and now I decided to set course for the second turning-point, and damn the consequences. Ten minutes later, of course, I passed over the first one, but it whisked by too fast for me to photograph it—if they hadn't observed me after that, it would be too bad.

The day was now virtually over, it was around 18:00 hrs and lift was dying. To hell with it, I *would* get round.

The southern rim of the Perugian plain is hedged by north-facing mountains, so in the north-west wind lift was not too hard to find, but it was not going very high. However, Spoleto landing field was for most of the time in range, and I caught up with one unfortunate who, being lower than me yet still airborne, put heart into me in the uncharitable way it always does.

I crossed the valley running north–south to Terni out of the south-west corner of the plain; now I had to get across the west wall of mountains out to the turning-point at their far foot—in a field near the foot of a range running exactly up and down the north-west wind. How on earth was I to keep going then? The only thing was to suck it and see.

The wind blowing down the Perugian plain was, of course, funnelled into the narrow valley running south to Terni, so there was no problem in getting enough height to cross the westerly range, and then I found a little tree-covered spur running out across the wind which gave me a beat of perhaps 200 yards to its summit at 1,500 ft. From this I managed to dash out to the turning-point, which I rounded at 1,000 ft, and flew back to my spur like a yo-yo, observing as I did a couple of gliders landed in a field whose hedges were so near their wingtips and tails that they looked as if they must have been planted after the aircraft had landed. The gliders looked gift-wrapped, like one of those Christmas boxes of handkerchiefs.

I plodded up and down my little spur, pondering the next leg. The straight line clearly wasn't on. It took one 10 miles over flat valley to Terni, power wires and all, and all thermal lift was gone—only sun-assisted slope lift remained. I badly needed an Idea myself.

An extra heave of lift gave me 2,000 ft, 500 ft above my spur, and I got it. I cut back on my tracks over the range, into the Spoleto–Terni valley, and turned south. At its southernmost point a 3,500-ft

L-shaped mountain (also called Mt Maggiore) obstructed its exit to the Terni valley, and I flew into its embracing arms with the near certitude that this was my way home. But there were still problems to overcome. The 'L' ran north–south, and then west–east. The sun was now so low that in the shadow of the north–south arm it was almost dark, whereas the north-facing stony slope of the west–east arm was a glowing gold. I reached this at about 1,500 ft and found gentle lift, but when I turned west at the end of my beat, flying, as usual, a few feet from the rocky wall, now on my left, I found myself flying at a black mass which could have been anything from 200 to 500 yards away. This constricted my area of operation more than somewhat, because the beat was so short and each turn away from the slope lost me lift. But patience did it, and perhaps 20 minutes later I topped my mountain at 3,000 ft and saw Terni, and beyond its southern mountains the gleam of the lakes in the Rieti plain.

More, I saw the smoke from Terni steelworks, huddled under the next mountain walls, rising in unmistakable lift, which made it a certainty that I could adventure over the town without having to risk a nearly impossible landing on its outskirts.

Which is what happened. I reached the smoke at 1,500 ft. It was the nicest horrible smell I have ever smelt. It was going up. It took me to 3,000 ft again, and a last fast final glide to Rieti, landing at 19:30 hrs. There I found Kitty hitched up and waiting for my phone call. Everyone else had been down for an hour and a half. An aeroplane had been sent out to locate the missing turning-point, and its pilot came up to tell me where it really was. I told him I had found out, the hard way.

But it was a wonderful day.

Speed versus romance

This last flight became most enjoyable because, although a set speed triangle, it came unstuck. But most speed tasks limit one's range of possibilities tremendously.

For one thing, there is no selection of the start time. All gliders are lined up on the field in a grid, the organiser decides when launching is to commence, and after becoming airborne everyone wants to wait around the start line until conditions are steaming and rush over it in a queue. Then, of course, the pilot is pinned to the set course together with everyone else, so flies round it in gaggles—only the leader of the moment is on his own. Climbing in a cloud of other sailplanes is a very beautiful experience, but does cramp one's style —the individual pilot who does something unexpected is apt to be unpopular and even dangerous. To me, a speed task round a set course is like corsets on a beautiful girl: it sets limits to one's imagination.

Yet, sadly enough, speed tasks are becoming the rule rather than the exception, and in some countries Free Distance is now altogether excluded in their competitions. For other reasons, cloud-flying is also becoming rarer—again in some countries it is prohibited altogether, on grounds of safety.

This is absolute nonsense, because in fact without cloud-flying, the risk of collision in contest flying is *increased*. The reason is that in such cases, every pilot will climb in clear air as high as he possibly can, and break off just at cloud-base. Thus one gets a large number of sailplanes all at exactly the same height and scuttering along in the ragged base of the cloud with very poor visibility.

I know this is against the regulation, which is that one must keep at least 1,000 ft below the height of cloud-base; but this is one of those scandalous rules which are made to protect the chairborne bureaucrat and not the pilot—for how can the pilot know when he reaches 1,000 ft below cloud-base unless he first climbs up to cloud-base to find out how high it is? The base of one cloud is quite often different in height to the base of the next one, and on most days cloudbase gets higher as the day goes on.

A curious feature is that it is the Anglo-Saxons who are still fighting against this castration of our sport, whilst most European countries are more or less willingly accepting these restraints: indeed in the 1970 World Championships in Texas there was very strong pressure put on the Americans by a majority of countries not to have Free Distance as a task at all, and they were successfully prevented from permitting pilots to select their own starting times, thus taking one more initiative from the pilot and putting it into the hands of the organisers.

One of the most popular competitions in Europe nowadays consists exclusively of speed flying round triangular courses, with no cloud-flying. If the pilot fails the course and lands out he is not permitted a second start, so there is no hurry to get back for a relight, consequently the retrieving teams can bask all day in the local swimming bath. I have no doubt this is good fun for some, but it bears no relation at all to the kind of fun Kitty and I have had over our gliding life: I would compare it as Coca-Cola to champagne, although admittedly it bears something of the same relationship in cost. Like any emasculation, it saves everyone a great deal of effort and trouble, at the expense of colour and romance. You will come back from such a meeting knowing little more about the country you have been flying over than when you arrived. You will not have experienced the friendly expertise of the little blacksmith in Grotta Minardo, who at 7 a.m. repaired your damaged trailer; you will not have met the Oklahoman farmer who, whilst you were waiting for Kitty to arrive, had discussed with you the differences between life in London and Hobart, whilst the cicadas chirped in the tree overhanging his farm and the warm grateful smell of his maize-fields expanding their lungs in the cool of the evening saturated the air. You will have missed being stabbed to the heart by the sad intolerable beauty of the girl in the funeral cortege in Roca di Botti, on a ledge overlooking the wide Italian valley lit by the westering sun, and the fugitive light in the cottage near Tuczna which was doused as you tiptoed up in the night to ask how to get to your Skylark stranded nearby in the Pripet marshes. Above all, you will not have experienced the warm glow of affection as the orange beams of the Standard's headlights suddenly lance the horizon after you have spent night hours dozing under your sailplane's wing in a far foreign field and you know that Kitty and your team have, in spite of all the confusions, found you again.

The dichotomy was trenchantly focused by Nick Goodhart, when at the 1970 Symposium of Competitive Soaring in Pittsburgh, Pennsylvania, he made this downright pronouncement: 'Let's face it, you are really only a computer sitting there, and your job is to assess all the inputs and outputs available. Some of them tend to be rather more interesting, but really not so valuable.'

If this is what we really want, we can bring this philosophy nearer complete achievement by:

(a) Scrubbing Free Distance and all open-ended tasks.

(b) Washing out pilot-selected starts.

(c) Sending up 'thermal-snifters' to explore the air before a competitor is allowed to take-off, to make sure no one starts before it is quite certain everyone, in lead-sleds or whatever, can stay up. This effectually knocks out the blighter who might enter with a low wing-loading aircraft and whisper off before the others on a hairline edge of skill and luck; it also distorts design, because no one is going to buy such an aircraft if it has no chance in contest flying.

(d) No tasks are ever set on doubtful days.

(e) Cloud-flying is prohibited.

(f) Second launches after an outlanding are forbidden—although I accept these should be prohibited for short speed-tasks, because these are computer-jobs anyway, so it is no good pretending otherwise.

You have then got everything set up for the human computer to win. But you would still be better off with the electronic variety, because the human one can still have two weaknesses. The first is that, hard as he tries, he may reduce his chances by being interested in something irrelevant such as the sheer joy of life, and the second is that, unlike the computer, he will *want* to win, and he might want to win so much that he might cheat.

The Modern believes that Genius is an infinite capacity for taking pains, whilst the Romantic agrees this, but adds a vital increment— an additional occasional flash of inspiration.

PART TWO

What it's all about

7

ᘛᘚ

The Romantic Air of Italy

Love at first sight

We came to Italy late in life, through an invitation to fly in their 1961 National Championships. It was probably General Nannini, the hero of a pre-war east–west Atlantic crossing with a number of Italian flying-boats, whose enthusiasm for gliding makes him in my view the father of Italian gliding in the modern sense, who had the idea of inviting a number of foreign pilots to fly in these Championships, and thus weigh up their skills and equipment against the home talent.

I like to think that this produced the same jump forward for Italian gliding that our own expedition to the German Internationals at the Wasserkuppe in 1937 had done for us.

The Italians have a Central Gliding School at Rieti, in the heart of the Apennines about 65 miles north of Rome, but in 1961 they decided to hold their Championships at Santa Egidia airfield, near Perugia, about 50 miles further north. So this was where the Wills family first came into contact with Italy and Italian gliding, and this opened up for us a new and serendipitous country, a host of new friends, and some of the most romantic and lyrical flying in the world.

Take a long peninsula 100 miles wide running north–south, arrange one or two chains of mountains running down its middle, surround it on either side with warm calm seas, cover the lot in dry, clear, blue and very stable anticyclonic air, and wait for the summer sun to climb into the sky, when the most delightful things will happen.

The sun shining on the land and the uneven escarpments of the mountains will force the air, however reluctantly, to start rising. Sea breezes will start to blow in from both sides at once. They will strike the mountain sides, be deflected by the unevenly distributed valleys and mountain spurs, and eventually start to form high shallow cumulus. Down in the valleys between the mountain chains the prevailing winds in the upper air will be deflected to run north–south or south–north along them, and the task of the sailplane pilot at low levels will be deliciously complicated. But once in the upper air clear of the mountain tops life will be gloriously easy. And some time in the afternoon the opposing sea-breezes will meet somewhere over the highest mountain chain and form nice digestible cumulo-nimbus clouds, with bases safely above the summits and tops running up to 15/20,000 ft. Then, as the sun begins to set, the basic stability of the air will begin to reassert itself, and waves will be superimposed on the slowly dying thermals.

Inhabit this country with a dynamic and friendly people with a 2,000-years history of artistic sensibility, stir well, and take your glider to Rieti in August. Then proceed with care, for the mountains are hard, ditto the rather few landing fields, and it is not gliding for children.

This is Italy, the paradise of the Romantic glider pilot.

One clue to the Italian character lies in the fact that, in the Middle Ages, every Italian town and village had to be in some sense a fortress, hence a very large number are perched on the tops of steep and precipitous hills. How they arranged their water supply I don't know, probably they needed far less water in those days than we can imagine. But with the coming of the 20th century, and the need for water, road and rail communications and the like, a very high standard of civil engineering became essential. We saw many of the ancient marvels of Rome, Venice and elsewhere, but one of the most abiding memories of the wonders we saw was the incredible new road from Florence, north across the mountains to Bologna. This fantastic highway runs for 60 miles and more, either suspended in space on viaducts and embankments or else diving through mountainsides in tunnels. It is one product of a race of engineering giants, fit successors to the creators of the vast architectural wonders of Rome.

The modern system of Autostrade is revolutionising communication in Italy, because they adopt the simple basic plan of running relatively straight and flat along the valleys, with spurs going off on each side to each mountain-top town. But the existing road-system does the reverse.

Gliding championships in Italy, therefore, present not only the most fascinating and beautiful flying for the pilot, but also the most arduous test for retrieving-teams and equipment. For road distances are up to *double* air distances, and average speeds of around 25 mph with the trailer are as much as can be achieved. Thus a flight of 100 miles may involve 400 miles for the retrieving team, in great heat by day, and it will be at least 16 hours, if all goes well, before the pilot and crew will reach home.

The longest flights of the 1961 meeting took place on 7 August, when we were set the task of flying as far as we could along a line to the south-east. We were told at briefing that if two pilots flew further than 200 km (120 miles), the following day would be a rest day, and if two flew more than 300 km (190 miles), the following two days would be rest days. At the time I was surprised, but in the event two of us exceeded the greater distance, and indeed it was the morning of the third day before we were ready to fly again, with over 750 miles added to the mileometer of the Vanguard that towed our trailer.

How to describe central Italy through the eyes of a glider pilot? It is a country of valleys, some wide and some mere clefts, and tumbled hills and mountains. The wider valleys are more or less densely cultivated, some so densely that a landing is literally impossible. In the whole valley of the Arno from the coast to Florence, some 50 miles, and for a radius of 30 miles round Naples, although the ground is flat there is literally not one single open field in which one can land. But although elsewhere the fields look, from ground level, too small and overgrown with olives and vines and maize, from the air one can see a fair number of possible areas. On the lower hills and mountains there are frequently much larger fields, but heaven knows how one's trailer would reach the aircraft if one landed there. The high mountains to the east, rising up to 9,000 ft in the Gran Sasso, are not of course landing country, but as long as one keeps sufficient altitude in hand to get away from them in case of need, they don't have to be.

The valleys are olive-green and brown, the mountains dark green and brown and grey. The summer air is hazy with brown dust, the sky overhead a dusty blue. The ground is dry and hard, and a field which looks smooth and friendly from the air will, on contact with your skid, give you and your glider's frame a severe test. After each day's flying, the repair hangar would be full of inverted fish-like hulls of gliders, holes being patched after minor landing mishaps.

The airfield of Santa Egidia is in the valley itself half way between the hilltop town of Perugia to the west and Assisi to the East, itself perched on a steep outlying spur of the 4,000 ft Monte Subasio. Little could St Francis have dreamed that his monastery and the adjacent town would in the 20th century provide the ideal starting point for Icarus in real life; for, baking in the sun, Assisi produced a permanent thermal in which each morning we were launched by aero-tow. Each morning 30 beautiful man-made birds, *una rombante e policromo carusella*, would circle and climb over Assisi, fly on to the vast slopes of Subasio, weave and rise above them, then set off on the flight of the day. But the saint's sympathy for flying things may have been called into play the first day, when two circling gliders overhead collided and plunged to destruction: both pilots miraculously escaped by parachute, and the machines—the Spillo and a Kanguro—missed the town and littered themselves harmlessly amongst the trees on the mountainside beyond.

This gave us all, at briefing on the second day, a somewhat uneasy ten-little-nigger-boys feeling, but turned out to be the only serious accident of the meeting. There were one or two lucky escapes, notably when one pilot took off without connecting his elevator controls. This is the accident which neither man nor God can usually forgive, but on this occasion God at least relented and the pilot—though not the unfortunate aircraft—escaped un-scathed.

The streets in the old walled towns and villages of Italy and the mountain roads, seem to have been built only for donkeys (and very wayward ones at that) so we felt with our car and trailer quite out of place and peculiar, like something from outer space, as we twisted our way along up to clusters of lights which looked like stars above us at night, because the only road inevitably went up to the little towns built on top for protection and then down the other side.

Vanessa, Justin and I were Philip's team and we were given an Italian boy to help with the language. Sometimes we shared ourselves out to Brennig James who had arrived relying on local help which could not always be spared from the hardworking organisation.

The Italians were charming and always very helpful, never made us feel out of place and everywhere coped with our requests and troubles sympathetically and efficiently. When our back light failed, the short was found and mended with enormous enthusiasm by half the town of Frosinone while we waited to get through to Perugia for news.

For our second retrieve, the task was a race to Pescara. We found no news at our first stop, Foligno airfield, but were given large slices of lovely cold water-melon by the family who were starting their lunch in the kitchen. On the next stretch to Rieti we fell in behind Brennig's trailer with Italo driving and Vanessa map reading.

At Terni there is a level crossing and as we came up to it the wooden arms began to wave violently. This is the Italian for 'here comes a candle to light you to bed' so of course we ducked and rushed across, but then to Justin's and my surprise the trailer in front of us suddenly reared up. The front had come adrift from the towbar, but this was nothing, we made holes in the wood and tied it down again. This was really nothing for later the mudguards fell off and then later still it suffered two caesarians, but our trailer also had its troubles, for on the Italian roads everything gets a good hammering. At Rieti we hear that Brennig has arrived at Pescara but that Philip is short. Never mind, we were in for the most wonderful drive, my only regret being that there was not much time to look out, what with twiddling the wheel, watching the temperature gauge and avoiding and trying to pass eighteen-wheel monsters which always seemed to come out in the mountains. To get to Philip the quickest way was over the Gran Sasso, the highest mountain in the Apennines and our car boiled repeatedly.

The country looked so wild when it became dark, that Justin and I shivered in our shoes expecting bandits to arrive at any moment during our repeated radiator-filling operations. However all went well and with luck we hit off the right small road at about 23:00 with a nice little crowd of children and the glider and Philip all waiting for us.

It would take too long to describe in detail each of the eight tasks
we flew, for although each had its own interests and glories, they
were basically in the same conditions. I won the first, a 100-miles
out-and-return race to Rieti and back. On the second, a race across
the mountains to Pescara on the Adriatic coast, I lost myself in the
high mountains and flew out east to safety but a low placing. This
gave me a lot of leeway to make up, which I did laboriously but
successfully, winning the fourth, fifth and seventh tasks, emerging
at the top, and holding it easily on the last day. This turned out to be
a valuable victory, for because of it we met the Orsis.

The Orsis

After the excitements of our fortnight's flying from Perugia, we
planned to spend a week having a more conventional look at some of
the beauties of Italy. So the four of us, Kitty, Vanessa, Justin and I,
towed the trailer up to Vergiate, the airfield then occupied by
the Centro Studio del Volo a Vela Alpino, north of Milan, left
it there, and ran east along the Autostrada for a few days in
Venice.

A week later, we arrived back in the evening light at Vergiate,
saturated with gondolas, St Mark's, Doge's palaces and all. We were
hooking up the trailer ready for an early start in the morning, over
the Simplon pass and back to England, when in the half-light a
short, square, dark man came up and introduced himself as Giorgio
Orsi. After a few minutes talk he asked us to his home for
dinner.

We had heard at Santa Egidia something of this unusual man, how
as a wealthy enthusiast he had set himself with intensity and genero-
sity to develop his club at Varese; how his wife Adele, also an enthusiast, had rapidly become the foremost woman glider pilot in
Italy. It did not take us very long to decide to accept his invitation,
unhitch the Skylark, and follow him in his Jaguar to his house on the
outskirts of Varese.

San Pedrino—we have been there since then, and it has never
lost for us the touch of magic. A three-storied L-shaped old house,
set on a low hill on the outskirts of Varese. From the terrace in
front of the west-facing wing, a view over the green tree-covered

plain, with a glimpse of the Lago di Varese in the middle distance. A quarter-circle of the prospect is bounded by the snowcapped high Alps, running up to Monte Rosa, furled in flame in the setting sun, thence the mountains diminishing in perspective over the horizon.

We came to it that first evening in the last light, and had hardly caught our breaths when we were indoors being introduced to Adele. I hope she will forgive me if I say she is like a small, determined fairy princess, and one can see her face in some of the paintings of the old Italian masters—one of her ancestors actually was one.

We—Giorgio, Adele, their children, the governess, and the four Willses—sat down to dinner amidst a stream of gliding talk, and towards the end, Giorgio turned to me and said, out of the blue: 'Now, Mr Wills, I am, as you know, doing all I can to develop Italian gliding, and particularly our club in Varese. I have made it possible for them to get a new airfield, we are going to equip it with a hangar and clubhouse, and a number of gliders and tow-planes. Adele has been doing well, and has just got her Silver C. But so far I haven't myself been able to get very far, and I think that what I need now is a really good glider. You have just shown at St Egidia that your Skylark 3 is an excellent machine, and what I wish to ask you is: will you sell it to me?'

There was an instant's petrified silence, then a babel of family protest. 'No, Daddy you *can't*! The Skylark is part of the family! We've just washed it and curled it and mothered it through the length and breadth of Italy and we *can't* leave it behind!'

I looked at Giorgio. 'You see?' I said.

'Oh dear,' he said, 'I really do mean it! Have some more Vino Sacro —it's from our own vineyard.'

The children went to bed, and the argument went on. Taking advantage of a minute whilst Giorgio was out of the room, I turned to Adele.

'Look, you can see that this is a little awkward and unusual. We haven't met before, and I can't tell whether or not this is the whim of a rich man, who would later regret it. I don't want to leave the Skylark, and above all I don't want to take advantage of such a man as your husband. Is he really serious?' She replied simply, 'Yes, he is serious.'

'Well,' I said, 'It is true that the Skylark is not only a good machine, but also one that is easy to fly. I can see that it is really important, if he is determined, that he should start with one that will be safe. So if you and he still want it, we will leave it for you.'

And that is what we did. In the Vanguard, next morning, no one spoke to me till, over the Alps, we were nearing Geneva.

But this was the beginning, not the end, of the story. For the following spring I started getting letters from Giorgio. The Skylark was wonderful. It had opened up to him the air. He had done his first cross-country flight. He had got his Silver C. He was now ahead of Adele. Finally—it was such a wonderful machine, he now wished to buy one for Adele.

I replied that production of the 3 had now come to an end, and Slingsby's were now building the Skylark 4. I had bought one myself and could thoroughly recommend it. Would he like to order one from Slingsby's?

Back came an instant reply—could he buy mine for Adele? *No*—I had just got mine equipped and instrumented exactly to my liking, please get a new one. Wise old Giorgio, knowing the difference, pressed me again. At last I weakened. 'Come and stay with us at Kits Close and then you and Adele can fly her, and if you like her we will bring her out to you in the summer.'

Just before they arrived, I had an idea. I wrote 'Please don't think me rude, but what does Adele weigh?'—'44 kilogrammes.' 98 lbs! No wonder Giorgio had outclassed her. I felt quite sure she had never flown a properly trimmed glider: she must have been flying with her aircraft's centre of gravity well behind the aftmost limit, and the handling qualities must have been abominable, quite apart from the fact that the stalling characteristics might easily be dangerous. I fixed a bolt in the nose of the Skylark, and bought four 4-lb lead weights. When the Orsis arrived, we went to Lasham, and put in the weights, and off flew Adele. When she landed, she confessed she had never flown so beautiful a craft.

So in August next we were once more in Varese. It was, I think, the Orsis' tenth wedding anniversary. Giorgio gave Adele a kiss and a Skylark 4. I made a speech to the effect that, if that was what he gave her after ten years, he was going to be in a spot as to what to give her on their Silver Wedding day.

The new club at Calcinate del Pesce was going strong. With the lake on the southern boundary, and the foothills of the Alps to the north, it is one of the most beautiful in Europe. We were all very happy.

A year later, Giorgio brought the Skylark over and flew in our Nationals from Lasham. I arranged for my cousins, Bill and Ferelyth, to crew for him with Adele. They got on famously. Giorgio escaped unscathed from an abominable landing in the midst of power wires. Their English stumbled over the night they all stopped on a retrieve for fish and chips in Ipswich.

Then, in 1966, came an invitation once more to fly in the Italian Nationals, this time from their national centre in Rieti. We went, we had the most wonderful fortnight's flying—and, five years after I had first met him at the bottom of the pilots' ladder, Giorgio became National Champion.

Rieti, about 60 miles from Perugia in the next valley to the south, gives gliding conditions which I have little hesitation in saying equal in strength of lift those met in Texas or South Africa (though over a smaller area), and which for variety of flying and beauty and interest of the country flown over, exceed both by a very wide margin.

And where Rieti, in August, beats every other site I know of is that in that month it has nearly 100% meteorological reliability; we could have flown every one of the 12 days. On rest days there are dozens of wonderful things to do, from bathing in one of the many lakes to expeditions to buildings and works of unrivalled beauty and history.

To beat our National (and even World) records, over triangles of up to 300 km, one need go no further than Rieti, and until you have learnt about mountain flying you are not a fully-developed glider pilot.

Although a lot nearer than Texas or Kimberley, Rieti is still a long way—three days, including the Channel crossing, the Mont Blanc tunnel, and a thousand miles motoring with the trailer, gets you there fairly comfortably. And the other thing to say is that flying over the Apennines is still a man's game: not nearly as dangerous as it looks (which is just as well), but still requiring skill, discipline and caution.

The risk is minimised by not flying except in conditions which, by our standards are absolutely roaring, and on no day did one launch into less than 3-knot thermals, which worked up to double that figure, and even then conditions were said to be subnormal.

The lessons to be learnt from mountain flying form a chapter in the behaviour of the air which to most British pilots is virtually unknown. One day, flying over the west-facing mountain south-east of Perugia, I saw factory-chimney smoke at Perugia blowing to the south, smoke from Spoleto, 20 miles south, blowing to the north. Cloud shadows, showing the upper winds, were coming from due west. My mountains had spurs facing north-west, and south-west. To which place should one go for lift? Without a relief map, it is difficult to answer this and the other hundred similar problems which present themselves, but I got very much better at forecasting the right answers before the meeting was over. The time of day, and hence the direction of the sun, of course came into the calculations, as did your own altitude when the problem presented itself. One day I was facing a landing in a valley, and noticed a small lake near the foot of the wall of mountains. A stutter of brilliance at one end of the lake showed that the air was cascading down the slopes at that point, and creating small ripples on its leeward side, thus showing the direction of the surface wind and hence my direction of landing.

In one day's task I used thermal lift, mountain-slope lift to 10,000 ft, wave lift and the roughest air I have ever met—I thought for a few minutes it might use *me*, but the Dart overcame it.

The furies of Mte Corno

The third task set at the 1966 Italian Nationals, on 4 August, was a 201-km triangle, Rieti–Funivia (ski-lift) Gran Sasso–Foligno airfield–Rieti. (See map, p. 152.)

The first leg of this course runs east from Rieti into the most dramatic region of the Apennines—the Gran Sasso d'Italia is the highest range of the system, forming the backbone of Italy, and the first turning-point was at the southern end of the foot of perhaps the most impressive soaring slope in the world—a straight line of steep mountains running perhaps twenty miles across the prevailing wind, averaging 4,000 ft in height, and at the northern end peaking up to Mte Corvo (9,000 ft) and behind that again, Mte Corno, nearly 10,000 ft.

This range forms the eastern wall of a wide central valley, containing the town of L'Aquila. It also forms the natural barrier between the Mediterranean and Adriatic Sea breezes, so that very often over its eastern slopes run a chain of cumulus and cumulo-nimbus clouds which can be seen from the air 50 miles away or more.

The course therefore runs east from Rieti, over the adjacent 7,000-ft Mte Terminillo, then a series of mountains and valleys to the first turning-point, thence north–west along the soaring slope described above, and a long series of lakes, mountains and valleys out to Foligno in the Perugian valley; the final southern leg being along the eastern side of the valley, over the southern mountains, over Terni in its valley, the mountains behind it, and back into the Rieti plain.

The weather on 4 August, though good by British standards, was only mediocre by Rieti ones, so the task gave competitors a lot of problems.

The first leg did not give much trouble. Slope-soaring on Mte Terminillo to 7,500 ft gave enough height to cross via Antrodocco to the northern end of the enormous slope of the Gran Sasso, and a southerly rush along this, holding the nose down to avoid gaining too much height, took me round the turning-point at the bottom of the ski-lift at its southern end. Then north again along the slope, climbing all the way at 5 knots, to the towering bulk of Mte Corvo.

I took this to the top—slope-soaring up to 9,000 ft—and then had to decide whether to set out on track from there, or to fly back east over a shallow rocky saddle to the still higher peak of Mte Corno.

I was with Vergani in his Dart at the time, and he took the first decision. It proved the wrong one, as he came to earth about 15 miles further north. I, on the other hand, allowed my greed for more height to win the day, and turned downwind for Mte Corno, less than a kilometre away. The profile of the two mountains is shown overleaf.

I had not flown 100 yards before I wished I hadn't: the air wasn't there. Instead, the saddle was filled with wild invisible devils, cavorting around, to and fro and up and down, as if they had gone mad at the invasion of their privacy. It was a vortex of the most vicious kind, unmarked by any cloud system, which might otherwise have made me wary. It was the wildest air I have ever met, even including the rotor cloud in the lee of Mt Cook in New Zealand, which, being in the lee of a 12,000-ft mountain, has far more excuse for its unkindness.

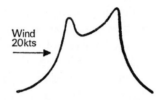

Figure 6   The profile of Mte Corvo (left) and Mte Corno

Before I knew where I was, I had both hands on the stick of the Dart, and was fighting to lift first one wing, then the other, as each in turn dropped precipitately into the invisible holes in the air. I dared not let my speed drop below 60 knots, because it was fluctuating wildly by as much as 20 knots, so, of course, the accelerations of the aircraft were all the more violent. There was not much margin for manoeuvre or error, since the walls of the two mountains were a few hundred yards ahead and astern, and the shale basin of rock between them was a few hundred feet below. No grass, nothing green, no kindness anywhere.

The sun above poured out of the blue sky on to what might have been a small area on the moon—perhaps that was why I was perspiring rather freely.

Thanks to the light and quick ailerons of the Dart, I fought her round, across the wind, so I was drifted sideways towards the slope of Mte Corno; then the inevitable upward sweep of the tortured air took hold and I was shot aloft, above the peak, into the blessed calm above. I took a couple of tacks to 11,000 ft, a long breath, and started to sort out the acid-drops and general clutter which had shot out of their pockets all over the cockpit.

Good for the Dart.

After this, the rest of the second leg was complicated, but relatively uneventful. It consisted of innumerable calculations of the effect on the wind of each mountain and valley ahead, so that course could be set for the most likely spot for the next upcurrent. The scenery below was of unsurpassed beauty: mountains, lakes, rivers, valleys, little villages, often clustered on hills under the shadow of a pinnacled castle or church. Then, out over the eastern mountain wall of the Perugian valley, over the turning-point on Foligno airfield— and, at 4,000 ft, into the unmistakable creamy calm and gentle lift of a wave.

I turned south and whispered for home at 40 knots, the Dart's wake lingering undistorted on air and silence. For 20 miles I flew, gaining height at half a knot, to 5,000 ft over Spoleto, everything so quiet that it was not the Dart which was moving, it was the dreamy earth below which was being drawn quietly backwards. I was not on the same planet as that which contained the fighting furies of Monte Corno.

So I landed at Rieti in a soothing frame of mind. Not so the next pilot of a M–100, who scrambled out of his cockpit, knelt down, and touched the ground three times with his hands before his team arrived to tow his aircraft in. I don't think any of the other pilots on that day took on my particular Gnomes of Corno, but they found plenty of other troubles of their own. But the hero—or heroine—of the day, to my mind, was Adele Orsi. She got her Skylark 4 round the course, in 4 hrs 38 mins. The 'Four' is perhaps the safest and steadiest sailplane in the world, but her very stability means hard work on the controls, and Adele is very small. She came in so exhausted she could hardly stand—but she came in.

To round off the day, we were all eating in the garden of the local hostelleria when, in the pitch dark, at 20:45 hrs, a whistle overhead announced the arrival of the final finisher. He had arrived after the turning-point and landing observers had closed down. But he also had arrived. Only seven finished; I had won in 3 hr 38 min, a minute faster than Giorgio Orsi in his SHK.

1966 Rieti Free Distance

The task I shall not forget was, of course, Free Distance. This is always the highlight of any Championships, but never more so than in Italy because, what with the roads, the distances, and the

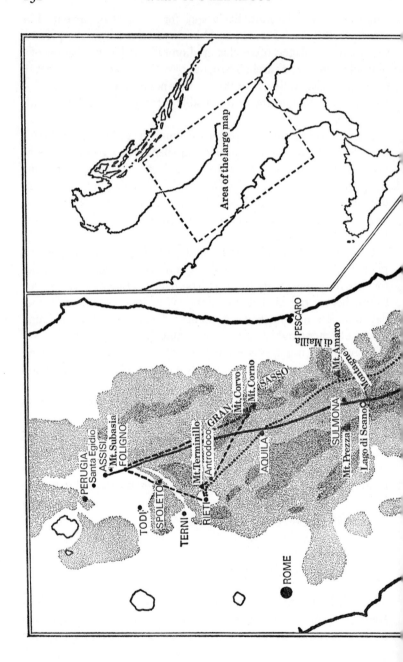

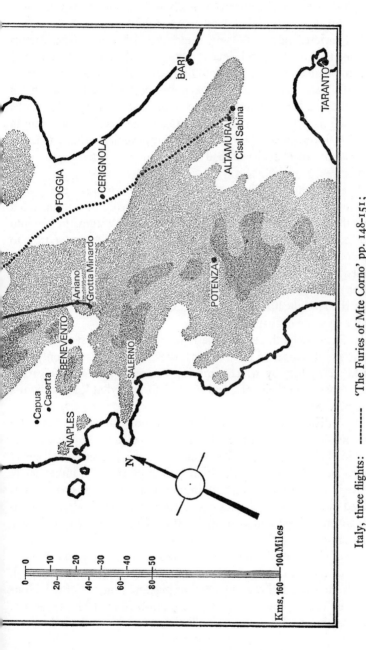

Italy, three flights:

-------	'The Furies of Mte Corno' pp. 148–151;
··········	'1966 Rieti Free Distance' pp. 151–157;
————	'Free as a Bird' pp. 218–229

telephone system, the retrieve is likely to be as big an adventure as the flight itself, certainly taking an extra day.

For various reasons, the only route for big distances from Rieti is the one to the south, and since the 'toe' of Italy is mountainous and said to be unlandable, up to now all distance flights have been made towards Taranto and the 'heel'. So it was on this day. The maximum distance available is just over 500 km, but as flying down the narrow sea-girt strip of land comprising the heel of Italy, late in the day, is obviously likely to run one into evening calm, so far the longest distance achieved had been Taranto airfield, just over 400 km.

The straight-line course therefore runs south from Rieti, over mountains which, as one goes on, get gradually lower, then out over the flatter south–eastern plain to the sea at Taranto, then on into the 'heel'. I, however, decided to start on a south–east course, to reach the giant soaring slope of the Gran Sasso near L'Aquila, and hoped to use this and a subsequent chain to the south to speed up my flight. This proved to be a wrong decision, since some pilots who took the straight line went further than I did, but it certainly took one over some enchanting country.

Unfortunately, there was a Designated Start, and first take-off was 13:30 hrs. I happened to be towards the end of the list, so only took off at 14:15 hrs, by which time lift was over 3 knots, the earlier starters were on their way, and we had all missed at least an hour's distance.

Immediately after release I turned on course, skirted Mte Terminillo on the south, and flew to a small cloud over 6,000-ft Mte Calvio, behind a deep valley containing the pinnacled village of Antrodoco; and one of the high points of the day immediately arrived. Because as I circled immediately over its crest I was joined by an orange and black eagle, who determinedly attached himself to one of my wing-tips and followed me round for at least a quarter of an hour. Fortunately I had my camera with me, and took a series of shots, of which two are the best I have in my collection.

From there to L'Aquila, and fast down along its eastern wall, which then was followed by another gigantic rampart of the Montagna de Mailla, towering up to the 9,500-ft peak of Monte Amaro. The sea-breeze fronts were conflicting over this and producing a

The Wasserkuppe: International competitions, 1937

Pilot and plane-makers: Philip Wills, Horace Buckingham and Fred Slingsby

The Weihe landing at Redhill, 1947
Sigma : a shot at the ultimate

truly impressive cloudscape, and there again I got a photo of a scene I shan't forget.

I avoided the cloud clamped on this peak, but took one a little further on to 12,000 ft, and from then on for a long way was in and out of cloud until, with the peak of Vesuvius just visible above the haze, nearly 75 miles to the west, I came out over the flatter eastern plain of Italy, west of Foggia.

The sky ahead was now nearly cloudless, but the sea-breeze front had moved east, and a big line of cumulo-nimbus, about 20 miles east of me, ran north–west to south–east along my track for many miles. So I flew towards it, and near Cerignola got under it, and in heavy rain found 5-knot lift. I turned on my oxygen, and climbed up into it. Here I made another mistake: I took it too high. At 13,000 ft ice started to form, and I went on to the top at 17,000 ft. I then turned on course, and flew blind for perhaps half an hour. Later, Vergani told me that, in this same cloud, he broke off his climb at 13,000 ft to avoid icing, and doubtless this made him many extra miles.

Fifty miles later I was on my final glide, and a slight complication intervened. Before take-off we had been briefed of a military zone into which were were not supposed to intrude. I was about to fly over a corner of it, and might not have enough height to overfly it, since no further thermals seemed in prospect. So I diverged to the east, following a long, straight road and railway line beneath. I passed over a tiny railway station at 1,500 ft, flew on a few miles, and it was clear I must land. Should I take the last mile or two, landing in the middle of nowhere, or go back to the little railway station, with at least a telephone? Remembering my last Free Distance effort in the 1961 Italian Nationals, where I landed in the wilds and subsequently when Kitty arrived couldn't even find my glider until 05:00 hrs the next morning (which led to a little justified criticism from my team as we rattled about through the night on fourth-class roads and walked around looking in vast ploughed fields with our torches), I took the easy way, turned back, and landed gently in a ploughed field by the station of the wee village of Cisal Sabina at 19:30 hrs.

The field erupted Italians of all shapes and sizes, and in no time I was whisked away in a battered car to a local café, where my forms and primitive Italian resulted in a lot of telephoning. Kitty's programme involved motoring down the Autostrada to Caserta, just short of Naples, calling in at one or two 'phoning points on the way, and then stopping at one of the Rovesi restaurants, spanning the motor-road, where she was to wait for my message. For here was the critical fork in her route, either across the tortuous and vertiginous roads over the spine of the peninsula to the eastern plain, or to keep to the western side if I had failed to cross the Apennines. When the call eventually came through, however hard I tried I could not get to speak to her myself (as a matter of fact she had been tempted away for a critical half-hour with the promise of better service in the local Post Office), but by the time my Italian friend hung up I was given to understand that my message would be given her. I had to hope for the best.

In the meantime the carabinieri from Altamura, 10 miles away, had arrived in force. I felt bashful at giving them so much trouble, but they were kindness itself, I eventually got the impression that this was a change from their ordinary routine duties. But it's just as well that up to a dozen of our police force do not have to involve themselves every time a glider lands in a British field.

Four guards were left on the machine, and I was whisked in a jeep back to the carabinieri-station in Altamura. Much activity followed. A sextuplicate report was typed to Rome, with copies all over the place, giving my name, age (a sore point: the local Rieti paper called me the '*piu ancienzo piloto*'), aircraft details ('What? No registration in your country?'), and, in due course, reason for landing.

Now, in a foreign language you can hardly speak, it really isn't possible to describe what Free Distance is all about. If you try and say you set out in the morning without the faintest idea of where you were to land, and here you are, you feel you may get yourself locked up as a lunatic.

So I compromised. I pointed to the military zone, pencilled on my map, and said I had landed where I had to avoid infringing it—which was exactly true, as far as it went.

Two days later, back at Rieti, the local paper had black headlines: '007 British pilot Philip Wills landed at a secret NATO airfield in Southern Italy and was immediately surrounded by armed carabinieri and Air Force Guards'. My horrified expostulations were met with bland assurances not to worry.

Then I was taken to a local restaurant, where I ate under the watchful eye of a junior carabiniere, back to their office, where I was given back my landing certificate covered with rubber stamps, to a local hotel, which the carabinieri opened up for me and where they obediently booked two bedrooms, although I said we would probably not arrive until around 4 am, then out and away through the sleeping countryside back to the Dart.

After trying to explain to all and sundry what gliding was all about, I got my sleeping bag out of the locker, spread it out under one wing, and lay down to doze until my team fetched me. The silence of the warm night was broken by the occasional cheerful chatter of the guards around my glider, and by the barking of innumerable dogs. The night sky was ablaze with a million stars.

I wished, sleepily, that some of the workers at Slingsby Sailplanes in Kirbymoorside could see some of the odd places where their craftsmanship took us, and how it was admired by the people who came to see it.

At 3 a.m. the headlights of the Fiat cast a yellow sword through the night from the horizon, and a few minutes later my team arrived. They had been misdirected, and had been nearly to Bari, when Justin managed to solve the somewhat garbled address they had been given. In ten minutes the Dart was in her trailer, and we were being led in triumphant convoy back to our hotel.

The only sad thing about the journey back next day was that we had no time to stop and look at the wonders on the way. Pompeii, Naples, Rome, and a hundred other marvels rushed by under the imperative necessity of our return. But I consoled myself: these would still be there another day, whereas with a glider you have a key to the way ordinary people live in out-of-the-way places which is denied to the tourist.

I had not done too well on this day—11 pilots had got beyond the Foggia barrier, and I was eleventh, with 366 kms, against Vergani's 440 kms, the longest flight yet made from Rieti.

8

The Weihe

The saga of a sailplane

Someone asked me the other day how long a sailplane lasts. I believe the official answer is, as long as the ply doesn't dry out, and I suppose this means that it depends very much on the climate in which it is kept; but the question set me reviewing the life history of the various aircraft which I myself have owned, and one thing led to another.

My first glider was the Scud 2, built for Mungo Buxton in 1932, and shared by me with him from 1933 onwards. Unfortunately, the identity of this machine has been lost. A Scud 2 is still flying at Dunstable, but whether or not it is my original one I do not know.

In 1934, Hjordis, designed by Buxton, was the first high-performance sailplane of British design to take the air. She was a prototype, heir to the imperfections of prototypes, but in her I learnt a great deal. After three years I sold her, rather unwillingly, to Andre Brink in Johannesburg. Unwillingly because, with no air-brakes or spoilers, and with rather poor and sluggish controls, she was unsuited to conditions on the high veldt of South Africa. I saw her last, a rather sad and dilapidated wreck, in the roof of a hangar at Germiston airport. Her days are over.

Minimoa, 1938. A beautiful, birdlike machine, with exaggerated stability characteristics, a very suitable machine to enable one to explore the difficulties of blind-flying in unstable clouds before the days of speed-limiting brakes. Taken over by the RAF in 1940, used for various moderately warlike purposes, including a tour of fighter stations to give fighter-pilots experience in the difficulties of getting their gun-sights on to such slow-moving aircraft (I believe no one ever succeeded). Then transferred to the nascent ATC, crashed in

1944, repaired after the war, owned by Sproule, Prince Bira, Lawrence Wright, and sold to Iceland, where I believe she was still flying after 19 chequered years.

The Weihe . . . ah, the Weihe! Let me try to record the history of the Weihe in more detail.

The actual time and place of her birth are shrouded in the fog of the war years. From the evidence of some of the materials used, Bolton had a theory that she might have been built in Czechoslovakia around 1942. In any case, I first set eyes on her, in sad disrepair, in a hangar on top of the Wasserkuppe in 1944, about the month of July. Little did I imagine her as the shining and graceful sailplane from whose cockpit, on 29 December 1954, ten years later and 12,000 miles away, I was to survey the astounding panorama of the New Zealand Southern Alps from a height of over 30,000 ft.

I was in a party, of whom Fred Slingsby was one, sent over by the Ministry of Aircraft Production to make a survey of any technical advances in glider design made by the Germans during the war, and we had authority to label any aircraft we thought merited investigation at home: the theory being that any machine so labelled would then be duly transported back for examination and flight-testing.

As I went round, one of the developments which seemed to me of great importance was in the field of stability and control. So rapidly does the science of aircraft design advance that many people may not realise that, up to 1939 at any rate, practically nothing was known about this all-important subject. Designers simply went on their previous experience; they had built a reasonably controllable aircraft with, say, a particularly shaped tail, so repeated the same general shape next time, scaled up if necessary. There were no design requirements covering the subject, and no measurable flight-tests laid down, since no one knew what to measure.

My first flight in an Olympia was therefore a revelation to me; here was a machine that seemed to fly itself in all circumstances, a machine in which blind-flying in all types of cloud assumed a new aspect. I had always shared the belief that Hans Jacobs was probably the world's most gifted sailplane designer, and here was proof of it.

So I decided that one machine to try and get over to England was Jacobs' latest design, and this meant the Reiher. Unfortunately we were only able to locate one of these machines (only three had been built) and we found it had been adopted as a pet by a certain Typhoon station in Northern Germany. Alas, our officially impeccable authority proved of little avail against the ancient right of possession. We pulled all our strings—they were made only of paper. The Typhoon boys couldn't actually fly the thing, but one day they intended to come round to it. In the meantime our beautiful Reiher lay out in the sun and rain for day after day, month after month. At last our slowly-grinding wheels brought it, over two years later, to Kenley, and when we inspected it, it was ruined beyond repair by mishandling and exposure.

In the meantime we had proceeded on our journey, and one day reached the Wasserkuppe. As we drove up its beautiful green and rounded slopes to the group of buildings on the top, I was remembering the last time I had visited this lovely place, the Mecca of all glider pilots, for the International Championships in 1937. What possessed this extraordinary people, with so beautiful a homeland, to go mad once again and destroy the world, themselves with it?

The group of buildings at the summit seemed much as I remembered, except for a large new swimming-pool in front of it. Evidently this had been the main block for whatever unit had been stationed there during the war. We started to wander through it, and in the centre came on a large chapel. Along both walls were yellow-pine pews, but the middle of the floor was taken up with a raised concrete platform, on which was reclining the more-than-life-sized concrete recumbent figure of—a dead pilot. His arms were folded on his chest, he was clothed in full concrete flying-gear, with an unopened concrete parachute on his chest. Wreaths of brown-gold artificial oak-leaves were propped around his plinth. At the far end of the chapel a stained-glass window, lit by the outside sun, representing the Angel of Death, complete with well-developed sun-bronzed private parts, lowered down on the absent congregation. It seemed, to put it mildly, an un-British way of stimulating the right outlook in an assembly of pupil glider pilots.

The Wasserkuppe was in the American sector, and hence occupied by a US Army unit, but embedded in this was a small RAF unit operating a radar station, and we were accordingly accommodated by our compatriots. As we walked round, we found ourselves in a veritable Golconda of gliders. Hangar after hangar was stuffed full of gliders of all types: if we could only have transported the lot to England, our home clubs would have been in full operation two years earlier than they actually were. Alas, our terms of reference were more limited. But in one hangar I found several Weihes, which had been Jacobs' last design before the Reiher. I had already an uneasy feeling about the possible future of that machine, and apart from that I was struck with the brilliant simplicity of the Weihe's rigging features, so I decided to label two of these aircraft.

But now I started making enquiries of our RAF friends as to the likelihood of our system working, and once more doubts began to creep in. It appeared that when the Americans first arrived at the Wasserkuppe, they had seen sailplanes for the first time in their lives. As might have been expected, they had joyfully accepted them as toys with which to while away the time. A sailplane—a Weihe of course, only the best would do—was dragged out, an American major strapped in, and catapulted off. The Weihe is a gentleman. It did its best. The major was in bed with a cracked spine; he was expected to recover. In the meantime a ukase had gone forth—no further glider flying for the occupying troops, and to make absolutely certain of no more trouble, all gliders on the field to be broken up and burnt next week . . .

I went and saw the Commanding Officer. I pleaded with him, I told him there were people in England who would give their right arms for his field full of gliders. In any case, I said, I wanted two Weihes, and had authority to arrange for their transport to Farnborough. I hoped, therefore, he would withdraw his order for their destruction, would think again; but I could see where his thoughts were leading him. If we wanted two Weihes in England, might not they also like them in the United States? I thought that just possibly I had saved the Weihes, but not for Farnborough. But there seemed nothing more I could do. Our trip came to an end, and we flew back to England.

Some months went by. We had made our report, and parts of it had been approved for action. But the official machinery of recovery had, as expected, failed to work, and no machines appeared in

England. Ken Wilkinson at Farnborough had confirmed that they would like certain aircraft, including the Reiher, Weihes, and a Horten IV tailless sailplane which we had discovered. This latter machine was on a proper airfield, and at last Farnborough, in despair, sent over a Halifax and carried it away in triumph. But the grass field on top of the Wasserkuppe was much too small for a Halifax, or even a Dakota, so the Weihes seemed doomed, the Reiher unobtainable, and my ideas about getting a jump ahead on stability and control doomed to failure.

Then one day my Air Transport Auxiliary freight section at White Waltham got a job to carry supplies to Prague. The route lay almost over the Wasserkuppe, so I decided to take one Anson-load myself, and call in on the return journey; the Anson, light, could easily make the landing.

Nothing had changed since our last visit. The same troops were still there, the same small British unit, the same gliders, undestroyed; so I had managed to achieve something in a negative sort of way. My two Weihes, with my dusty labels attached, were still in their hangar, where it seemed probable they would stay till Doomsday.

Other German pilots I had interrogated had confirmed their excellence, and I felt more than ever sure that, if Farnborough could test them and put the results at our disposal at home, we should be able to use them as a basis on which to lay down our post-war requirements and ensure a new generation of British aircraft of the first quality. (I was not to know that, a little later, Dudley Hiscox was to ensure a great step forward in the same direction by arranging for Chilton Aircraft to build him an Olympia from the pre-war German plans. The Eon Olympia, which resulted from this, ensured that once for all we at home came to know what constituted a first-class sailplane from the handling point of view.) I resolved on desperate measures.

I had a long talk with the RAF Flight Lieutenant in charge and told him my problem and he assured me that if I could get a Queen Mary trailer to the Wasserkuppe he would arrange somehow that the Weihes would be put on it. I had a friend in the shape of a Group Captain in charge of an aerodrome in Belgium where we used to refuel our freight Ansons, and I determined to put my case before him and see if he would play. After all, if Farnborough had sent a

Halifax, what was a Queen Mary? Calculation showed that a trailer of this size should be able to accommodate not only the two complete aircraft, but also a spare pair of wings, so I labelled a pair for luck. Then I took my courage and a saw in both hands, and set about one of the worst tasks of my gliding life. I sawed up a beautiful Weihe. I sawed off the wing-roots and the centre-section fittings, and put them in the back of my empty Anson, together with a complete tailplane. At least we should be able to examine the brilliant detail design of the rigging features, and if I left the machine there it would do no one any good. But it was a cruel job.

On the way home I called in to refuel, and found my Group Captain friend in his office. To my joy, he agreed to help. He would do his best, and send me a signal at White Waltham if and when the aircraft were ready to collect at his airfield. And so back to White Waltham, feeling that I had done what I could for the time being, but of course the chances were slight. The radar unit at the Wasserkuppe, on whom all depended, might be moved at any minute, or any other link in the tenuous chain I had tried to lay down might vanish without warning.

In writing up a history like this, it is easy to give the impression that all my attention was focused on getting hold of these Weihes at the time, but of course this was far from the case; in fact, I had almost forgotten about the whole thing when, a couple of months later the signal arrived and I had to look at it twice before I understood it. 'Goods arrived, awaiting collection.'

By now, the war in Europe was nearly at an end. Aircraft were still flowing out of the factories and across the Atlantic, and all piling up in store. The storage units were by now only running a five-day week, and at weekends many aircraft were ferried in by us to our home aerodromes, and on-flown the following Monday to their final destination. So I went up to Prestwick one Friday and brought a Dakota down to White Waltham which was allotted for storage in a nearby Maintenance Unit. I measured up its hold and the size of its door. It seemed Fate when I discovered that, as far as I could see, the Weihe wing would just go through the door, and just fit in the hold with two inches to spare. And so it proved. Furthermore, the Dakota just took one complete Weihe and one wing over, and in two flights, by Sunday night, the job was done.

It was more than a year later when the next fortunate chapter opened. One of the Weihes brought over had proved to be fairly badly damaged, but the RAF had duly repaired and tested the other. The civil gliding clubs were slowly struggling back to life, and the British Gliding Association had started to function again. Dudley Hiscox was Chairman, but I had taken on a more than full-time job in British European Airways, and had little time to spare for gliding affairs. However, I still managed to attend Council meetings, and at one of these it was reported that Farnborough had finished with the various sailplanes brought over from Germany, and it was proposed to transfer them to the Association.

The damaged Weihe seemed to be a problem, as no one knew what it would cost to repair it or even if it was repairable at all, whilst none of the clubs at that time had any spare funds to undertake such a doubtful project. I therefore proposed that, if the Council approved, I would purchase the remains from the Association, and this was agreed. This was at a time when people were still thinking of high-performance sailplanes in terms of £300 apiece, so when I got a bill for repairs of £250 I did not seem to have done so well. However, the work was done, and I never regretted it. For two years I had much joy from her, and did many flights, including a height record in a gigantic cumulo-nimbus near the Long Mynd.

Just after this flight she again went in for a renewal of Certificate of Airworthiness and my feelings were indeed mixed when it was found that previous inspections had not revealed what may have been a deliberate piece of sabotage by those who had been originally forced to build the aircraft for their German masters. The spar-booms and webs were hardly glued together at all, and when the wings were completely unskinned each spar peeled down to four almost undamaged pieces of wood! Yet in this condition she had uncomplainingly carried me through extreme turbulence and many hours of flying over a period of two years. This is the sort of thing that makes one believe in high safety-factors.

As for the other aircraft, the second Weihe went to the Surrey Club, and is now at Dunstable where I flew her in 1971. The spare pair of wings and the sawn-off fittings and tailplane were rebuilt into a complete machine by Bolton and, as was the Horten IV, sold to the United States, contributing their small share to the dollar shortage.

A small grant from the Ministry enabled us, amongst other things, to finance the flight trials necessary to plot a polar curve for the Weihe, and everyone knew how good an advanced sailplane had to be to be good: it had to be better than the Weihe.

When eventually the Slingsby Sky appeared and proved to be the best 18-metre production sailplane the world had yet seen, my Weihe, from which so much benefit had been derived, went off to start a new life on the other side of the world. Painted a brilliant red, maintained by Dick and Helen Georgeson with loving care, now being reconditioned by a new owner in the North Island, I can see no reason why she should not continue to grace New Zealand skies with her slender beauty for another decade or more. Born in the dark days of war under the tyranny of repressed Central Europe, now with new worlds to conquer in the extraordinary air of free New Zealand, what could be a more unlikely or a more romantic history?

9

The High Air of New Zealand

Altitude in undress

The Mackenzie country in the South Island of New Zealand is an extraordinary oval, flattish plain, at an altitude of between 1,500 and 2,000 ft above sea-level, almost entirely enclosed by a ring of mountains, running between 5,000 and 6,000 ft high except in the north-west corner, where the mountains tower up to the majestic pyramid of Mt Cook, 12,340 ft high, surrounded by dozens of other snow-capped peaks. (See map, p. 169.)

Originally the whole plain must have been one vast field of ice, fed by the huge glaciers of the Mt Cook system, for in this range the rainfall varies within a few miles from 200 to 400 inches a year, and the glaciers move down from it at enormous speeds compared with their counterparts in the European Alps.

The Mackenzie plains are covered with sparse brown tussock grass. At first sight they seem dry and waterless, but in fact the whole terrain is laced with a network of clear, fast-running streams, and inset in it are three large lakes, Tekapo, Pukaki and Ohau. Lakes and streams contain large numbers of enormous trout, running up to over 18 lb in weight.

Beyond the eastern rim the country slopes down to the green Canterbury plains, but westward and south-westward range after tumbled range of mountain, partly unexplored because of their fantastic ruggedness, stretch to the coastline, at its nearest only 40 miles away. It is a country of great beauty and fascination, of sudden, local and inexplicable changes of weather; in fact, the air over it must be as complicated and interesting as anywhere in the World.

With the prevailing wind blowing from west and north-west, tumbling abruptly over the main mountain wall of the Southern

Alps into the Mackenzie basin, it is quite obvious that conditions are ideal for the formation of standing waves going to probably unprecedented heights; indeed on many days this is made obvious by the appearance of lenticular clouds at enormous altitudes all over the sky. After the flight I am now going to describe, it became clear that waves of the first order of magnitude also exist in absolutely clear air, of a size which I think had previously been thought not possible.

The Canterbury Gliding Club held its Christmas training camp on a splendid site called Simons Hill near the south-western corner of the basin, and perhaps 15 miles from the western mountain wall. Here an isolated hill, rising perhaps 1,500 ft above the plain, provides hill-soaring in nearly all wind directions, with good landing fields at the foot. The friendly owner made available his sheep-shearing accommodation, near a large flat field suitable for both aero-towing and winch launching onto the neighbouring brown slopes. Here, Dick Georgeson and his wife took the Weihe which I shipped out to him in 1954, and which they allowed me once more to fly.

I had my first flight on 27 December 1954, on a quiet day with numerous dry thermals to 6,000 ft above take-off. I had decided to try to stalk Mt Cook, 45 miles to the north. It was necessary always to keep within range of one or other of the homesteads sparsely dotting the plain, because each of them had one or more ploughed paddocks in which a landing was possible; a landing in the tussock plain itself would carry a risk of damaging the keel of the aircraft, apart from the difficulty of retrieving out of such rough country.

The upshot of this flight was that I got within about eight miles of the mountain, just over the first scattered patches of snow; but then the air became rough and untidy, and at 6,300 ft I thought it wise to retreat home.

On 29 December there was a light westerly wind, and Dick Georgeson came down from a flight around midday saying he had found a wave to 11,000 ft, some way to the east of the site. But as there was a cloudless sky, except for a low cap of cloud blanketing the westward mountains, I did not expect anything very big when I took off at 16:15 hrs, and so did not dress for height, although Dick insisted on giving me a barograph and oxygen mask. As the ground temperature was nearly 100°F, one did not dress for altitude unless one had to.

At the last minute the towing aeroplane found it was out of petrol, and though this still further reduced the chance of more than a few minutes' descending flight, I decided on a winch-launch on to the hill, thinking it didn't matter anyway. In the event, this fortunate happening resulted in my eventual gain of height being considerably greater than it would otherwise have been.

I was winched to 550 ft, and turned back to the hill, which I reached at about 450 ft; the site at Simons Hill being 1,600 ft above sea-level, this gave me a low point on my flight of just over 2,000 ft above sea-level.

I found fairly good hill-lift at one point, and soon climbed up to the level of the top. Here I immediately found a thermal upcurrent, in which I circled up to 6,500 ft about four miles downwind of the site, over the pebbly channels of the Tekapo River.

From this point I flew north-westwards towards where Dick had previously reported a wave, and in a very few minutes found myself climbing at 5 ft/sec. Incidentally, to fly down from a thermal up-current into a wave upcurrent a few miles away was then thought to be a meteorological impossibility, but meteorological impossibilities are two a penny in the Lost World of the Mackenzie Basin.

Presumably I was in the fourth or fifth wave in the lee of the mountain, and each wave would run north and south parallel to them. Mt Cook lay due north, so it became obvious that another attempt on it was possible. The lift was not strong, so careful flying was necessary as also a constant endeavour to picture the shape of the air in which I was flying, in the absence of any cloud to show the lie of the waves. I crabbed northwards until my wave seemed to peter out, then turned and flew upwind at 60 mph through the compensating downcurrent until, sure enough, I found myself in a slightly stronger one.

In this way I slowly dog-legged myself northwards and westwards until I was at 14,000 ft at the very mouth of the gorge leading up to the mountain. I tried to determine the distance between each wave and it seemed very short, until the following day I remembered that the speed shown on one's airspeed indicator grows progressively less with height. Thus to maintain an indicated 36 mph as I climbed,

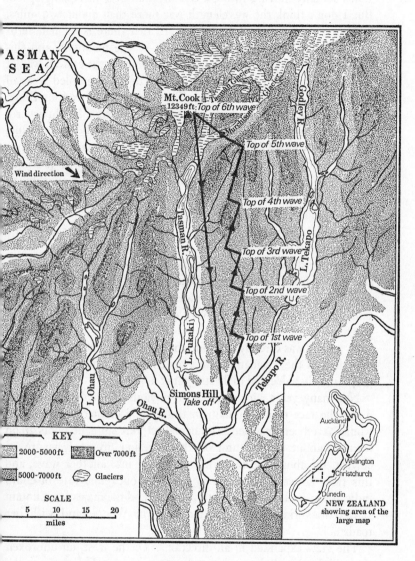

Mount Cook

I was actually moving through the air at an ever-increasing speed. But I don't think the wavelength was more than about two miles.

After my first flight I had discoverd that there is a small aerodrome in the valley almost at the foot of the mountain and this knowledge gave me courage to continue flying up the eastern wall of the tremendous valley which here slopes up in a tumbled scree of rocks to the huge Tasman glacier. Then I noticed an exciting thing, which for the first time made me think of a possible height record.

Overhead and to the east, the sky was a clear and dazzling blue, but as I have said before, the mountains to the west were completely hidden by an unbroken sheet of cloud clamped down on their summits. I now noticed that where this sheet of cloud came to an end, over the east-facing wall of mountains, it was curling over and descending like a waterfall down the slopes, evaporating into nothing after falling a few hundred feet. And Mt Cook itself had a similar waterfall-like cap.

From the altitude I had now reached I was looking at this cap from above, and from this angle it looked irresistibly like the top of a lenticular cloud. The conclusion was that downstream of the mountain, even in clear air, the air itself might be rebounding in a wave-like form.

By now I was directly opposite the eastern face of the mountain, the width of the Tasman ravine away from it. I took a hasty photograph and then decided to fly straight at it.

Not many years ago, to fly at an obvious downcurrent pouring down the face of a mountain in the middle of inaccessible peaks would have been regarded as a suicidal act, but sailplane pilots go on learning about the air, and on this occasion my analysis proved correct, for about two miles from it I flew into another wave, and this time far stronger than my previous one. The rate of-climb indicator moved smoothly up to 20 ft/sec, and the majestic mountain started to shrink below me like Alice in Wonderland with her toadstool.

The view expanded in all directions. To the west, an unbroken sheet of cloud with, beyond it, a glimpse of the sea. Below me, to the south-east, the whole Mackenzie basin lay like a huge, oval irregular brown frying-pan; beyond it to the east, the country sloping down to the sea, visible 100 miles or more away. To the north-east, end-

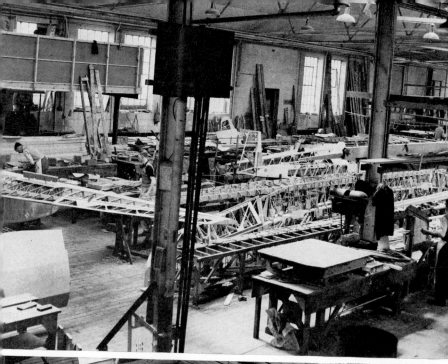

Old and new ways: Slingsby Sailplanes
Manufacture in wood, 1956, and manufacture in resin-bonded glass fibre in 1971

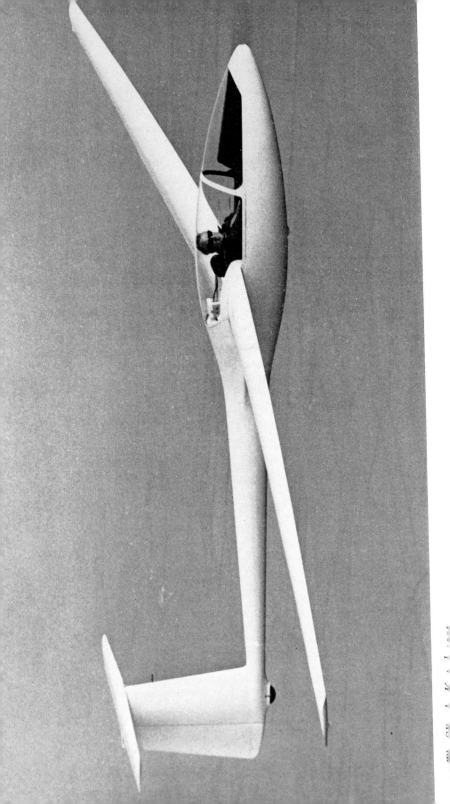

less snow-clad peaks and glaciers peering out of the edge of the cloud-sheet. Overhead, nothing but cloudless blinding blue.

The altimeter wound itself up to 20,000 ft, then 25,000 ft, and I moved up almost directly over the big mountain, now sadly diminished in size, the Weihe hanging apparently stationary in smooth space, facing into wind. I tried the controls to see if increasing stiffness might be apparent, due to the grease freezing or control-cables shortening in the cold; but packed with anti-freeze grease, they seemed entirely unaffected.

The cold—suddenly I became aware of it, and then was amazed that I had not felt it before. For I had taken-off clad for the heat of mid-summer, and was wearing nothing but an open-necked cotton shirt, grey flannel trousers, a sports coat, light city walking shoes and a pair of thin nylon socks.

This rather dreary sartorial revelation now became a major factor in my future course of action, although I later discovered that my increasing numbness was being assisted by the fact that I did not fully understand Dick's oxygen system, and so was considerably under-feeding myself with oxygen.

About now I began to feel rather vulgar stomach pains, caused by the expansion of the stomachic gases in the low pressures of this high air. I began to wonder when to leave off.

Twenty-eight thousand feet above sea-level, and still going up. I had long ago broken both the British gain-of-height and absolute altitude records. Well, let's go for the height of Mount Everest. Twenty-nine thousand: done it. What about the round thirty thousand? Probably fortunately, I forgot that at 33,000 ft the world gain-of-height record would be mine.

A number of small, sharp splintering sounds from the thin Perspex canopy of the cockpit made me sit up; it was showing signs of cracking, due to contraction in the cold. Supposing it cracked enough to break up?

The possibilities after that were uniformly dreary in the extreme. In my light clothes, I could stay in the machine, but I could not hope to lose height nearly fast enough to avoid being overcome by the cold long before I got down to a safe height. I could jump overboard with my parachute. This would mean leaving my oxygen supply, and I would then have a few seconds before losing consciousness.

If I pulled the rip-cord at once, my rate of descent would be so slow that I would be frozen as stiff as a log long before I reached the ground. If I left it folded, I might expect to come round again around 10,000 ft, but it would take at least two minutes falling free to lose the four miles down to this height, and, I would by then be far too frost-bitten to have any fingers left for pulling the rip-cord, if I hadn't already hit a mountain top.

The spectacle I presented was, in retrospect, not without its funny side. A very dusty middle-aged gentleman, in light summer clothes, spun between ecstasy and torture, nursing an uncomfortably bloated and borborygmal stomach, suspended in space in a small thin plywood cigar at a height considerably greater than Mt Everest (for the altimeter now showed we were approaching 30,000 ft), staring anxiously at a miserably thin bit of celluloid-like sheet a few inches in front of his face, which had almost certainly never been selected with a view to carrying such an onerous responsibility as that of preserving him from a rapid end by deep-freezing. The outside temperature was around 50° of frost.

This is 20th-century fun with a vengeance.

With quite a sharp bang a three-inch crack suddenly appeared just in front of my nose, and I came out of my reverie with a start. This was the signal for home. I turned down-wind, the rate-of-climb indicator swung to 'down' and we were on our way.

The inside of the cockpit cover misted over with frost, and I put out my bare fingers to scrape a patch clear. My fingers stuck lightly to the transparent panel, and I felt as if they were being burnt. I snatched them away and rubbed them in the palm of my hand.

I put out my air-brakes to hasten my descent, but found that, even at 60 mph on the clock, I hardly seemed to be moving. As I had 45 miles to get back to base, I put them in again and put my speed to 75 mph, which must have been a true airspeed of around 150 mph. At last we moved back into the downward part of the wave, and began to lose height at a round speed. My feet were lumps of ice. I took them off the pedals and left the rudder to itself and stamped a small tattoo on the floor of the cockpit.

Slowly we edged our way home, and at last we were down to 10,000 ft. I turned off the oxygen and took off the mask with a sigh of relief. There was the landing field, Dick and Helen still waiting patiently by the silver trailer. I had been away nearly four hours; it seemed longer.

I landed, still cold in my bones, but very, very happy.

Had the barograph worked? Glory be, it had. My lucky day.

The height achieved was officially confirmed as 30,400 ft Absolute Altitude, 28,200 ft Gain of Height—both British records.

Mountain rescue

My next visit to New Zealand was seven years later, and once again, as if fate had ordained it, I was plunged into gliding of dramatic order.

I took off from London Airport at 15:15 on 28 December 1961. It had been freezing hard for days and I had just started one of my earth-shaking colds. The sun was setting in an icy and smoky haze. Kitty had to stay at home to cope with schools. I was off to New Zealand and Australia on a rushed business trip, with perhaps a little gliding on the side. It should have been a time of glad anticipation. I felt thick in the head and miserable as hell.

In those latitudes the fleet 707 nearly kept up with the sun. It had been about to set in London; finally it inched over the western horizon when we were over Newfoundland. It was still 28 December 1961, when 18 hours later we dropped wearily on to the runway at Honolulu. Here a merciful airline decrees a 24-hour stop to give the confused and tired passenger time to try and catch up with himself, to accustom himself to having breakfast at dinner time and waking up when his whole being is insisting that it is time to go to bed. The attempt, though no doubt well meant, is a very partial success. At midnight on 29 December, a small gaggle of somnambulists stalked into another merciless 707, and five hours later by the clock were decanted at Nandi, Fiji. It was 31 December—the conjuring trick of the International Date Line had seen to it that in my personal calendar there will never appear the date of 30 December 1961.

An hour later we were sitting, our eyes on stalks, in a TEAL Electra on the penultimate leg of our flight to Christchurch. A brisk New Zealand air hostess came by handing out the daily newspapers. The first headline I saw—I found my neighbour giving me the disapproving glare of an Englishman who has caught one of his compatriots expressing emotion in a public place—'Elderly glider pilot crashes on mountain . . . Matthew Wills, aged 61 was seriously injured yesterday when . . .'

Cousin Matthew—elderly my foot! great big burly Matthew, he may have been 61 by the clock, but the clock, as I had recently been finding, can be a liar. But Matthew, with whom I was going to stay in his caravan at the gliding meeting at Omarama in the Mackenzie country near Mt Cook, had yesterday crashed in his Skylark 2 on top of a 5,000-ft mountain. The Electra droned on at a miserly 400 mph towards New Zealand carrying one passenger who felt very miserable indeed.

At Christchurch I was met by Fred Dunn, who told me the story.

Matthew had been quite determined to attain the final leg of his Silver C before my arrival, by doing five hours on the mountain. This he certainly achieved, but not in the way he had intended. He had taken off on aero-tow at about 10 a.m., and near the top had become worried that he was being towed too near the mountain side for comfort. He had therefore pulled his glider away from it, but as he was still tied to the tug this had turned the aeroplane's nose further in towards the hazard. Too late, the tug pilot had realised the dangers of the situation and had dropped his end of the rope. A moment later Matthew saw the mountain top rush at him. He too pulled his release and a second later the crash came. There was a stiff breeze blowing up the mountain and the Skylark's airspeed indicator was found stuck registering 70 mph. Flying down-wind, it must have struck at nearly 100. This particular mountain is wickedly steep and ridged up to within a quarter-of-a-mile of the summit, but for the last stretch it is a gently rounded slope covered with rough brown tussock grass. Matthew found himself dazed but miraculously conscious lying with the splintered wreckage all round him. The wind was cold, but the clear New Zealand sun blazed down from the dazzling sky. His back and his ankle hurt pretty badly and he put his hand to his forehead and it came down wet and sticky and red. The straps had broken on impact, and he had been hurled through the perspex canopy, which had shattered and had gone some way to scalping him. He realised that something must be done if he was not to bleed to death; the central part of the fuse-lage was quite near and he managed to crawl round it and drag out the first-aid kit. He got out the bandage and laboriously wound it vertically round his head and his jaw to hold his scalp in place.

After its release the tug pilot had landed at Omarama, but as soon as he had stopped his engine the realisation of what might have happened came to him; he rushed to the propeller and swung it again, took off and climbed full-throttle back to the point of release. He saw the wreckage, and Matthew, seeing him, gave him a wave. The Tiger Moth streaked away out of sight.

Now Matthew was attacked by a fierce thirst. After the blood he had lost, he realised the vital necessity of a drink. In the splintered cockpit of the glider, next to him, was a bottle of lime juice, but he was quite incapable of standing up to lean inside and get it. He picked up a piece of jagged wood under his hand and banged it against the plywood shell. At the second or third attempt it broke through with a crackling sound, and then occurred the second miracle of the day: the bottle of lime juice lay inside the hole he had made, unbroken. He dragged it out and took a long drink.

Now he had at best a long wait, so he managed to drag a spare coat out of the cockpit and painfully crawled under the remains of a wing, covered himself as well as he could, and settled down to wait for rescue. A few minutes later the Tiger again buzzed overhead but could see no sign of Matthew or of life.

Down in the gliding camp his friends had sprung to fierce action. New Zealanders know their mountains and they knew it would require a major effort to beat time if they were to get their friend down to safety before nightfall. Bruce Gillies was fortunately one of the most experienced mountain rescuers in the South Island. All his instincts were to drop everything and lead a party in a wild dash up the mountain. All his training told him that he must stay at base and organise the others. He stayed, and in so doing undoubtedly saved Matthew's life.

A first party of twenty men set off. It was impossible to make a straight attack up the west-facing slope because from the gliding site a steep ridge ran up to be interrupted by a chasm running athwart the mountain face. So the party set off by Land Rover round the south-western flank and then took to the climb from that direction. Dr Ferner, carrying his bag, led the way. It is not every doctor that can climb a steep 5,000-ft mountain in walking shoes and get first to the top, but Ferner did it, in two-and-a-half hours. He found Matthew under the wing and in a couple of minutes realised he would have to be carried down. He diagnosed possibly a broken back, ankle and hip; he dressed the forehead as well as he could. Prearranged signals were laid on the ground and seen by the hovering Tiger. Matthew was a big man—he must weigh over sixteen stone. Bruce had foreseen all this, and called up an aerial ambulance from Queenstown and in a short time a special stretcher had been dropped beside the waiting group of men.

The route by which they had come was far too steep and rugged for a descent carrying a heavy man on a stretcher, and a second one had been planned, descending the summit along a spur running down to the north-west. The party set off in this direction, but as soon as they left the relatively smooth plateau and started the descent proper they realised that four men on the poles of the stretcher could not possibly hope to carry the burden. A member of the party clambered back to the Skylark and with a saw cut out lengths of the wing-spar; they were lashed to the poles and with eight of twelve men carrying it the descent commenced.

The going was wickedly rough and some of the men's light shoes began to break up. The sun drained the moisture from them and thirst became an increasingly intolerable burden. Matthew had been given one injection of morphia, but refused a second, asking Dr Ferner to keep it until the pain became insufferable.

The day wore on and complete exhaustion relentlessly stalked the rescue team. Finally they came to the end of the ridge they had been descending and saw that the last thousand feet consisted on each side of a nearly sheer shingle slope. It was utterly impossible in their exhausted condition to hope to get the stretcher, sliding and slipping down the shaley cliff, to safety. All seemed lost. The crawling beetle on the mountainside came to a despairing halt.

At that precise moment there came a hail from below and a second beetle appeared scrambling up the declivity. Bruce Gillies, foreseeing everything, had organised a second rescue team of some twenty men and sent it up to meet the first. Watchers below saw the two insects meet, coalesce, split up again. Over ten hours after the accident, a weary but triumphant party of nearly fifty men staggered into the yard of Omarama Hotel, where an ambulance waited for the injured man. Matthew had been deaf since birth, but he could communicate well enough. From his stretcher he pointed at his dusty, parched exhausted friends standing round him, then at the door to the bar, then to himself. I suspect that with this single gesture of unselfish gratitude each one of his rescuers felt the ardours of the day had been adequately recompensed. As the ambulance disappeared in its cloud of dust down the road to Oamaru, they turned into the bar to have the drink which Matthew had offered them.

World record

By 4 January my cold was on the mend, but one's ears do not like rapid altitude changes with a thick head, so I decided against going to the gliding camp, and instead motored to Oamaru to see Matthew. He was coming along well, nursed by his wife Jan, and in excellent spirits. The day did not look anything special from the gliding point of view (at any rate, to my eye, unversed in the extraordinary atmospheric phenomena of New Zealand), and when I got back in the evening to my cousin's homestead at Irishman Creek I was astounded to hear the news that Dick Georgeson had broken the World Out-and-Return record with a flight in his Skylark 3F of 400 miles, from Omarama north along the famous North-West Arch to Hanmer and back again. God moves in a mysterious way— thank heavens for my cold, which kept me away, for if I had been there Dick would quite certainly have put me in his aircraft for a local flight, and the record would never have been achieved.*

The glider site at Omarama is a huge, flat, brown grassy plain, near the head of a valley running out of the south-west corner of the Mackenzie country. High mountains hedge it in to the west, south and east; to the north the valley runs round a spur of Mount Benmore into the oval Mackenzie basin, surrounded in its turn by a ring of mountains, snow-capped to the west and north-west.

But round Omarama itself the adjacent mountains are not quite high enough for snow in mid-summer, and seem to be made of crinkled brown velvet. In the evening the setting sun lights the

---

* Whilst going to press, news has come through that Dick has done it again, with a flight on 7 September 1972 of 1003 kilometres along the same wave system, Hanmer-Mossburn and return in eleven hours fifty-five minutes.

sunward slopes to a living golden colour, and the shadowed sides become a true deep purple.

Along the eastern side of the field a small, straight brook of clear, sweet water has been cut, and along the bank of this is a single line of trees perhaps a mile long. The caravans and tents of the gliding folk are pitched in their shade. At their back the brown mountain springs steeply up into the sky.

On the morning of 4 January 1962, the pilots were preparing for the day's flying. The conditions did not seem unusual, and Dick Georgeson was planning his flight, when a few minutes before take-off a telegram arrived for him from Fred Dunn in Christchurch reading 'Arch to Mt Torlesse occasional but increasing lenticulars northwards.' For long Dick had planned a record out-and-return flight along the front edge of this vast wave cloud known in New Zealand as the North-west Arch, to its known northern edge at Hanmer, 200 miles away, and back again. Fred's telegram provided the clue to possible success. Dick leaped into action. (See map, p. 180.)

His Skylark 3F was a machine specially built for the British Team at the 1960 World Gliding Championships in Germany. After this, I was due to buy it, but just then Dick wanted one, and I transferred my option to him. I have not regretted this, because in January 1961 he achieved the World Gain-of-Height record with a climb of 34,300 ft near Christchurch, and in January 1962 this further World Record also fell to this formidable combination of man and machine.

His aircraft was ready, with two separate oxygen installations and all the equipment needed for a long flight at great altitudes. In fortunate New Zealand, the ether is not over-crowded as elsewhere, and an HF radio frequency is reserved for glider pilots. This gives a range of several hundred miles, and so it was possible for the pilot on this flight to remain in contact with his base throughout, though at one point a second glider, airborne over Omarama, was used as an intermediate re-transmitter.

The most important preparatory task was to arrange for photographic evidence of his declared turning-point at Hanmer. Dick put a new film in his camera, which was then sealed. He then took a photograph of a blackboard having the message: 'Ja. 4th 1962, pilot S. H. Georgeson, Skylark 3F, course Omarama–Hanmer–Omarama.' In his haste, he failed to wind on the film correctly, and only a small fraction of the right-hand side of this photograph materialised— but just enough to fulfil the requirements. On such small mishaps may a world record hang! The subsequent photographs include three taken of the turning point at Hanmer and two final ones of the same blackboard taken that evening, thus locking the film within the timespace of that day.

Dick was eventually towed off at 11.05 hrs, and released five miles away at 3,000 ft. The main first problem on these wave-flights is usually to get up through the weak mixed thermal and wave lift to the critical altitude above which the wave takes firm hold of the air. This proved so difficult that on this day Dick alone succeeded and then only after nearly an hour's struggle. Finally, helped by radio advice from Bruce Gillies, who was also struggling in a Skylark 2, he found himself quite suddenly in the typically smooth lift of a wave at 6,500 ft west of Benmore mountain, climbed rapidly to 14,000 ft and set off northwards. The three beautiful lakes of the Mackenzie Basin, Ohau, Pukaki and Tekapo, showed up well between the formations of cloud, but all the New Zealand Alps to the west were completely blanked out. In these conditions it was hard to locate lift, but if it became weak, he first turned and flew into wind for a time, and if this failed, he would circle and be carried downwind until he was brought back into the rising part of the wave.

At 20,000 ft over Irishman Creek he called Bruce Gillies again, who said he was still struggling over Benmore, and then flew on into the never-never country of the Two Thumbs. The wave formation was completely jumbled in this area and the country below absolutely inhospitable. Wind direction was 290° and the course around 030°, so he decided to do a long glide down-wind to the first of the series of lenticular clouds reported in Fred Dunn's telegram. Sure enough, he found it, over Methven, and at 18,000 ft ran into smooth wave-lift again.

Now over 100 miles away, he called Bruce Gillies again—Bruce had struggled up to 14,000 ft and then lost it all again and sounded frustrated in the extreme, but full of encouraging words. He called Christchurch Airport and got clearance to pass through Red 1, the airway to Australia, and eventually reached the Hurunui River at 25,000 ft. Ahead he could see the end of the arch and beyond it a

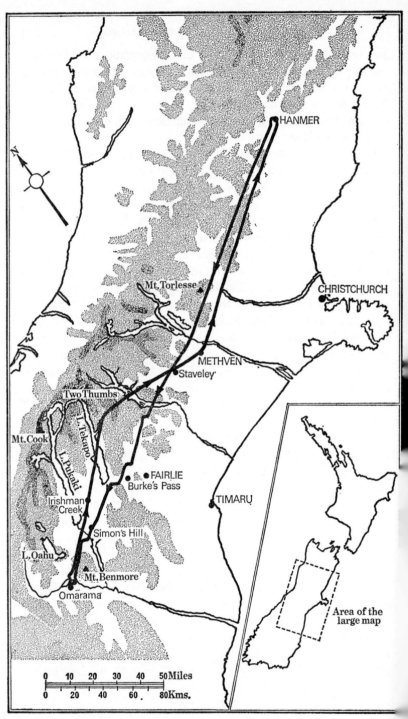

Omarama–Hanmer–Omarama world record, 1962

low-down sheet of cloud covering the whole northern end of the island. It looked quite possible that Hanmer was just too far north to be visible from above; if it was under this cloud it would, of course, be quite impossible to photograph the turning-point, and the whole enterprise would be vitiated. But fortune (aided by experience) smiled, and the turning-point was just short of the cloud sheet. There seemed no chance of covering the last 25 miles, as the air was clear, but extraordinary luck continued and a lenticular tongue formed under his starboard wing and kept pace a little ahead of him—a guardian angel leading to his goal.

Two-and-a-half hours after getting away, he photographed Hanmer, having travelled 200 miles—a startling average speed, aided by a favourable wind component and the increased ground-speed achieved at the great altitudes at which he had been flying. The inside of the cockpit was a veritable icebox and he had to prise open the window with his finger-nails to see where he was and to take his photograph. He tried to call up Bruce Gillies again, and also Stewart Cain, who was flying the Eagle. He got no reply, but gave his height and position in case they were still receiving him (which they were).

The return journey was, of course, much harder, with the wind now adverse. Unless he maintained between 80 and 100 mph, he seemed to make little headway; the downdraughts between the waves were up to 3,000 ft per minute, so in spite of his great altitudes, a single mistake could have had him on the ground in a few minutes. At the southern end of Lees Valley, he again called Christchurch control for clearance. A TEAL Electra was climbing out to 24,000 ft. By now the Skylark was at 28,000 ft, so obviously the Electra was in no hazard.

He was beginning to feel the need for food. On a flight a few weeks before he had taken a thermos-flask of hot coffee, but the low pressures at altitude had caused the cork to lift, and the coffee had frozen solid and hence been useless. So on this occasion he had taken a bottle of lemonade and some sandwiches. Both were useless —the lemonade a mass of ice-crystals and the sandwiches triangles of frozen rock. In the rush of the take-off he had not put on his full kit and the combination of cold and hunger began to present a serious hazard.

About now, at an altitude of over 28,000 ft, he began to fee
decidedly odd; he found himself busy trying to call Omarama, but
on the Christchurch tower frequency. His previous experience immediately led him to suspect anoxia, and a glance at his blue-finger-
nails confirmed the suspicion. He grabbed the oxygen valve and
found himself turning it the wrong way—to the 'off' position. The
shock of this realisation aroused him; he turned it full on, took
several deep breaths, then opened his airbrakes and dived down to
25,000 ft and promptly felt better. Investigation showed that his
oxygen mask was not fitting tightly, having lost much of its elasticity
in the cold.

Six hours after take-off he was over Staveley. The cirrus arch
was now above him, cutting off the sun, and the cold was intense.
He found himself rubbing first one leg and then the other, muttering
'The cruel cold, the cruel cold.' This kind of flight can be a solitary
experience, for the sky is so vast and one is so insignificantly embedded in it.

Now he had to move to the west, upwind, and so leave the comforting line of the wave he had been following for over 100 miles. He
dived into wind, found the next wave at 18,000 ft and repeated the
manoeuvre a second time. At 18:00 hrs he was half-way across the
Fairlie Basin at 13,700 ft. In most parts of the world this would
indeed be a comforting height, but not in these great wave systems.
He thought of abandoning the record attempt, running comfortably
along the wave and landing at Timaru with his 500 km easily in the
bag. But world record winners are made of sterner stuff than that.
He rejected the temptation and, although there seemed no visible
support to the south, he set off on course and arrived over Burke's
Pass at 12,000 ft. At 10,000 ft over the Tekapo River he encountered
unmarked and entirely unexpected lift and for the first time in the
whole flight realised that there might be a chance of success.

At 19:00 hrs he was past Simons Hill at 12,000 ft and had only
to make a final up-wind dog-leg into just one more wave, when he
could turn along it and it would lead him back to his starting point.
Marking its position was a roll-cloud, that indication of the violent
turbulence that frequently underlays wave systems. The Skylark
crept up behind it, and suddenly the thrashing came. The aircraft
bumped and banged, wings veering and clawing the insane air.

His camera hit the cockpit roof with a bang magnified by the cramped size of the cockpit.

But Dick was ready for this; he put up his speed to the maximum permitted in rough air, and suddenly was through it and at 8,000 ft found himself rising, swiftly and smoothly. At this moment he knew he had won the day.

It was now 19:30 hrs. He had eaten nothing all day and was feeling cold and sick. But he reached Omarama at 10,000 ft and touched down shortly afterwards with all the camp surrounding the aircraft. Since they had heard his transmissions throughout the entire flight and there had been silence for the last half-hour, the excitement when he landed victoriously can be imagined.

Bruce Gillies expressed his mixed emotions of congratulation and frustration by seizing Dick and ducking him in the creek, whereupon the entire camp threw themselves on Bruce and reciprocated the operation. But Bruce put himself to rights the very next day when in the high wind and almost total cloud-cover he set off and triumphantly achieved his Gold C in his Skylark 2.

These were great days.

∽∽∽

10

Which Sailplane is the Best?

Well, which?

Pilots are always dashing up to me asking 'Is your sailplane better than mine?' as if there was a monosyllabic answer.

The other awkward question is: 'My best gliding angle is 36—what's yours?' To which the answer is (a) how do you know, and (b) do you mean—the gliding angle I buy it on, or the one I fly it on if I want to win? This does not imply that anyone is trying to be dishonest, but because no one really knows (or hardly ever knows) what is the exact performance of a sailplane, all designers have to make estimates which naturally tend to be optimistic.

To take these problems in order: What *is* a 'better' sailplane?

Let us first be quite clear on the question of span. Given the same degree of sophistication, and up to a span where structural limitations become serious, a larger-span machine must have a better performance than a smaller-span one. But performance is far from the only criterion. Stability and handling is another thing, and on the important question of manoeuvrability, it is easier to get, e.g. quick rates of roll and lighter controls with a small machine than with a larger one.

Let us therefore, in our search for the 'better', put down first our specification of the perfect.

1 PERFORMANCE

    a) A low minimum sinking speed—say 2 ft/sec.
    b) A good maximum gliding angle—say an L/D of 40.
    c) Good penetration—say an L/D of 20 at 90 knots.

2 HANDLING AND STABILITY

    a) Positive stability at all speeds.

b) Light and responsive controls at all speeds; quick rate of
roll.
c) Limiting airbrakes.
d) Good cockpit—good view, draught-free, silent, good instrument panel, adjustable seats and pedals; adequate width
for broad pilots—in one word—comfort.

3 PRICE

In these inflationary days, it is impossible to define the word
'cheap'. But it is possible to select a machine that will be cheap
and easy to maintain and to repair. Very few pilots take this
into consideration, yet even in competitions, the ability to
carry out a quick repair will often make all the difference to the
final result.

4 WEIGHT

Light, say 300 lb, to facilitate rigging, handling on the ground,
and trailing. Quick and easy to rig.

5 RUGGEDNESS

This is not the same as strength. All aircraft have to meet
strength requirements so that they don't break up in the air,
but the rugged aircraft stands up to the knocks of real life,
which take place on the ground.

Having set down the specifications for a perfect glider, it will
be clear that we shall have to wait for the next world before we can
hope to get one. The best any human pilot can do is to decide what
he wants most, how much he is prepared to spend, and then—buy
whatever machine most nearly fits his desires and his pocket.

If he wants to win records, he must go for a fast machine above all,
regardless of price, for he is only interested in good days with strong
lift. If he wants to win championships he needs a wide spectrum of
performance. Weight and ease of rigging are secondary. If he wants
the maximum of fun, he will go for the performance spectrum but
price will be a factor, and so will weight and general ease of ground
handling, for the most fanatical glider pilot wants to keep at least
a small circle of friends.

The aspect that costs least is good stability and handling, for this is a function of design skill. So if everything else is equal, select the machine which is best in this field. If a machine handles well, you can centre in a thermal and outclimb another which is, on paper, better, and you can tackle cloudflying and rough air conditions with safety and confidence. You won't get so tired, so will land safely and fly better next day. You will have much more fun.

So the first answer to this first awkward question is: 'Better for what and for whom?'

On the second question, of performance, the main problem is the great difficulty of accurate measurement. About once in ten years one particular type may get reasonably accurately measured. With an almost audible thump, everyone comes down to earth. Then year by year new types come along with estimated performances that creep higher and higher. Everyone naturally tends to optimism in their estimates, and I suppose no one is much the worse off provided relative estimates remain roughly proportionate. Machine A claims 37; machine B 40. If the figures, on test, should come to 35 and 38, relatively speaking the pilots of each will not be misled—unless they base their speed charts on these figures, but even so a few sad experiences will lead them to discount them downwards in actual flight.

Performance : the elusive polar

Performance is generally assessed on the polar curve (see Fig. 7), and the choice here lies in general on deciding how much importance is attached to the left-hand sector—the climbing regime —and how much to the right-hand one—the cruising regime.

Until recently, the emphasis, performance-wise, in this country has been on getting to the top of the thermal as quickly as possible, with some sacrifice of speed to the next one. This presumably because of our temperate conditions. Now fashion is swinging towards wearing the polar more to the right.

Of course, designers attempt to get the best of both worlds, but this all too quickly leads to extremes in complication, and hence price, and consequently to the sacrifice of a good number of the other requirements.

Looking south over Mt Cook to the Mackenzie country

Matthew Wills, Peter, Dick and Helen Georgeson, at Simons Hill, 1954

The Skylark 4 landing at Lasham
Justin Wills in the Dart, Lasham, 1967

Unfortunately it is extremely difficult to obtain real cast-iron polar curves for sailplanes. The reason is not far to seek—the work involved is expensive, time-consuming and even dull. Until some-one thinks of a better way, what is required is a large number of

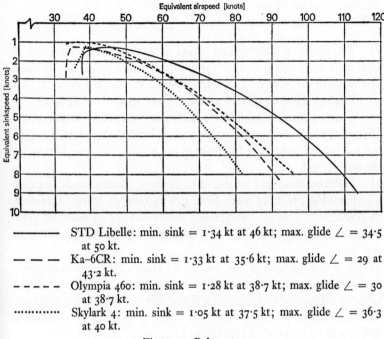

STD Libelle: min. sink = 1·34 kt at 46 kt; max. glide $\angle$ = 34·5 at 50 kt.

Ka–6CR: min. sink = 1·33 kt at 35·6 kt; max. glide $\angle$ = 29 at 43·2 kt.

Olympia 460: min. sink = 1·28 kt at 38·7 kt; max. glide $\angle$ = 30 at 38·7 kt.

Skylark 4: min. sink = 1·05 kt at 37·5 kt; max. glide $\angle$ = 36·3 at 40 kt.

Figure 7   Polar curves

aero-tows to considerable heights with specially instrumented sail-planes in calm air—usually therefore at unearthly hours in the early morning—followed by hours and days of dull mathematical com-putations.

We really must try and overcome this problem, and not only in this country, but in the meantime the—very second—best is to indulge in comparison flying—flying two different types of sailplane side-by-side over a range of different speeds. Since even this involves at the very least one aero-tow to 5000 ft for each of the two gliders concerned, it is not cheap, but it is interesting enough to expect a number of pilots to try it out, and even a number of single reports coming from several different pairs of pilots from different parts of the world, will, taken together, give some reasonable idea, not of absolute, but of relative performances. If these reports are sent to the manufacturer concerned, it would enable him to produce something at least likely to be more reliable than the third, least satisfactory, method of all—calculated polars.

The following notes may help:

1) The thing is enormously easier if each glider concerned is equipped with radio, so that the pilots can talk to each other and one of them can give data (heights, speeds, etc.) to the ground.

2) The test must be carried out above any unstable layer of air.

3) The two aircraft should fly approximately level with each other, about a span apart. If one is up to 3 yards behind the other, it helps; but not too far, otherwise the wake of the leading one may advantage the one behind.

4) There is a tendency for one or both pilots unconsciously to apply a little rudder, to keep away from the partner. It is wise therefore to put a wool-tuft on the perspex cockpit-cover in front of your nose, as this very sensitive slip indicator will immediately show this up.

5) It is best to start in the low speed range, for obvious reasons. A comparison at this end takes longer than you would think. Given a minimum sink around 2 ft/sec, five minutes flying will cost 600 ft, and if by then one aircraft is 25 ft higher than the other, this indicates a superiority of 4%. Quite a lot.

6) The start of the test should be signalled to the ground observer, with the speed and height, who then presses a stopwatch. The best measure of height difference is the fuselage-length of the glider— say 25 ft. When both parties agree that one machine is around one fuselage-length higher than the other, tell the ground, giving altitude, which then stops its watch. The speed and time will give approximately the air-distance flown. Tap the altimeter before giving starting and finishing heights.

From these data, the distance, time and height-loss, an approximate comparison will emerge, which should be quoted as a percentage.

7) Do *not* think this will give anything like a figure of true corrected

sinking speeds. The two ASI's may read slightly differently, due either to different position errors, or one being out of calibration. The air is almost certainly not truly stable, and is certainly not a 'standard atmosphere'. The wings of each aircraft may be covered with dust or squashed flies, accreted since take-off. Dozens of calculations are required, and dozens of readings, before a true corrected point can be plotted on the polar. But the figure you get may be of *some* direct use: you may get some idea of the real performance you can expect in real air from your actual glider when covered in real dust and squashed flies. Come to think of it this may matter more than anything else.

8) If the original aero-tow is 5 miles down-wind, the end of the first test (up-wind) may bring one over the airfield again with, say, 4000 ft to go, and still 2000 ft of stable air below. The pilot slightly to the rear will have been 'in charge' (because he can see more of what is going on), so it is useful then to use airbrakes to level up the aircraft again, go straight ahead and repeat the test with the previous leading pilot dropping slightly back and taking charge.

9) If there is still useful height available, turn down-wind towards the airfield and do another test in the higher speed range. Here the differences in performance are likely to be larger, so although height is lost more quickly, a fuselage-length height-difference will be achieved more quickly.

It is not much good going on after this amount of height difference has been established, because thereafter the two pilots' estimates of the difference will vary wildly.

10) When sending in your results, include any substantial differences in the configuration of each glider—viz. differences in pay-load (difference in pilot weights, weight of instrumentation such as one machine having accumulators installed for electric services, the other not, etc), any non-standard features on either machine likely to affect the drag, one machine being old and wrinkled and the other spanking brand-new, etc.

If we have so far had to buy gliders based on performances calculated in optimistic designers' heads (for if a designer was not an optimist he would commit suicide), the remedy lies partially in our hands.

Example of what kinds of report *not* to send:

1 The last thermal took me to 5000 ft after which I glided 40 miles. Your glider is *wonderful*.

2 Ditto . . . ditto 10 miles. Ditto . . . ditto . . . lousy.

3 At 70 knots its sinking speed is only 1 knot. Marvellous!

4 Ditto . . . ditto 6 knots. You should be shot.

Such information is not sufficiently full to enable anyone to form any conclusions on it, except possibly some tentative ones about the sender.

Cold feet

I have written above that pilot comfort is one of the most important features of a good sailplane. However good a pilot you may be, if you sit for up to ten hours in a cramped or uncomfortable cockpit, your flying will progressively deteriorate, and the very last moment of the flight may call for a difficult landing involving maximum skill just when you are most tired.

An altitude record to 30,000 ft in New Zealand in 1954 was limited, amongst other things, by the risk of losing my feet through frostbite; for at that height the heat of the sun through the perspex cockpit cover was still sufficient to keep my body warm, but in the shadow of the nose my feet rapidly froze and lost all feeling. It was thus quite impossible to tell if they were so frostbitten as to be permanently damaged.

So before a second trip Kitty and I did a lot of work trying to think up some device to keep them even slightly above freezing point. At first we tried electric socks. An American friend sent us some special resistance wire, and Kitty knitted it into a pair of socks. These were the days before most gliders carried wet batteries, so the only easily available source of power was a nest of dry batteries, to be carried in one's pocket. Alas, it proved, as was to be expected, that dry batteries did not hold enough juice to keep one's feet warm for more than a very few minutes.

Then I ran to earth a firm making some chemical powder, which produced large amounts of heat when water was poured on it. I got them to make up a number of bags full of this stuff, small enough to fit under my insteps when wearing a somewhat oversize pair of shoes.

Then complications started building up. How to introduce the water when needed? It was no good putting it in before take-off, since once in, the chemical action was irreversible, and it was obviously necessary to keep one's powder dry until it was actually needed. So rather sinister long rubber tubes were inserted into each bag, and run up inside my trousers legs, out of the top, through holes in the pockets of my flying overalls, and so ready to hand when needed. A plastic bottle full of water in the cockpit pocket completed the plot.

On a second visit to New Zealand in 1957 the day came at Simon's Hill, in the Mackenzie Country, when once more the Mount Cook wave was blowing. Jon Hamilton and my son Chris set off in the Eagle, and landed later at Christchurch with five New Zealand two-seater records. But I stayed behind in the Weihe, to have a shot at another altitude record in the lee of the big mountain.

The vast rotor cloud was churning away over Lake Pukaki, and the wave above was obviously going to enormous heights. Somehow I could not achieve enough height to surmount the rotor, so rashly decided to enter it. Before doing so, I poured some water down each of my two tubes, and felt the comforting warmth stealing into the soles of my feet. Then, in we went.

I suppose, in retrospect, this was a silly thing to do. Rotor clouds of this order have been known to be so violent that aircraft entering them have been broken up. But, through keeping the speed of the Weihe well down, I emerged unscathed half an hour later, after the second roughest flight of my life, but much too low to attempt a further shot into the wave. Alas, by now, my feet were roasting. Heat sufficient to keep them warm at 30,000 ft was superabundant in midsummer at 4000 ft, and there was no way of turning it off.

At last, it was too much. I turned and landed back at Irishman Creek. When I got out of the cockpit, stood up, and put my weight on my feet, the heat was such that I gave an involuntary shriek. I nearly blistered them and could have been laid up for days.

This is, I regret to report, *not* a solution to this serious problem.

Future trends

The polar curves on p. 187 are, I hope, self-explanatory. The very big jumps between the performances of the Olympia 460, Ka-6CR, Skylark 4 (the old generation of wooden aircraft), and the glass-fibre Libelle show the enormous technical strides which have taken place over the past few years. These sudden jumps are similar to those which took place in powered aviation between say, biplanes and monoplanes in 1930–1935, between piston and jet-engined aircraft in 1946–1950, and now possibly between subsonic and supersonic aircraft.

Each step-jump is followed by a slow improvement as detail design is polished up, then another step comes into sight.

This latest leap forward has been foreseen for some years: it is based upon the application of an entirely new basic structural material. Resin-bonded fibreglass has taken over from plywood. This has made it possible to achieve profiles of such accuracy that we can make use of wing-sections and shapes which are not efficient when subjected to the slight wrinklings and distortions unavoidable when using the previous materials. In addition, it has produced much lighter gliders: my new Libelle is nearly 100 lb lighter than my old Dart, and has a much better performance. It weighs 400 lb against 490 lb, and has a span of 15 metres against the Dart's 17 metres. A dramatic improvement indeed!

Where do we go from here? In the immediate future (1972) we have now approaching completion in this country the advanced Sigma project, a design initiated by Nick Goodhart and a distinguished band of colleagues.

This is a concept which has been waiting for a design group with the courage to attempt to overcome the detail engineering difficulties inherent in trying to get the necessary machinery into a wing of variable camber and variable area—one which with flaps retracted gives a small area and hence good high-speed performance and with flaps extended a larger area and a slower speed for the climbing regime when circling in thermals; in fact, to achieve the benefits of two wings in one (or four wings in two, if you want to be pedantic). The performance gain on existing advanced sailplanes could be as much as 15% at the high-speed end.

Further ahead we have yet another new material in sight—carbon-fibre. This could produce a further dramatic saving of weight. It is likely to be 5 or even 10 years ahead, for at present the cost is prohibitive.

On about the same time-scale is yet another development of even more dramatic possibility—a thermal detector. We have had several shots at it in past years, but all have failed. But the big boys—the airlines—are now after an instrument to detect at a distance what is called CAT (Clear Air Turbulence)—the high altitude rough air that is met in clear air jet-streams. No doubt the first instruments will be much too heavy and expensive for our use, but once the basic problem is solved, we may expect cheaper solutions in due course.

To be able to detect rising air from a distance will transform our sport. Some would say for the worse, but alas, we cannot help that.

11

The Charms of Radio

Small beginnings

For years two-way radio in gliders was an impractical dream. The Air Traffic Control authorities used to press us to install it, to which the answer was that there were no sets in existence light enough, cheap enough, small enough, or which consumed sufficiently little electricity, for it to be anything but a beautiful idea.

It was around 1952 that Pye produced the first practicable equipment, which we used in the World Championships; but then and for some years afterwards the sets were so delicate that they were virtually only usable if you were a radio expert, or had one in your team who would be constantly tuning them up and maintaining them at a useful level of efficiency.

In the early '60s various American valve sets appeared which were both reliable and could be powered by dry batteries, and in 1963 I installed one of these. Nowadays they are outclassed by small, light transistorised sets, operating on three separate frequencies.

This is nothing like enough to make it possible to communicate with the ATC authorities, but is extremely useful both as a means of communication between sailplane and retrieving car, and also as a method of reducing the collision risk between sailplanes in the same cloud.

Radio has very much altered the entire flavour of soaring flight; whether for better or worse depends, I suppose, on your temperament. Without it, you were romantically on your own—so was Kitty. Now you live in a babel of voices, and if you make a mistake and have to own up, the whole world hears of it. 'Philip's come unstuck and landed at Basingstoke again!' goes from Land's End to John o'Groats in 60-mile jumps from pilot to pilot.

Certainly nowadays you hardly ever land in Cornwall to find that your trailer has gone to Liverpool, but even when that happened your wait was tinged with a kind of romance: and in gliding, as I have said, it is the romantic which has always appealed to me.

But I find it sad that Free Distance flying, which is by far the most romantic and subtle task of all, is rapidly becoming despised as too chancy in favour of the mechanistic attractions of closed circuit racing, a kind of feverish fishbowling around frenetic triangles.

But it is no doubt now on its way out, aided by the increasing restrictions on airspace and the really staggering distances which modern sailplanes can now cover, which can make a retrieve *en masse* a major exercise in logistics.

Let me describe two flights in the pre-radio days, and some just after radio came in, but before it became the almost tyrannical device it now seems to be.

Bramcote–Dunstable, June 1947

This was a flight of a mere 56 miles, carried out in my immediately post-war Weihe. It was a very odd flight indeed.

The weather was grey and the air apparently stable. A light wind from west of north drifted across Bramcote airfield from the smoky regions of Birmingham, Lichfield and beyond. Occasional drops of rain showed, however, that instability existed in the upper air, and this had been forecast. In fact it sounded as though, if one were lucky and hit a means of getting above say 3,000 ft, something might be done.

Various other competitors on this day, the first of the 1947 National Gliding Competition, had been aero-towed up, but had all come down again, one or two a few miles away.

When I took off at 16:30 hrs there was no special reason to hope for anything better, though occasional irregularities in the cloud overhead, and patches of watery sun, were to be seen.

I asked my tug pilot to tow me straight upwind to 2,000 ft and on the way up we passed through only very mild patches of lift. At 1,800 ft over Nuneaton, I thought we struck a rather better patch, and released. I soon found I had been optimistic and turned downwind to fly back to the airfield. Not a wrinkle in the sky all the way back, and I crossed the upward boundary at 600 ft, and circled to land.

At the last moment I came on a slightly brighter patch, where the sun was struggling weakly through the overcast and shining on the mown hay over the starting point, and the tea-tent in the spectators' enclosure. And then I saw a couple of hundred feet above me a Weihe just winch-launched, and circling!

Simultaneously my variometer shook itself, the red ball dropped for the first time and the green ball opened one eye, gave a sort of elfin hiccup, and flopped back into its seat again. At 400 ft I started to stooge about in an erratic circle after the green ball. She's up—she's down—up again—no she isn't—yes she is.

After a few circles the altimeter showed a slight gain, and the Weihe above me a bigger one. We struggled round and round, and the tent enclosure drifted away gradually upwind, 600 ft—700 ft—900 ft—and it looked as if we had a hope.

At 1,000 ft I saw, above the other Weihe and further downwind, an Olympia, perhaps 1,500 ft up, and still circling. If only I didn't fall out of the bottom of the thermal! At 1,700 ft I was nearly up to the other two machines, when the Olympia went off south, and the other Weihe east–south–east.

Away in this latter direction were distinct signs of a rain-cloud of fair dimensions, so a little later I followed, and Bramcote soon disappeared. Down at 1,200 ft I caught up with the other Weihe, circling under an outpost of the larger rain-cloud, and I followed suit. Shortly after the other machine went off eastwards towards the large cloud, but I felt suspicious, and hung on to what I had got for some time longer. At 2,200 ft I saw a quite hopefully gloomy-looking chunk of murk to the south–east, and although I didn't know where I was, my goal was Dunstable, so this was the right direction, and I set off for it.

Rugby wireless masts soon hove up through the greyness, and the greyish blackness above it was emitting bits of drizzle. When I reached it I found gentle lift, and circled up into it.

Inside lift was neither strong nor constant, but with the splendid stability of the Weihe and my specially damped turn-and-bank indicator, I found I could chase round in ellipses or figure-eights almost as well as in clear air, and so climbed to about 6,000 ft.

Further efforts seemed to produce as many downs as ups, so I straightened on to my course of 150° and set sail for Dunstable.

Bits of ups and downs were met, but for about 20 minutes nothing was to be seen, then I came out of actual cloud at around 4,500 ft and dimly could see the ground through the grey haze, not however well enough to locate myself.

I was again in a patch of watery sunlight, and now away to the east saw something that looked quite active, a greyish and messy mass of cumulus rising from the mist below. This was off my course, but I didn't actually know that I was on the darned thing anyway, so set off for it. At one point I could detect a kind of cauliflower, at which I steered.

Ten minutes later I flew into the side of the cloud, on a compass course for the cauliflower, and shortly afterwards rattled through the usual down currents into quite good lift—for the day. Broken lift of 10/12 ft/sec took me up to 8,000 ft and then it got pretty rough. I couldn't manoeuvre back into smoother lift, so again set course. As I had flown east of my track, I added 10° for luck, and hung on to 160°. Such is sailplane navigation!

After a while I came out again, to a very drear scene. Below was grey haze, and a very faint shadow of the earth. Behind and to one side was a mess of cloud, and above a sheet of stratus. No sign of sun or life anywhere, and the air as dead as ditchwater. It wasn't the sort of day a chap expects to find himself around in a glider at all.

I sailed on again, sticking to 160° for want of anything better, and soon saw ahead a large grey column of cloud appearing out of the haze below, its top disappearing into the stratus overhead.

I tooled inside and after a few minutes struck good lift. By fiddling around I reached 20 ft/sec, and the altimeter started to wind itself up in a forthright manner. At 9,000 ft a bit of ice started to form, and in a fit of optimism I put on my oxygen mask (1947 improvement) and turned on the gas. But at 9,900 ft I again entered rough air and although I persevered in fairly brisk ups and downs, made no more height, so set off again.

Even on the Weihe, holding a course on a magnetic compass and a turn needle is not a very exact proceeding, so when a while later I again came out above the haze and below the stratus, I hardly knew which sheet of my map I had better turn to.

I sailed on however, and when down to 6,000 ft came to the edge of a sheet of stratus below me. Just under this edge I thought I could see through the haze faintly white geometric lines, which I took to be the concrete roads of the outskirts of a largish town. This I thought could only be Luton, no other town of this size being near my course; so I turned, in order to avoid the sandwich of clear air ahead between the top and bottom layers of stratus, and circled down until at 3,000 ft I came to the lower level of the stratus, and there, sure enough, was Luton, in the haze below. It was like a conjuring trick. Nothing up my sleeve—absolutely damn all.

After that of course, it was easy. In dead still air I flew to Dunstable arriving at 1,800 ft and circled down, landing at 19:25 hrs. The inmates were as surprised to see me as I was to be there.

The Killing, June 1962

You are standing in front of the Ops Room map the morning after a competition day. It is dotted with pins each bearing the number of one of your opponents' sailplanes, marking its landing place. Far out in front of all stands one lone pin. It bears your own number.

This is a flight we have all made hundreds of times. Then we have woken up. On 6 June 1962, it actually happened to me.

The combination of circumstances was unusual. I was flying my new Skylark 4. It was, as everyone now knows, a really splendid machine. But everyone was waiting for it to show its paces. And on the very first day of the 1962 Nationals, held at Aston Down in the Cotswolds near Cirencester, I had fallen flat on my face. I had just taken delivery, had only flown her three times before the Champs, and my variometers were still in a mess. On the first day's task of a 300-km triangle, 28 pilots finished, and I collapsed on the second leg. I started with the undistinguished placing of 31 out of 40—176 marks out of 1,000. Everyone, including myself, thought that was the end of it. Modern pilotage is of such a high standard that one can't hope to catch up after such a calamity.

The only hope was a really tricky day in which one could take a desperate chance—having nothing to lose—and by success turn the tables on the rest of the field; but the weather was doggedly consistent—day after day of anticyclonic thermals, either with shallow cumulus or blue—producing triangular races and the like with no chance of a break through. Came 6 June, and a poor forecast—light easterly wind, no cloud, hot blue day, low inversion, thermals starting late and low, working up to only around 3,000 ft by the mid-afternoon. Ann Welch gave us Free Distance. It was the only possible task, and my only possible chance.

The pundits, secure in their lead, would not risk cutting themselves off from the airfield by going away too early and risking an early collapse. My 4 was exceptionally good at holding on to low broken gentle upcurrents.

The possibilities were to go north-west to Anglesea, around 140 miles, or south-west for Land's End, nearly 200 miles. Down the narrowing Cornish peninsula the obvious risk was sea-breezes coming in and killing the lift. But Met had uttered some magic words —'possibility of sea-breezes from both coasts.' A sea-breeze coming in from the south with the wind might obviously meet, somewhere near the north coast, with its opposite number from the north, and something must go up. Met didn't think so, but it was a chance. (See map, p. 201.)

I told Kitty I was going to try for Cornwall, and took off at 11:00 hrs. On release, I saw a number of gliders circling in weak thermal a mile downwind of the airfield, about 1,500 ft above it (Aston Down is 600 ft up.) I joined them, and sure enough, reached the bubbly top at 2,100 ft above sea-level. Soon everyone else abandoned it for another, as the wind drifted us away from base. I hung on, endlessly, drifting across Nailsworth until I was irrevocably committed. Downwind slightly to the south was Nympsfield, the home of the Bristol Club, on top of its ridge with the Severn Valley to the west and the sun beating down into a deep cleft to the east. If there was going to be another thermal anywhere, it must be there. I straightened up, reached it 1,200 ft above the field, and nosed around. Over the north-west slope I found another gentle upcurrent, and inched up to 2,100 ft again. Next please.

The glory of the country around Aston Down is that it is full of incident—hills and valleys, woods and fields. South of me, Dursley basked in its steep valley running west to the Severn plain. Another natural. I drifted down to it, reaching it at 1,500 ft. Again, a shy and gentle heave. I circled—I couldn't quite locate it. Over the town, over the golf-course on top of the southern hill, back to the town. Down to 1,200 ft, up to 1,400, down again. Humphry Dimock joined me in his 3F, and struggled lower and lower to a landing. But in these conditions a margin of performance—allied to a big improvement in aileron response—makes the difference between failure and success. At last I got my half-knot circle complete, and gently reacquired my pathetic ceiling of 2,100 ft.

Kitty and David in the meantime had hooked up the trailer and rushed to a hill near Avening, to make quite sure I was going to Cornwall instead of North Wales. Dennis Burns didn't do this, and when he phoned that evening from Devon found Ann had landed 350 miles away near Liverpool! When Kitty saw me struggle away from Stroud she knew my die was cast, and set off gallantly for the far southern seaside.

Two hours later I was exhausted but safe, in the lee of Filton, circling up in the first reasonable thermal of the day. There had been one or two scarifying moments on the way. At one point I was circling low down when a sudden shriek, as of a maiden suddenly pierced to the heart (or something), came apparently from the fuselage behind my head. It turned out to be the whistle of a train passing on the line just below. Possibly the driver hooted to get me out of the way. Possibly not. But I was certainly pretty low.

But coming off the vast Brabazonian concrete of Filton was, at last, a man-sized thermal, in which I climbed briskly to the unbelievable height of 3,500 ft; and downwind of Bristol itself was another similar gay fountain of rising air.

My course now ran south-west, out to sea beyond Weston-super-Mare, and back to the North Devon coast near Watchet. I had assumed that here I would have to make a long tack to the east, to get round the flat wet country of Taunton Vale, but just as I was about to set off in that direction I saw, out to sea beyond Weston, the faintest hint of a flat white cumulus cap sitting on top of the brown haze marking the limit of the inversion. Almost certainly, a sea breeze, cutting in from the west, was lifting the easterly wind over its invading wedge of cold stable air. It was a bold decision, but then it was a day for bold decisions. I set off along track, losing height fairly rapidly, out over the coast, over the miles of flat brown greasy

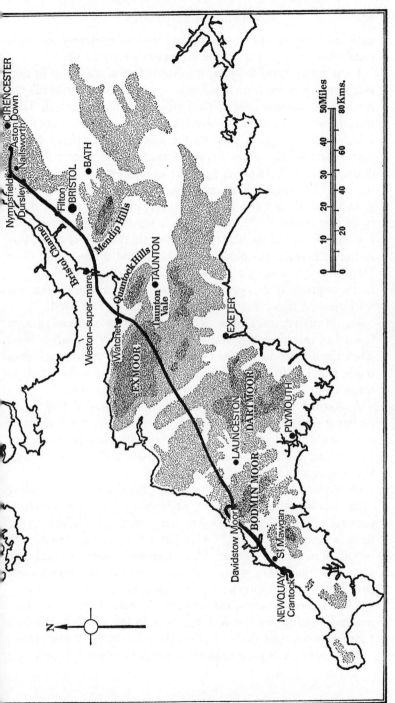

Aston Down to Crantock, 1962

mud until, beyond all reason, beyond hope of retrieving the flight should the guess go wrong, the variometer swung to lift.

I was up to 3,000 ft again, the North Devon coast was in easy reach, my recovery from the depths was definitely a possibility. I reached the western edge of the Quantock Hills at 2,000 ft. They ran east–west. The wind was along them. But by now I was in form. I knew where to go. A bowl on the southern side offered a good source for a wind-shadow thermal. I reached it at 1,500 ft. It was, of course, there. Up again at 3,000 ft I set off on the long grind across the edge of Exmoor towards still distant Cornwall. Four hours had gone by. In the first two I had covered 24 miles, in the second two twice that distance. Two-and-a-half hours later I was in sight of Bodmin Moor, and the blue sea to the north. A billow of smoke just in from the coast was blowing strongly inland to the south. Over Davidstow Moor airfield I circled up in lift which took me to the north, in precisely the opposite direction. The sea-breeze effect was working—the upper wind was opposed to the surface wind.

For 20 miles or more I flew along, parallel to the coast and perhaps five miles inland, gently climbing or descending the whole way. Then the day definitely began to die. St Mawgan aerodrome was in reach, and I got there with 1,200 ft to spare. It was too much to throw away. My killing must be as complete as possible.

At 800 ft I whispered over the roofs of Newquay, dozing in the declining sun, hardly losing height, over the river, a low range of hills, another creek showed ahead. On my right a caravan park, next to it a long narrow field of cut hay, up-hill and into wind. Safe home, after an eight hours' flight.

Quarryfield Caravan Park, Crantock, proved the perfect landing place. Kind and helpful folk, tea, a telephone. A quarter of an hour later Kitty phoned Aston Down. 'Any news of Philip?' 'Yes,' came a lugubrious voice, 'you've got a long journey I'm afraid'. —'Oh dear, North Wales?'—'No Crantock, near Newquay, in Cornwall.' She looked at her map. 'As a matter of fact, it's six miles from where I am!' Kitty's telepathy had done it again.

I had flown 158 miles, the runner-up's marks were in the four-hundreds against my 1,000. I was back in the running. Would I have taken these chances if I had not started so badly? I don't know.

With this flight my log-book showed that I had just topped a total

Primary trainer, Dunstable, 1933
Falke powered trainer, 1971

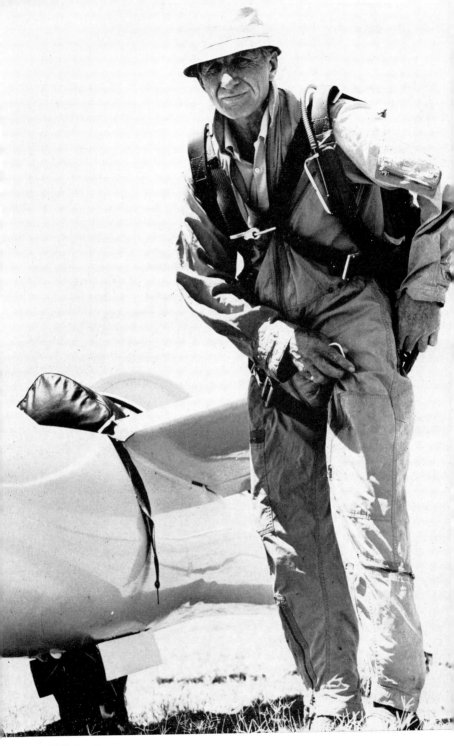

Heli Lasch

of 25,000 miles cross-country flying in sailplanes. Once round the world. It sounds a lot, until one confesses it took 30 years to reach it.

Mallard to Drake—Do you quack?—April 1963

In 1963 I fitted radio into my glider after resisting the temptation for fifteen years because I am not an electronic expert and cannot understand anyway why a radio transmitter should need more looking after than the home wireless receiver. But at last a friend assured me that a set was available which you could fit and forget. So I fell.

The main idea was to make it more fun for Kitty, who had for thirty years chased me with a trailer when I fly across country, fished me and my glider out of the field I land in, and brought me back. She had by now exceeded 100,000 miles in this open-ended egg-and-spoon race, so it was possible to think she needed a break.

Pre-radio, the form was for her to set off when I did, along my line of flight, telephoning back to base every hour. No news, and she carried on. When I landed I rang back to base, so the next time she 'phoned she got my message. It meant a lot of small change for Kitty, to activate roadside telephone-boxes.

With radio in car and glider, all this is different, for (in theory anyway) she can keep in touch as I go along and follow on (or under) my heels. But there are snags.

In the first place, the Post Office at first only offered glider pilots one wavelength on the VHF band. This had two main effects. First, every other glider pilot with radio was on your wavelength, so the air got pretty crowded with chatter, which had to be kept to a minimum, or life became too confused altogether. Secondly, range is limited, like a searchlight, to 'line-of-sight', so that the higher you are the further you can communicate.

This of course means the converse—the lower you are the less far you can talk, and as you really want to get through to Kitty most of all just as you are down to a few hundred feet, and finally committed to landing in a field near Nether Mudwallop, it is most frustrating that at that very moment you are both struck dumb.

Nevertheless, car and glider were equipped, and we set off on our first cross-country. Airborne, I switched on. The loudspeaker is concealed behind my instrument board. Up to now one of the charms of gliding had been that you were alone, very much on your own. But now the nose of my glider became filled with voices.

Suddenly a girl's voice said very rapidly, 'Beep-beep!' and a man replied 'Beep-beep!' This somewhat Martian exchange apparently conveyed all that was needed, because that was the end of that conversation.

Then Peter Scott was in the cockpit with me. 'Mallard to Drake, do you quack? Over.' Philippa replied 'Loud and clear. Over.' Peter—'2,500 ft, A20 over.' Philippa—'Am approaching position K. Out.'

Heavens! What could I say? No prearranged concentration of coded messages. No esoteric interchanges. I was the new boy, on his first day at the bottom of the fourth form.

'Philip to Kitty. Am at 3,000 ft over the western outskirts of Norwich, Over.' Kitty—sounding rather miserable and unhatched: 'Thank you, Philip.'

But she cheered up when she rounded the next bend of the road, to find Philippa and trailer waiting by the cross-roads—the mystery of position K out of the bag.

The flight went on, and eventually I came unstuck. Too busy to get through to Kitty, I selected a large muddy field and landed. It was drizzling. 'Philip to Kitty—do you read?'—No reply.

An idea! Born, perhaps, of Telstar. 'Does anyone read poor Philip?' A comforting voice from a glider, still airborne: 'Humphry to Philip—loud and clear.' 'Humphry, could you contact Kitty and ask her to come to a point three miles south of Aylesham?' The reassuring sound of Humphry relaying my position to Kitty, whose reply was still inaudible to me.

About now three would-be-rescuers came squelching through the mud and ran and peered through the streaming perspex of my cockpit at me. 'Can we help? Are you all right? Can we give you a lift to a telephone?' 'It's all right thanks,' I replied from my haven, comfortably lighting my pipe, 'I'm just waiting for my wife to come in range, then I can direct her here'. 'Lord,' I heard one chap mutter to his friend, 'wish I could treat my missus like that!'

Ten minutes later Kitty said: 'Am now three miles south of

Aylesham. Where are you?' and five minutes later car and trailer drew to a halt by the gate in the hedge near by. Radio is fun.

From powder-monkey to admiral, May 1963

On the third contest day of the 1963 Nationals the Wills team's fortunes were at a pretty low ebb. I had completely fallen down on the first two tasks, and my score was only 460 points.

Ann set us a 300-km triangle: Lasham–Sherborne–Nympsfield–Lasham. It was a hot blue easterly day, with a forecast of dry thermals at first, occasional high cumulus expected during the afternoon as the ground heated up.

Around 1 o'clock there was plenty of dry thermal up to 3,000 ft and I decided, having little to lose, to cut away before most of the others. For ten miles or more I bumbled along the top of the haze layer, losing practically no height. To the south, over the coast, cumulus started to form—clearly some sort of sea-breeze front. But it was too far to reach it, so I carried on. And came unstuck.

The wide area of gentle up-current was succeeded by a similar area of down. Lower and lower I sank, until it became clear that I was lost. I just managed to radio Kitty that I was landing by the Pheasant Inn, a few miles east of Salisbury, Peter kindly repeated this message to Kitty, and then I was in a large field, listening to the approaching chorus of my more successful competitors, taking advantage of the improving conditions.

Within a quarter of an hour Kitty and David swept up and drove the trailer right up beside the Skylark. Working on our own, we had her packed up in another quarter of an hour: fortunately the farmer arrived and so saved us the time necessary to find him, and we shot off back to Lasham.

It was a hectic drive, not made any the more pleasant by the hordes of outward bound trailers we swept past on our way, each of which gave us a commiserating wave. Poor us.

Back at Lasham, the field was empty of gliders, save an Austria rigging madly at the launch point after a similar collapse. As we drew up, the crowd belched eager assistants. We arrived at 15:05; at 15:10 I was in the air, and at 15:15 was released in 5 knots up. No time to go back and cross the starting line: for us there was now no question of finishing the course; we were in for a rescuing operation, saving what we could from the wreck.

Conditions were fizzing, upcurrents up to seven knots, cruising speeds up to 70 knots. Once more Hampshire streamed past below, Kitty thundering along the now empty road underneath. Gradually distant voices started coming through again on the radio, and near Salisbury, only 25 minutes later, I saw a glider circling ahead. Joy! So after all we might not be the last.

Kitty and David also started overtaking trailers waiting by the roadside: things were looking up.

Twenty minutes later I was able to tell Kitty to start heading north. I was certain of turning Sherborne, and an hour after take-off I was round the point: several more gliders were around and ahead. The sea-breeze clouds had now moved inland and I was in clear air, whispering along at max. glide speed to try and catch them up. Any attempt to hurry now would be disastrous—and was for those who did.

I headed for a large cumulus which had now built up over Glastonbury, and caught it at 2,000 ft. Cloudbase by now—17:30 hrs—was over 5,000 ft, and on reaching it I switched on the turn indicator and climbed up into the cloud.

At 9,500 ft I ran into trouble. My Cook compass had been showing unaccustomed signs of sticking, and now refused to give me a clear lead out of the cloud on course. Eventually, however, I emerged, but the haze and cloud below were too thick to enable me to make a course other than on my dubious compass. However, I set sail as well as I could on track, and some 20 minutes later Bath appeared ahead to starboard. I gave Kitty my position and was greeted by encouraging noises from her.

West of Charmy Down the scenery below suddenly caused my heart—hitherto somewhat subdued—to leap. 'Kitty from Philip: lots of beautiful sailplanes in the fields below!'—'Philip from Mallard (Peter Scott): where are you?'—'Mallard from Philip: 2,000 ft 14 miles south of Nympsfield'—'Well done, I am on my way home, having landed near Bristol'.

Could it be a dream? No—lots more gliders on the ground slid past underneath. We whispered on, pretending to the air that we weren't there.

'Kitty from Philip: just passing over some sort of monument job, Will land at the bottom of the hill, and phone Nympsfield.' 'Philip from Kitty: why can't you make Nympsfield? Go on!' But at that moment I sank below the hilltop and my reply—which might have been a bit acid—was cut off in its prime.

I landed at 18:30 hrs in the prettiest, tiniest village in England: Wortley, near Wotton-under-Edge. I went to the nearest thatched cottage, where my unexpected hosts welcomed me with elderberry wine of such excellence that Kitty has tried (and failed) to equal it ever since.

I had beaten the field. Radio and the quick rigging of the Skylark 4, plus the lion hearts of Kitty and David, had made the difference between a zero score and 1,000 points.

And the sticking compass, but for which I might have done even better? I had at last agreed to carry wing-pickets, and they had been stowed in my map pocket, just aft of the Cook. They were magnetic, so of course the needle tried to point itself at them regardless. No comment.

Radio location

One of the main uses of radio is for the pilot to tell his team where he is. It is important therefore to devise a scheme enabling him to do this quickly and with fair accuracy; and if he wants to, to keep the information private between himself and his team. (I am a little against this, except possibly in World Championships, but no matter.)

To have no system at all can be catastrophic. After a feverish search on his map, at a time when he is desperately struggling above the middle of nowhere, he may declaim (I have declaimed) he is landing two miles south of West Wanborough, and his team may rush to a point two miles south of West Warnborough, which is 30 miles away. Kitty and I have also had our misunderstandings between Newbury and Blewbury, but managed later on to patch our marriage up again.

A very good and foolproof scheme is based on the use of the BGA plotting tape. This consists of a transparent cellophane adhesive ribbon, with a red line painted along one edge, marked 1 to 10 at inch intervals. (Sorry about the inches, but we live in a barbarous country which is only just coming round to the metric system.) Immediately the course for the day is announced, say a triangle from A to B to C to A, the tape can be stuck in automatically straight lines (no ruler required) along the three legs on the map. To preserve anonymity, A can be located at any required number on the tape, say number 2. Then, on a quarter-inch map, A3 will be four miles on course on the first leg. The retrieve-car map (which must, of course, be the same projection) is taped in identical fashion.

From now on life is easy. 'Four miles south of B6 3,000 ft climbing' is an instant location. Also it clutters up the ether for the minimum of time, and gives one's team all necessary information.

Stripping the tape off is not 100% successful, unless the map is varnished or otherwise surface-protected: it should be tried immediately the day is over. If the surface starts to peel off, one has to stick the tape back in place, and leave the line on the map. But maps are relatively cheap, and change so rapidly that this is not too serious a drawback, compared to the very great advantages of the system.

Whether or no radio is a Good Thing, it has its points. It has saved at least one life.

During the National Championships at Lasham in 1967 we were set, on 29 May, a triangular race from Lasham to Bicester, South Marston, and back to Lasham. Near Oxford some of us ran into a cumulo-nimbus cloud which (as is the way of cu-nim) looked comparatively digestible, and a number of us climbed up into it.

Amongst us were two gliders, one a Ka-6 flown by Tony (Major-General) Deane Drummond, the second, an SHK by Paddy (Air Commodore) Kearon. Unfortunately each was operating on a different radio frequency (we have altered that since) so neither knew the other was in the same cloud.

On the ground, suddenly the message came through from Paddy: 'I have been struck in cloud.' This was heard both at Lasham, and at nearby Bicester, the home field of RAF, gliding, where the chief instructor of RAF gliding, Sergeant Andy Gough, was listening out. Andy: 'By another aircraft?'—Paddy—'I don't know, I still have control, I think, but aircraft is vibrating. I am straightening up to come out of cloud ... I am now out of cloud; there is a large dent in the upper surface and leading edge of my starboard wing.' Andy: 'How far out is the damage?' Paddy: 'About two thirds of way out. The tip is still on . . . is there any way out if the wing comes off?' Andy: 'The main thing is to get your legs from under the instrument panel.' Another pilot chipped in: 'Be careful when you jettison the canopy that the drag on your chute doesn't pin you in your seat.' Paddy: 'I have slackened my straps and can now see that the under surface of my wing is also cut to about half-way back; it gives the impression that it is waggling.' At this moment yet another, unrecorded, pilot cut in and almost certainly saved Paddy's life. 'On no account open your divebrakes.' Andy: 'You must abandon task and land at Bicester.' Paddy: 'I don't like to do that.' Andy (Sergeant) to Paddy (Air Commodore): 'It might save your bloody life; we can always get another SHK—but not another Paddy Kearon.' Long pause. Then, Paddy: 'I didn't know you cared, Andy.'

However, he took his advice, glided gently back to Bicester, and landed, without the normal use of divebrakes. If they had been opened as usual, low down on the last stage of the approach, thus throwing most of the weight of his aircraft on to the tips, the damaged tip must have broken off, and Paddy must have lost his life.

In the meantime, Tony Deane-Drummond had continued on his way, thinking he had suffered a minor lightning strike. When he was clear of cloud, he saw he had lost the outer 3 ft of his starboard tip, but he still carried on until brought down by poor conditions. In the bar that night, he was heard to remark to Paddy that he really thought this sort of thing was carrying inter-Service rivalry too far.

As a result of this incident, we passed a rule that, when entering cloud, all gliders must listen out on the same frequency and report their position before going in, and their height whilst inside.

Lightning strike and collisions in cloud—two of the most dramatic hazards of high-performance gliding. We had better look at them a bit more closely.

Within the past six years I can recall at least six cases of lightning strike in cu-nims in this country. In these, five aircraft were damaged, one destroyed, four pilots fairly seriously shocked, one killed.

The curious thing is that, prior to that, I cannot remember any cases of this sort in this country at all, but I conclude this is simply because only in the last few years has there been any sufficient number of flights in cu-nims for the actuarial consequences to show themselves.

I must do some wildish guesses here, but I should be surprised if during this six-year period there had been more than an average of 100 flights a year in cu-nims. If this is so, the risk of a damaging strike in these clouds is of the order of 1%. This risk is reduced in a metal aircraft, and by bonding the controls in a wooden one, but nothing can avert catastrophe in the event of a direct strike. Although the single fatality we have experienced is insufficient to form any conclusions as to the order of catastrophic risk, it seems to me that this sort of general risk figure is altogether too high, and nothing can be done about it except to keep out of cu-nims.

Lightning strike can have some very devious effects on the structure of wooden aircraft. It has been known to explode the wood internally, rather like a grain of puffed wheat, so that externally everything looks all right, but inside a spar the wood may be almost powderised. It can also run along metal stranded cable and burn out a number of strands in places far away from the strike, which may be difficult to inspect.

Justin was once struck at 21,000 ft in my Dart, the lightning striking the tip of the metal web of the metal/wood bonded spar about 5 ft from the wing-tip, burning a small hole through the underside of the ply bottom surface of the wing, running along to the opposite tip, and burning its way out at the identical point there. The spar had to be virtually sawn to pieces, only to find no serious damage. Kitty and I were so pleased to have him back that the damage to the Dart was almost a pleasure.

Probably because all our aircraft's controls are now bonded, Justin had only experienced a mild shock, but whether or not the aircraft and pilot are physically damaged, the flash and bang associated with a strike are alarming enough to carry the possibility of affecting the pilot's judgment and capacity to carry on in difficult conditions without loss of control.

Let us be clear about this however. If you get in the way of a *direct* strike—whether in a glider, an aeroplane, or sheltering under an oak-tree on a golf course—you are almost certain to be killed.

Coming back to cloud-collision risks. I think we have had about a dozen such collisions since the war, one aircraft lost, no casualties. In this time there have certainly been tens of thousands of cloud flights. So the risk is much smaller than that of lightning strike in cu-nim. But in this case it is possible to reduce it still further by sensible use of radio, and the BGA acted accordingly.

The Gliding Type

Powered gliders

The kind of people making up and running the British gliding movement has been rigorously controlled by the severe demands hitherto made on time and enthusiasm owing to the crudity of our training methods and equipment.

When a new Club starts off on a windy hill-top with no hangar or clubhouse, only the most dedicated fanatics can survive, and the amount of work and organisation required for each achieved hour of flight can be laughable. To find the most charming and competent folk in the world, tight-knit in their struggle for survival, you must go to a distant and newly formed gliding club.

Increasing growth and success then inevitably dilute this pristine band, but nevertheless our freedom to control our own affairs has maintained a very high standard of human being in the gliding world, because it requires a high degree of self-reliance and technical knowledge in different fields. But a recent new development is almost bound, eventually, to produce a change in the spirit of gliding. This is the powered trainer.

Ever since I started gliding the stock silly question from the outsider has been 'Why don't you put a little engine in it?' and for over forty years designers have tried to do just this. For reasons I simply don't understand, until a few years ago all such attempts failed to produce a practicable aircraft; but suddenly, with no noticeable technical advance to explain it, but with perfectly conventional airframes and engines, a number of sensible powered two-seater trainers have come on the market, and the whole picture is in process of transformation.

No longer is it necessary to go week after week to your club and hope, with luck, to get in two or three four-minute training circuits on the two-seater, a hope more often than not dashed by bad weather, mechanical failure of the launching apparatus, or a queue of twenty or thirty aspirants lined up before you arrive. With a powered trainer you can book your half-hour or hour's training at a specific time on a specific day, and unless the weather is quite hopeless only a single other person—your instructor—needs to be on the field when you arrive.

Now this clearly has enormous advantages. Training times will come down from months—or even years—to weeks. Each instructor will produce two or three times the number of trained pilots in the same number of working days, and membership will increase because the factor of frustration which previously limited it will be enormously diminished.

But since the shape and structure of the sieve, which determines the kind of people who have until now formed our movement, is in a very short time undergoing fundamental alteration, so will the nature of the folk who will make up the future be changed. No doubt in the past we have lost some excellent men and women who literally could not spare the time involved, but even more have we automatically lost anyone who was not prepared to join in the communal labours of a gliding club. Our remaining safeguard is the tradition we have built up, which will take some erosion.

There cannot be any direct competition between a motorless glider and a powered one, for a rather subtle reason. Unless it is made impossible to restart the engine after the initial take-off climb, the very ability to do so in an emergency makes it possible to take risks, by flying over unlandable country in search of lift, which it would be too dangerous for the true glider to accept. Of course, if the pilot of the powered glider fails to find anything, he simply restarts his engine and flies back to base. He hasn't scored, but lives to try again.

It could be that the kind of people who don't want to go on from powered training to the still fairly frustrating sport of pure gliding will graduate to powered single-seater gliders, and hence leave us in possession of our own particular field. If so, there is a new exciting sport opening up to them. I look forward to the day of a London to Cape Town 'race' for powered gliders, where time elapsed and fuel used might be the parameters of a really exciting contest, as full of adventure and romance as anything we have done before.

Heli Lasch

Heli Lasch is a thin, dark man of medium size. He has a spare face, quizzical eyes, an enormous beak of a nose, a quiet slow voice, and a humour all his own. He married Orcillia and has three stunning daughters who in their time (they are now all married) turned the heads of all pilots as they walked down the rows of sailplanes at the launch point. On earth, Heli is an engineer with at once a brilliant imagination and a precise mind. But in his gliding he has a curious lack of precision in details such as his instrumentation.

In 1967 Orcillia gave him a beautiful new glider, one of the first of the new generation of fibreglass construction, whose German designers had been encouraged and financed by Heli.

One morning Heli set out on a flight, and when he got home that night Orcillia noticed he had not brought back the trailer. She asked him where it was and he said he had left it in a field.

At breakfast next morning, just before she opened her morning paper, he said gently: 'I'm sorry, Orcillia, but when I said I left my bird in a field last night, I didn't tell you, I left it in little pieces scattered all around.'

He had nearly got back from a cross-country flight, and whilst diving to lose height, he had lost sight of the needle of his Airspeed Indicator, because it had disappeared behind a small piece of paper, which, for no known reason, was stuck onto the glass face and obscuring the top range. The next thing he heard was a small noise like a rat gnawing on timber, and then he saw his starboard wing folding back like a jack-knife.

He managed to bail out and parachuted down amidst the bits of his aircraft, landing in a tiny field just big enough to take his parachute and him, surrounded by trees.

Heli is one of the great romantic pilots. Whenever I go to Johannesburg I go and have a draught of Heli and Orcillia and get him to tell me his latest adventure.

The last time I saw him, he had just returned from one of his many shots at flying the 300 miles from Johannesburg to Durban.

This means taking off from Johannesburg at 6000 ft, flying 200 miles over the flat high veldt, then crossing the mountains of Lesotho which eventually tumble down to Durban at sea level. The flight has so far defeated him because on approaching the sea one invariably flies into stable and contrary sea breezes. So it ends somewhere in the mountains, which in parts are very mountainous indeed.

On this particular occasion, Heli said, he got trapped on a precipitous slope in the midst of the mountains with no possible landing within reach anywhere, so started plodding up and down waiting and hoping for a thermal to come along before the sun set and extract him from a sticky end. After a short time, he told me, he was joined by two vultures, Hans and Lena, and a few minutes later he distinctly saw Hans' head to towards Lena, and heard a voice saying: 'Let's stick around here dear, here's our dinner.'

Fortunately (else I should not have heard the story), the sun obliged, and half-an-hour later Heli was able to circle up and away, leaving his two disappointed companions to look elsewhere for their next meal.

Women pilots

Dr Johnson once said of women preachers that they were like dogs walking on their hind legs: they did not do it well, but the remarkable thing was that they did it at all.

In spite of all the evidence to the contrary, it infuriates me (as it must infuriate the ladies) that this is still the general attitude to women pilots.

Frequently I have pointed out that the very existence of world records for women is a clear restatement of the Johnsonian attitude. Oddly enough, the strongest feelings on this thorny subject come from Iron Curtain countries, where women engine-drivers and even women judges are taken for granted. The Russians for some time have been pressing for a special women's class in World Gliding Championships, and when I expressed my personal reactions to this at a CIVV meeting I ran into very heavy weather indeed.

For reasons I have never been able to fathom, it is a fact that far fewer women *want* to fly than men, but of those who do, the proportion of good pilots is I think as high as for the other sex. I have written before that our 100 ATA women pilots produced results identical to our men pilots, in technical skill, pilotage, accident records and all the rest of it.

Hanna Reitsch, Amy Johnson, Sheila Scott, a number of women Air Transport pilots quietly flying around today, equate with any male pilots I know.

For some curious reason (holding the views that I do) I am today Chairman of a committee which recommends Annual awards to members of the British Women Pilots Association, and each year we get citations apt to include some innocently-meant eulogism like 'even our men pilots are full of admiration at Doris's (or Dora's) piloting skill and ability'. Dear little things.

I suppose, to do a bit of self-analysis, my fury on this subject roots back to the fact that this attitude is just another expression of the old-fashioned reaction to flying, that it is difficult and danger-ous, only to be performed by strong hairy men with outstanding qualities of bravery and intellect, that it is quite right to pay the driver of a jumbo jet a salary in five figures whilst a nurse or a probation officer is lucky to get £1,000 a year.

I know, when we get to the very top of the tree, that Shakespeare, Leonardo da Vinci, Beethoven and Einstein were all men, and again I am not sure why this should be so. But to equate aerial navigation with this order of genius is absurd.

It must have been some time in the summer of 1941. I was then Officer Commanding No. 1 Ferry Pool ATA White Waltham. One morning we were told to be available in the Operations Room at 11:00 hrs, as we were to be inspected by Mrs Eleanor Roosevelt.

So there we were, myself, my two Operations officers, Captain Pauline Gower (our Chief Woman Pilot) and one or two pilots who, having been on leave (we ran a thirteen-day fortnight, two-day leave system so as to rotate the days of leave) and hearing of the excite-ment, had come in to see the sights, in our Ops Room with its big wide windows looking out onto the concrete apron and the grass airfield beyond, sodden with good British rain.

Pretty well on the dot the door opened, and in came our Com-manding Officer, Gerard d'Erlanger, with Mrs Roosevelt, a stringy elderly lady with a lined kind face wearing an extraordinary crumpled flat dark green beret, a number of US high-ranking army officers with chesty acres of medal ribbons, our Pool adjutant, and numbers of other seniors. Pops d'Erlanger introduced us, and I showed her our system, designed to solve our daily crossword puzzle of how to ferry up to 100 aircraft of all types from and to airfields all over the country, with a strength of around forty pilots.

I showed her the pilots' blackboard, each pilot marked with his ferry class (from Class 1, limited to light aircraft, to Class V, capable of flying everything from a Tiger Moth to a four-engined bomber), each shown as on duty, leave or sick. I ran through the Daily Operations Book showing the type, location, delivery point and priority for each aircraft, and how we endeavoured to couple up each delivery with another collection so that a single pilot might ferry up to five aircraft in a day.

I showed her our taxi programme, so that our Anson and Fairchild taxis could deliver each pilot to his starting point for the day and collect him from his final destination, perhaps five deliveries later. I described our growing system of transit ferrying, so that we could take an aircraft to another Pool on the route, hand it over and collect a return machine.

Mrs Roosevelt took it all in, had a word with each of us, and then standing in front of her retinue, made us a little speech.

'Thank you so much for all you have shown me. I have been particularly impressed at the extraordinary scope of the work done in ATA by women. They not only fly your aircraft, they help in the engineering shops, and the hangars, they drive cars, and even run their own Ferry Pools entirely staffed by women. In fact, I am told that in ATA women do no less than *forty-eight different things!*'

There was a loud crack, and the floor shook ever so slightly; it was a pin dropping. About a year went by, then a gentle breeze rattled the windows as everyone let out their breath at once. I glanced at Pauline: she was looking straight ahead with a slightly strained expression on her face. A gallant girl.

We shook hands all round and the visitors left us. It was up to me. For want of a nail a shoe was lost—for want of a horse a battle was lost. The whole future of ATA was at stake. I turned to Pauline, and my voice sounded hoarse in my own ears.

'Pauline—you MUST tell us—*what are the other forty-seven?*'

Free as a Bird

I have tried in this book to show the synthesis of technical and practical work involved in the maintenance and growth of our sport with the non-dimensional values of companionship, of discovery, beauty, freedom and adventure, which to me at any rate gives an intrinsic worth to the art and science of soaring flight. But for these qualities, life would be only a matter of eating and earning, of putting one foot in front of the other, step after step, whilst time passes and the uncommiserate wind whispers through the drying grass.

In previous chapters I have recorded instances of the kind of hard slogging work that has to be done, so in this one, I will end with the story of the sort of flight which shows why it is all worth doing.

On 7 August 1961 the task set for the contestants in the Italian National Championships was free distance along a line south-east from Assisi through Potenza and as far as possible beyond to the southern coast of Italy. (See map, p. 153.)

The surface wind was light and north-westerly, the usual hot blue day. A surface temperature of nearly 80°F was needed to break down the inversion and give us lift to 4000 ft, and our ceiling would rise with the sun, eventually over the mountains reaching perhaps 10,000 ft under the mountain cumulus.

It was useless to take off too early, so it was 13:15 before I was released over Assisi, to circle and climb with my friends and competitors over and above the slopes of Monte Subasio. At first, below the treeline we dodged into and out of the bays and crannies of the lower slopes; then we climbed to the grass-covered heights, Assisi became a cluster of white spots on its spur far below, the mountain itself was overtopped and we set course east of south for the high mountains and our goal.

By now I had become accustomed to the look and layout of the country below, and had no hesitation in leaving the safe wide valley running south from Perugia to Spoleto on my right and setting course over the tumbled hills and valleys leading to the main high wall of the Apennines. The first 50 miles went by, a perpetual feast and wonder to the eyes, but without difficulty, for as the ground below rose, so did the height of the thermals, and high flat cumulus forming overhead made easy the location of the upcurrents beneath them. By 14:30 I was running down the wide central valley in the heart of the Apennines, from L'Aquila to Sulmona; on my left the giant wall of the Gran Sasso d'Italia Mte Corvo, Corno, Paganica, 9000 ft and 10,000 ft giants; on my right, and almost as high, the chain including Mte d'Ocre and Mte Sirente. My own height was 10,000 ft, plenty of lift, no worries in the world. As I flew south the valley wall of the Montagna del Masure on my left coalesced into the most gigantic soaring slope I have ever seen. From the valley the mountainside sprang up in a 45° slope for some 6000 ft, running on ahead of me for miles, and since this slope faced not only the wind but also the sun, I flew eagerly towards it, certain of finding miles of strong and friendly lift.

One of the rather surprising features of soaring on steep mountain slopes is that the upcurrent, though often strong, is only to be found very close indeed to the face of the mountain, so that until one gets used to it, it is quite alarming to be flying along with one wing practically scraping a rock wall some thousands of feet high. But on this occasion I suffered one of the rudest shocks of my gliding career. Never have I been so certain of finding lift, and I had expected a climb of up to 1000 ft/min. Instead, as the trees and rocks ahead swung into close focus, the air beneath me seemed to open up, and I found myself plummeting down at the fantastic rate of 1200 ft/min. The mountains ahead and above seemed to leap up into the sky, the trees and cliff in front swept up like a rising theatre curtain, and I put the Skylark into a vertical bank, turned back to the valley, and rushed away from the invisible Niagara as fast as I could.

Clearly I had been caught out by the Adriatic sea-breeze, which must have been penetrating inland and cataracting over and down the mountain range into my valley. By the time I had escaped from its clutches, I was down to a mere 3000 ft over the valley north of Sulmona, with mountains ahead and right and left towering far above me. Unless I could find lift somehow, somewhere, I must land with only around 100 miles in the bag, which would almost certainly put me out of the running.

If the air was cataracting down the eastern valley walls, it was at least likely that the compensating upcurrents were to be found to the west, so I flew in that direction and soon found myself flying up a steep and narrowing side valley with a small stream running down it, round a right-angle and then south up to the little Lago di Scano. I was down to 2500 ft; to the north was the 3000 ft Mte Prezza; the valley got narrower and I got lower; we came to the right-angle bend, and I got a whiff of rising air. I circled tightly and looked back. If all went well I could just get back and out to the main valley. If I hung on to my lift and it turned bad on me it might be doubtful. A single-line railway had twisted up the little valley to just below, then it saw what it was facing, did a 180° turn, gave a gasp of horror at what it saw behind, turned a further 90° and dived straight into the mountainside, from which, as far as I could see, it never emerged. I wished I could follow suit. But slowly the tumbled air sorted itself out, slowly I climbed, and at last the air solidified into a coherent thermal. The valley below diminished, hope became certainty, and I was up and away again on my course, little daunted by the sight of another white sailplane, the Skylark of Brennig James, sailing overhead fast and free.

After this there were no more troubles for a long time, and as I flew on south-east past Campobasso the mountains became lower and less imperious. As the sun set, a strong sea breeze from the north-north-west came to help me on my way, but at the same time increasingly cut down the thermals. At last, around 6 pm I was flying over a country of wide valleys and low hills with large stubble fields, and every now and then a grimmer higher ridge with the inevitable town perched on top of each. This was bound to lead to one final balancing decision, and in due course I got so low that it just was or was not possible to surmount one final rough and un-landable ridge ahead, to reach the next wide valley beyond. On top was the town of Ariano. I took it on, and cleared its roofs with perhaps 200 ft in hand. Ahead in the next valley lay my inevitable landing. I swept on down the slopes, over the valley, over a road, along the banks of a small river; a ploughed field offered a good landing place. I turned and approached it. Two feet above it I realised with horror that a ploughed field in Italy bore no relation to its featherbed counterpart in England, for this one was comprised of enormous chunks of earth, the size of paving-stones, baked as hard as rock. I prolonged my glide as well as I could to its far edge, but it got if anything worse, and we subsided onto it with a series of shattering jolts. I scrambled out and took a too-brief look at her (she seemed all right) and turned to meet the Italians pouring at me through the maize-field between me and the road.

Ten minutes later, and I was on the pillion of a small motor-cycle buzzing along the straight road running for some miles parallel to the river, with fields of maize and roots and stubble on either side. A half mile or so down I had seen a farmhouse, and had assumed that there we would find a telephone, but we whizzed past this and went on and on. I tried to find out from my driver how far we were going, but could not understand his reply. It was half past six and suddenly I realised that it might well be dark before I could hope to get back to the Skylark—and, in the dark, could I find it? From the road, it was on the far side of a field of tall maize, and by day a glimpse could be caught of one wing-tip. But by night? However, there was nothing to be done, the telephone was the priority object- ive, so that Kitty and the trailer might find me before the night was out.

After some six or seven miles our road joined another, turned left and crossed the river, and wound up to a large village called, I found, Grotta Minardo. In spite of urgent appeals, I was whizzed past the telephone exchange in the main street and ushered into the presence of the chief of the carabinieri. After examining my papers, he put through a phone call, talked rapidly for a few minutes, and before I could stop him, hung up. I asked anxiously, 'Perugia?' and then was made to understand that this wasn't the form at all. The nearest village to my landing point was Castel Baronia, and it was the carabinieri in that area who must receive my report, sign my landing certificate, and presumably take me under their wing. It might take anything up to two hours to get through to Perugia, and before this I must be clocked in in the correct quarters. Nothing I could do prevented me from being dumped once more on the pillion of my friend, and buzzed back to the road fork by the river bridge, where we sat, fuming, for half an hour. Then a jeep drew up with no fewer than five carabinieri on board. After more explanations, my papers were signed, the Jeep disappeared down the road in the direction of the Skylark—I thought, incorrectly, to guard it until we turned up—and I was whizzed back to Grotta Minardo. In the office of the carabinieri there, I found Biagi.

Biagi is a redoubtable French pilot, who was also flying in the Italian Championships. He is large and very dark and Southern, has a loud grating voice which is almost always in use, talks very colloquial French, and is unexpectedly one of the kindest of men. Unlike me, he also speaks Italian, so his path had been much smoother than mine. Alas, he had just rung off after giving his position, a few miles short of mine, to Perugia. I must start all over again. He took me to the central exchange, and I put in my call. A query as to how long I might have to wait was answered with a shrug.

The telephone exchange at Grotta Minardo consists of a dark room which one enters from the street. On the left is a phone box. At the far end is a counter; behind the counter sits (or sat on this night) a very active, very cross, boy of apparently about fifteen years operating the actual phone board. He was—or looked—very cross because our half of the room seemed entirely full of Italians all talking at him or with each other at the tops of their voices. How through this uproar he could carry out his job was a mystery.

A few hard benches stood around, and I sat tiredly on one to wait. Soon I was surrounded by a ring of curious faces. 'Inglesi?'—'Si.' Thank heavens, this is a passport to friendliness in many countries. 'Piloto aliante. Telephono Perugia fur mein'—dammit, I was breaking into German—'mia moglie con macchina.' Pretty well the end of my vocabulary. It was now dark, with the suddenness of those parts. Biagi had gone, he was fixing a bed for the night—did I want one too? Before I had contacted Perugia, I could not know, for I had no idea when the team would arrive to pick me up.

All the lights went out, except for the ghostly working of the green and red indicators on the switchboard. There was a moment's silence, then the scratch of a match, and the switchboard boy was unconcernedly lighting a candle and sticking it to his desk. The uproar broke out again, as loud and friendly as before. This, I thought, will be the moment when my call comes through, and I will be shut in a Stygian box unable even to read my map. But no, the lights went on again, and another hour passed by. I began to be glad we had been given two days for our return.

At last the boy looked up, pointed first at me and then at the phone box and said, 'Perugia'. I dashed inside with my precious map, shut the door (the glass immediately becoming smudged outside with a dozen breaths) and picked up the receiver. A distant feminine voice said something incomprehensible (but which I took to mean, 'Are you there?' and I replied 'Si') then 'Wait', or words to that effect. I waited, for some 20 minutes, standing cramped and airless in my vertical coffin, with occasional words of hope and cheer from afar, 'Pronto' or 'Subito' or similar words. Then all the lights went out again.

Immediately my door was opened and half a dozen friendly hands came through, holding half a dozen lighted matches. As these burnt out, the smouldering ends were dropped, some on the floor and some on my feet, and others were lighted. In no time I was stamping around in my box like a performing bear, extinguishing incipient conflagrations and begging my helpers to desist until I had actually established communication, but it was a nervous while before my anguished message penetrated the language barrier. Suddenly the lights went on again, and ten minutes later—about 9 o'clock—Perugia, a faint and far off Perugia, came through. They were as relieved to hear from me as I was from them. I tried to shout (a) the whereabouts of my glider, in a field near Castel Baronia, and (b) my location in Grotta Minardo, and I understood in return that Kitty and the team were at the Albergo San Bartolomeo at Benevento, 20 miles away to the west. But I couldn't be quite sure that my message had got through, and asked one of my audience to take up the cudgels on my behalf. He took over the phone, shouted at it a lot, and then abruptly hung it up. All was well, he said; but somehow I doubted it. Anyway, the next thing was clearly to ring Benevento, and see if I could talk to Kitty.

This would have been a good plan, but alas the telephone book and finally the Benevento carabinieri both confirmed that that town boasted no Albergo San Bartolomeo, so once more I was suspended in uncertainty. Grotta Minardo exchange now showed signs of packing up for the night, so I was reduced to relying, as sometimes before—and never in vain—on Kitty's telepathic powers in finding me. But this was not the end of my problem, for on going out into the street I found the night was growing colder. I was wearing only a pair of shorts and an open-necked shirt, insufficient to keep me warm through a night in the open air waiting for an indefinite rescue.

The little town was bright and gay with cafés, and stalls selling slices of water-melon; a few neon lights overwhelmed the myriad stars and the pale new moon. In one of the cafés I found Biagi drinking a glass of beer, and talking volubly about his flight of the day. He had found an inn, would I come and eat with him and share his room? As I had eaten nothing except a few biscuits in the cockpit since breakfast, I gladly accepted the first offer, but was still undecided about the bed. Any moment the trailer might arrive, and no sailplane pilot likes to be found by his exhausted and hungry crew comfortably abed.

We were now in the southern part of Italy, where the 'economic miracle' had not yet started to catch up. The inn was just a poor little house in a row of poor little houses, and we ate in a dark room on bare benches off a board table. But the kindliness and interest were there just the same. By midnight Biagi and I were drinking a last cup of coffee in the last café to stay open, then we repaired to a water-melon stall, which kept us going (and on my part shivering) till 1 am, watching every oncoming vehicle for the tell-tale yellow headlights of the Vanguard; but they did not arrive. At last, there was nothing for it, and I followed him back to the inn, up a dark narrow wooden stair into a tiny cell with two truckle beds. I took off my shoes and lay down and tried to doze.

Half an hour later there were steps on the stair, a knock on the door, and the landlord's son, half asleep, peered in and said, 'Camion—moglie.' They had arrived. By one of her usual feats of second-sight, Kitty had found Grotta Minardo, wakened the carabinieri, and they had led her to my door. Outside I found the silver bulk of the trailer and the Vanguard with softly glowing yellow lights looming enormous between the sad stone houses under the stars. The first stage of the retrieve was over, pilot and team were reunited. We thanked the half-awake carabinieri and set off to find the third essential component, the Skylark.

It was very hot, an Italian heatwave. The task was along a line to the south-east. We got round Rome and under Cassino tried to phone back in an awful dead-beat café with an old juke-box going. The brand new monastery was sitting above us and the place seemed full of ghosts. After two frustrating hours of not getting through we suddenly realised that our only hope was a dash to a main exchange in a large town as everything would shut down at midnight. It was 11 pm and 60 km to go. However, we arrived at 11.50 and got the call through, getting a rather vague message that Philip was at one of two villages.

It was then while trying to tiptoe through the sleeping towns that we noticed the embarrassing squeak. We greased the towbar, but it still went on. As our ideas about what to do then ran out we battled on on the mountain roads. At one point we just found out in time that an eighteen-wheeler and us wouldn't fit together on to a bridge. The eighteen-wheelers are driven very fast and well by young men and the lorries make a wonderful sucking noise when braking as if they are trying their best to make themselves smaller.

At last we arrived at one of the villages we had been given and at 2 am the only person about was a little girl putting out her melons for the morning market.

We battered at the carabinieri's door, endless trouser putting on, then they appeared and we set off walking much farther than we expected, till at last a dishevelled house with No. 100 roughly painted on in red, looking like blood. More trouser putting on and the whole household seemed to be getting up. At last Philip appeared and we trudged back.

He, to our surprise, was horrified by what we now considered our tame, rather comforting squeak.

We had not gone a hundred yards before we went over a minor bump in the road and the trailer behind emitted an agonising metallic screech. I uttered a yelp of horror, but the team (Kitty, Vanessa, Justin and an Italian young man, Italo Nannini) were unperturbed. 'It started doing that miles back,' said Kitty, 'and we got out and greased everything we could think of, but it still does it. It doesn't seem to matter.' We were all too tired to mind, so I decided to go on the remaining few miles to the glider and then have a good look. In another three miles I knew I had taken the wrong road. We pulled into a side lane and laboriously reversed. We drove back to Grotta Minardo and started again. This time the river bridge and fork duly turned up, but the screeches wore me down, and at length we put Justin in the trailer and drove on, so that he could locate them. He reported that they came from the starboard springs, so I got out and examined them. They seemed to be all right, but I put the grease-gun on them, and then, for luck, went round to the other side to do the same. Immediately the cause of the trouble was out: one of the shackles had come adrift and, with both shackle pins, was missing. The trailer was resting directly on the rear end of the spring. I looked at it; there was nothing to do. It had lasted for some miles, we must try and see if it would carry us for a few miles farther, to the glider, and then back to a village for repair. At ten miles an hour we squeaked despairingly on into the night.

The road went on straight and uniform, with maize and stubble on either side. At last I thought we must be near the machine, and we stopped. With our torches we scattered into the fields on our right and started searching. The hills bordering the valley to north and south loomed faintly in the starlight, and a few lights marked a small village here and there, but no Skylark was to be found. We went back to the car and drove on until some trees loomed up which, I felt sure, meant we had gone too far. We reversed again, and went back for another fruitless search. After this, we uncoupled the trailer, turned east again, and drove for miles, with me trying vainly to find some landmark. At last we had clearly gone too far, and again, despondently, we turned back. It looked as if we must simply stop and await the sunrise, now only an hour away, when in the glow of our headlight ahead we saw a small boy, trudging along the road with a loaf of bread under his arm. We stopped, and Italo eagerly asked him if he knew where was the *aliante*. 'Si, si,' he said, and we hauled him aboard. He was barefooted, had a rather nice grubby smell, and a lurcher dog who ran on behind us. In a mile or so he stopped us, and dived into the fields on our left. We followed him; no glider. So again we spread around with our torches, and at last looming ahead I saw a group of trees bordering the river, which gave me a picture of my landing approach. Surely I had come in round them? I broke into a run and there, shining in the light of my torch, was the upflung wing of the Skylark. I shouted and waved. The pinpricks of torches centred on me, and soon the team were round her. We walked back to the road and, leaving one member marking the spot, drove back to the trailer, manhandled it round, hooked it up, and ran back to the goal. Again we unhooked it, turned it round,

jacked it up, and stumbled with our torches through the maize field to the Skylark. I shone my torch on her to start dismantling, and it lighted on a sinister crack in the underside of the fuselage. With a cry of horror I got down on my knees and played the beam along her keel. On either side the brick-hard ploughed earth had punched a number of remorseless little holes, and towards the stern was a large and ominous broken panel of ply. We were out of the race.

Or were we? We still had a day to get home and another for repair, if such was possible. The glider was damaged, the trailer was broken, and the car was giving signs of trouble. But we were at least all together again in one spot. The sky was lightening, dawn was on us, and with it our hearts rose, in spite of everything. My team was dauntless. I had first broken and then lost our aircraft, but their spirits were undimmed, and I certainly was not going to let the side down. We had won the day, as I had flown the farthest, and we would win the rest as well.

Getting the parts of the dismantled machine out of that field was a nightmare. In the half-light we stumbled and tripped our way with each succeeding component back to the road, desperately careful to damage her no more. But at last they were in, and we were ready to start back on the long road to Perugia. We crawled off, dropped our ten-year-old saviour, still clutching his loaf of bread, at a solitary farmhouse, and squeaked our way cautiously through Grotta Minardo, beginning to wake up, and on to the next village. Here, at seven o'clock in the morning, we found a small garage and with the extraordinary engineering facility of all Italians, the proprietor rigged us up a new shackle within an hour.

The rest of the day was just an interminable battle against heat, dust, and the desire to sleep. We ran up Italy through Caserta, Capua, Cassino and round Rome, through names that echo in history both ancient and modern, but we were too tired to take much notice. At 7 pm, just as the sun was setting, we were back at the home airfield. A night's sleep, a day with the cheerful and hard-working repair team, and on the morning of 10 August, we were lined up for the next task.

∞∞∞

Memories? We brought back too many to record. One day we saw the beautiful frescoes of Giotto in the incredible Franciscan Monastery of Assisi, and the next I was looking down at the white town ridge-backed on its mountain spur. There came an unforgettable moment when three Skylarks met and circled over the wonderful peak of Mte Cucco, two Englishmen and an Italian pirouetting together god-like over the beauty of the Appenines. At the end of our last task, I landed at the foot of a tiny village called Roca di Botti perched on a mountainside overlooking a valley, closed to the east by the towering mountains: before landing I had flown up to the far end, but the dying evening lift would not give me enough height to overclimb them. Just before I turned back for my landing I flew over an outlying spur of steep and craggy rock, as hard and sharp and lifeless as a moonscape. On the very razor back of the spur, 2000 ft above the valley, I saw what looked like a tumbled ridge of immense teeth, like the armoured back of some vast prehistoric monster. As I whispered a hundred feet over them, I saw they were the incredibly remote remains of some long-forgotten mountain fortress or village, looking down on either side on nothing but boulders and rock and scree, no blade of vegetation, no water for miles. What sort of people could have possibly lived, 2000 years ago, in such a gaunt and unforgiving eyrie? Whoever they were, they could never have conceived that a man from a far northern country, then consisting of bog and swamp and inhabited by savages, would one day sweep silently over what remained of their roof-tops in a man-made bird, wondering about them and their harsh lives.

A little later, I stood and waited on the ledge on the mountainside which is the main street of Roca di Botti. Behind was a row of rough stone houses. In front, over a low balustrade, was the darkness of the valley, a few twinkling lights, the dark outlines of the mountains opposite and to my right. The warm night was full of the chirp of crickets; the villagers were strolling up and down their little street, untouched by the glories with which they lived. Overhead glittered the Milky Way and a million stars. The pale road corkscrewed down to the valley at my feet and then ran off to the left, where lay the world. Again I was waiting for the far gleam of yellow headlights. For the hundredth time I pitied the folk who cannot understand why we are fascinated by our sport. For all its discomforts, its stresses and occasional despairs, it leads us again and again to moments like these, when we get an unforeseen insight into the world which is going on, living its quiet and only slowly-changing life throughout the centuries, behind the cities and the H-bombs and the flickering glare of the television screen.

Roca di Botti and Rome, the Autostrada from Florence to Bologna and the surging skies of the Appenines, all are part of Italy and of the world we live in.

∞

Appendices

Appendices

I

THE BRITISH GLIDING ASSOCIATION

STRUCTURE

MEMBERSHIP: Consists of Full Member Clubs and Individual Associate Members.

STRUCTURE: Control is exercised by the Executive Committee of Management which is elected by Full Member Clubs, with the Chairmen of the various Committees. The Association's headquarters takes the form of a permanent secretariat of twelve under a General Secretary.

The Executive Committee delegates authority in specified fields; the main structure is as follows:

Patron: HRH Prince Philip, Duke of Edinburgh, KG.

President: Philip Wills, CBE.

Vice Presidents: Basil Meads, MBE; Air Chief Marshal Sir Theodore McEvoy, KCB, CBE; John Furlong, MBE, DFC; Peter Scott, CBE, DSC, LLD; Dr A. E. Slater, MA, FRMetS; K. G. Wilkinson, FCGI, FRAeS.

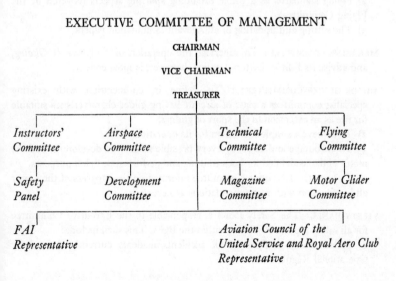

EXECUTIVE COMMITTEE OF MANAGEMENT

CHAIRMAN

VICE CHAIRMAN

TREASURER

Instructors' *Committee*	*Airspace* *Committee*	*Technical* *Committee*	*Flying* *Committee*
Safety *Panel*	*Development* *Committee*	*Magazine* *Committee*	*Motor Glider* *Committee*
FAI *Representative*		*Aviation Council of the* *United Service and Royal Aero Club* *Representative*	

TERMS OF REFERENCE OF THE COMMITTEES

AIRSPACE COMMITTEE: To maintain a continuous watching brief on all matters concerning controlled airspace and to advise the Executive Committee on important problems as they arise. This includes liaison with the Department of Trade and Industry over proposals for the revision and extension of controlled airspace.

DEVELOPMENT COMMITTEE: 1) To investigate the possibilities of obtaining grant aid for gliding clubs from the Department of the Environment under the provision of the Physical Training and Recreation Act 1937 as amended in May 1963 to include single sport activities.
2) To advise clubs in making applications if they were found to be suitable.
3) The Development Officer is responsible to the Executive Committee for promoting increased efficiency and the future expansion of the gliding movement.

FLYING COMMITTEE: The Flying Committee is responsible to the Executive Committee for all sporting aspects of gliding. This shall include all matters associated with the badge scheme, all forms of competitions, records, cups and awards for sporting gliding and for the FAI Sporting Code (through the BGA/CIVV representative).

INSTRUCTORS' COMMITTEE: The Instructors' Committee is responsible to the Executive Committee for:
1) Administration and practical aspects of the rating of instructors.
2) Flying standards as a whole excluding sporting aspects (covered by the Flying Committee).
3) The setting and updating of all relevant examination papers.

MAGAZINE COMMITTEE: To supervise the operation of *Sailplane & Gliding*, and advise its Editor. Editorial policy, however, is independent.

MOTOR GLIDER COMMITTEE: 1) To define in co-operation with existing specialist committees a class of aircraft having glider characteristics suitable for use as an extension to the sport of gliding.
2) To achieve a simple legislation for its operation.
3) To encourage and assist by every possible means the development of the motor glider as defined for both training and performance flying purposes.
4) To keep the Executive Committee informed on the progress of the motor glider situation with recommendations as necessary.

SAFETY PANEL: The Safety Panel is responsible to the Executive Committee for all safety aspects of gliding within the BGA. This shall include:
1) Collation and analysis of all accidents/incidents currently defined by Operational Regulations.

2) Production and publication of statistics and safety information.

3) Liaison with the Department of Trade and Industry Accidents Investigation Branch.

TECHNICAL COMMITTEE: To advise the Executive Committee on technical matters; in particular to supervise the airworthiness scheme:

1) Supervision of the issue of Certificates of Airworthiness.

2) Supervision of the approval of Inspectors.

3) Consideration of all technical problems.

II

GLIDER REGISTRATION

Very noticeable on all British gliders is the absence of long and disfiguring registration letters and numbers painted on wings and fuselage. Instead, most of us have simple one or two-figure numbers on our wings and fin, which we need for our competitions.

Just after the war, the Ministry of Civil Aviation required us to fall into line, like other aircraft, and we nearly agreed, but the Yorkshire Gliding Club objected so strongly that we went back and argued our case.

The only necessity for State-issued registration is for police purposes; particularly so that an aircraft may be identified from a distance should it be engaged in smuggling or in other ways breaking the law. But a glider can hardly be used for smuggling from or into the UK nor can it land in a field and take-off in a few minutes before anyone arrives on the scene.

Once more, the Ministry accepted our argument, and has left us to look after ourselves; another instance of the co-operation which generates self-responsibility and hence safety.

III

GLIDER PILOTS' MEDICAL STANDARDS

Some people may think this Appendix is tiresome and dull, but it is a good example of the sort of tiresome and dull work that has to be done if we are to retain our freedom.

In the UK we have never suffered from officially imposed medical standards for glider pilots, whereas in most other countries (the USA being a conspicuous exception) varying—and sometimes absurdly stiff—examinations are required.

By the late 1960s some bureaucratic pressure was building up to 'bring us into line', so it was desirable to examine our record of the previous years in order to produce proof, one way or the other, of whether or not our freedom from official controls had produced satisfactory results in comparison with other nations.

In the USA, the March 1965 issue of *Aerospace Medicine* published a paper by Dr R. L. Wick, Flight Surgeon of the Research Branch, Research and Education Division, Office of Aviation Medicine, Federal Aviation Agency, titled 'A Five-year History of Sailplane Accidents'.

This paper was based on a total of 12 fatal accidents and approximately 110 serious accidents reported in that country over a period of five years, and the following is an extract:

'The hazard which a sailplane presents to persons on the ground is one which must be considered. The following study covers a period of five years and, although more glider flying has been done during this period than during any similar period in the past, there is no incident which involved injury to anyone on the ground. Property damage during this five-year period was limited to several telephone wires which were inadvertently pulled down, a number of fences—mostly in the vicinity of airport runways—which were also knocked over, and one outhouse which had its door knocked from its hinges when a glider came to rest with the nose just inside the doorway. The risk to persons and property on the ground from sailplaning is apparently negligible.

'It is significant that, for a training flight in a powered airplane during early phases of pre-solo training, one hour is used as a standard instruction period. A student may make as few as one take-off and one landing during that time, particularly if airwork is practised during the hour. In a sailplane, however, a flight of ten minutes or less is common. Therefore, per hour of flying, the number of take-offs and landings is much higher in the sailplanes. This is reflected in the Civil Aeronautics Board figures for accident rates. Single-engine airplanes have approximately 40 accidents per 100,000 flying hours, while for sailplanes the rate is approximately 64. However, fatality rates show a different relationship. The rate for these is 3·41 and 2·56 respectively. In fact, the fatality rate for sailplanes is lower than for any other type of aircraft except multi-engine fixed-wing airplanes, which rate approximately 2·05 per 100,000 flying hours. Sailplanes are largely flown by amateur pilots and multi-engine airplanes generally are flown by professional pilots. The trend seems to indicate that sailplanes are far safer than any other type of flying by amateur pilots.

'In view of the vicissitudes of sailplane flying, a question arises concerning the medical status of the individuals involved in fatal accidents. During the period under review, most of the fatal accidents happened to pilots who did have medical certificates. (Actual figure seven out of 12 accidents.) Post-mortem examinations were performed on only two of the pilots involved and neither of these revealed any evidence which might point to physical incapacitation on the part of the pilot. Ample causes for the accidents were demonstrated.

'In a recent letter sent to all airmen in the United States, the Administrator of the FAA pointed out that 68% of all accidents were caused by faulty flying technique and 31% were caused by careless or reckless operation. This leaves only 1% of the accidents which can be attributed to either a mechanical failure or physical incapacitation on the part of the aircraft or pilot, respectively. Therefore, in the entire five-year period only one would be expected to have been a result of a physical deficiency of the pilot. It is doubtful if requiring physical examinations of almost 1000 pilots for those five years would be worth the effort, since it is by no means certain that the physical examination would have prevented the one expected accident among glider pilots. Furthermore, since we are really speaking of the glider pilots without physical examinations, the time period could be extended to as long as 20 years.'

In most countries—including the UK—serious glider accidents have to be investigated by the official Ministerial body concerned. In the UK, however, the major responsibility for safety is delegated to the British Gliding Association.

As I have written before, 'in the field of accidents, remedial action can only be securely founded on an analysis, not only of serious accidents but of all accidents and near-accidents (or incidents). This is because, after an initial mistake or failure, it is often pure chance whether a fatal, serious or minor accident—or even no accident at all—ensues. If, therefore, an incident is reported, remedial action can often be taken in time to prevent a repetition and thus avoid a subsequent serious accident.' By achieving a high standard of self-discipline amongst its pilot members, the BGA has managed to get them to report a much larger number of such minor accidents and incidents than, probably, in any other country in the world, and thus can produce statistics more informative and accurate than are available elsewhere.

The following table shows the total civilian launches carried out in the United Kingdom over the ten years 1959–1968 inclusive, and the number of accidents/incidents reported and analysed each year.

	Civil Launches on Club Sites	Accidents/ Incidents
1959	121,196	90
1960	122,557	84
1961	139,826	70
1962	163,313	113
1963	152,676	79
1964	170,535	92
1965	183,527	98
1966	204,881	102
1967	195,610	106
1968	218,358	104
	1,672,379	938

Of these 938, 180 accidents were sufficiently serious to be legally reportable. This is a good measure of the degree by which the BGA analysis forms a reliable basis for accident prevention measures as compared with analysis based on accidents officially reported. Four of these accidents/incidents had a conceivable medical causation, of which two were suffered by pilots holding Private Pilots' Licences with the official medical standard involved. The medical deficiency discovered in the other two accidents would not have been detected in a PPL medical examination.

The following table gives the details:

	Nature of disease	Medical standard
1	Epilepsy	Private Pilots' Licence
2	Coronary artery disease	Private Pilots' Licence
3	Coronary artery disease	Service Officer
4	Coronary artery disease	BGA declaration

In relation to Nos. 3 and 4, the evidence available indicates that examination to PPL standard would not have revealed either defect. In none of these four cases can it be said that the medical defect was the certain cause, but that it was a probable or possible one.

In the classes of accidents/incidents other than fatal accidents, there were no reported cases indicating medical causation. This does not, of course, prove that medical causation was entirely absent, but simply that it was not detected. However, any such cases must have been very few.

Dr Wick's paper concluded with the words '. . . there is no evidence to indicate that requiring (glider) pilots to possess medical certificates would lower the present accident rate.'

The BGA analysis of over 900 accidents/incidents arising from over 1·67 million flights gives a sufficiently large statistical base on which further to strengthen this conclusion. There is now positive evidence to show that the imposition of medical certificates for glider pilots is unnecessary. Any such imposition simply restricts development and expansion of gliding with no compensating reduction in the accident rate.

The tendency amongst Ministerial medical experts throughout the world is to try to anticipate possible medical causes of future accidents and then to impose medical checks and restrictions to avoid their possible future occurrence.

The correct attitude, I submit, is the reverse—to investigate and analyse closely the actual occurrence over the past ten years, and draw conclusions from the *facts* thus revealed. These facts are now virtually established—no medical certificate is necessary.

Unfortunately, this is not the end of the problem. Hard as we try, neither Ministries nor the public can be made to realise that a sport involving the use of the air is no different from one taking place on the sea or on land. Although no Ministry requires medical certificates for underwater swimming, ski-ing or mountaineering, the ordinary man takes it for granted that some standard should be required before a man is permitted to fly. It would, in fact, be immensely more sensible if medical examinations were imposed for the issue of a car driving licence.

However, to preserve the good name of the sport, the British Gliding Association require certain minimal procedures, particularly for instructors and pilots carrying passengers (see p. 241).

1 An analysis of past accidents/incidents shows conclusively that:

   (a) The imposition of compulsory medical requirements for glider pilots does not beneficially affect the accident rate.
   (b) Accordingly, such imposition does not beneficially affect the risk to persons and property on the ground, which in any case is exceedingly small.

2 In view of this the imposition of compulsory medical requirements for glider pilots is unnecessary and undesirable.
3 Therefore, in the case of pilots flying solo, all that is needed is to advise them—before starting to glide—of the general nature of medical disabilities which might increase the risk so far as they personally are concerned, and leave them as in other sports, to decide whether to accept it or not. It is, of course, up to each club or association whether or not to permit a medically deficient applicant to use its equipment.
4 Nevertheless, for political reasons, it may be desirable to require some logically defensible medical requirements for pilots carrying passengers and/or instructors, particularly professional instructors.

In a thesis entitled 'The Medical and Pathological Investigation of Fatal Civil

Aircraft Accidents', published in 1970, Wing-Commander P. J. Stevens, OBE, MD, PCPath, of the RAF Institute of Pathology, Halton, adds to my schedule of the fatal accidents experienced in British Civil Clubs those experienced by Service Clubs and the Air Cadets, and has extended the time scale to the eighteen years 1950 to 1967 inclusive. This produces the staggering total of 4,473,275 flights, including 35 fatal accidents.

His conclusion is as follows:

'In my opinion, the latest regulations on medical standards imposed by the British Gliding Association are likely to result in an acceptable level of medical fitness among those who glide in this country; medical investigation of 14 of the 23 fatal gliding accidents that have occurred in the last 8 years, has not provided any evidence to show that a system of licensing and medical examination of glider pilots would materially increase the safety of the sport.'

We still maintain our freedom from official control of pilots' medical standards, but in most other countries the bureaucrats and the professional aviation medical experts have so far proved impossible to dislodge even in face of our virtually unarguable evidence.

BGA MEDICAL STANDARDS

PART ONE

A. *To be signed before starting to fly as pupil or solo pilot*

I hereby declare that, I have never suffered from any of the following, which I understand may create, or lead to, a dangerous situation in flight.

Epilepsy, Fits, Severe Head Injury.

Recurrent Fainting, Giddiness or Blackouts.

Unusually High Blood Pressure.

A Previous Coronary.

I am not regularly taking Insulin for the control of Diabetes.

I further declare that, in the event of my contracting or suspecting, any of the above conditions in the future, I will cease to fly until I have obtained medical opinion.

Signed.............. (Name caps)................... Date ....

If you cannot sign the above declaration, you must, before flying, obtain the signature of your *regular* GP, or that of an approved Department of Trade and Industry PPL Examiner, below:

I am the regular GP of the applicant. }Delete as appropriate.
I am a DoTI PPL Medical Examiner. }

I understand that the applicant wishes to fly in sporting gliders, but has been unable to sign the above declaration. In my opinion, it is safe for him/her so to fly.

Signed .... Date ....
Name/Address .... Applicant's name ....
....

B. The following may cause you difficulty while flying. If you suffer, or have suffered, from any of these, you are advised to take medical opinion:

Chronic Bronchitis.

Severe Asthma.

Chronic Sinus Disease.

Chronic Ear Disease.

Eye Trouble (e.g. Inability to read a car number plate at 25 yards—corrective glasses may be used)

Regular, Severe, Migraine.

Diabetes in any form.

Rheumatic Fever.

Kidney Stones.

Psychiatric Disorders.

Severe Motion or Travel Sickness.

Any condition requiring the use of drugs. (Includes any medication whatsoever.)

You are further advised that:

a. If you normally wear spectacles, you should always carry a readily accessible spare pair.

b. Minor illnesses, drugs, and the donation of blood, will probably make you temporarily unfit to fly.

PART TWO *Passenger Carriers or Instructors* (*Excluding Professionals*)

Before commencing to carry passengers, or instruct, in sporting gliders, the certificate below must be signed—in addition to the signature required at Part One. The certification must be renewed as indicated.

Doctors may use the conditions listed in Part One A & B as a guide to the requirements.

I am the regular GP of the applicant ⎫
I am a DoTI PPL Medical Examiner ⎬Delete as appropriate.

I understand that the applicant wishes to carry passengers, or instruct, in sporting gliders. In my opinion, he/she is not suffering from any medical condition which might make him/her unfit so to do.

Initial/Renewal Certificate (Delete as appropriate)

Signed ....   Date ....

Name/Address ....   Applicant's Name ....

....

(For Club Use) Valid Until ....

PROFESSIONAL INSTRUCTORS (Defined, for this purpose only, as any person receiving wages/salary, excluding expenses, for Instructing in gliders for any consecutive employment period, of 12 calendar weeks or more.)

Evidence must be provided, before commencing to instruct in a professional capacity, that the normal PPL Medical Examination has been passed.

RENEWALS

The PART TWO Medical Certificate (or PPL Medical for Professionals) must be renewed as follows:

1. Up to and including age 40—Every Five Years.

2. Age 41 to 50—Every Three Years.

3. Over 50—Annually.

Clubs should calculate the renewal date, using the relevant periods, to the nearest next date of the BGA Annual Return.

NOTES

1. In all cases, possession of a *valid* PPL, CPL, or equivalent Service Document, will override the BGA requirements.
2. Foreign Certificates may be accepted, provided there is proof that the standard is at least that of the BGA.
3. Clubs may demand a *higher* standard, for any of their members, at their own discretion.
4. In the case of defective vision, hearing or physical disability, a Club waiver of demonstrated ability may be operated.
5. When a signature is required at PART TWO, PART ONE must also be presented, signed, to the relevant Doctor, for his information.
6. In cases of doubt, or non signature of the certificates, the applicant should be referred to the BGA for final arbitration.

IV

THE AIRMISS WORKING GROUP

In the UK we have a very good—I think unique—tool for measuring the approximate risk of aerial collision in the Airmiss Working Group, which represents the technical rather than the emotional approach to the problem.

All pilots are required to report airmisses, which are then analysed and split into three categories. Category C is where no significant risk is involved—one pilot sees another aircraft whose presence has not been reported to him, but neither aircraft has to change course to avoid risk of collision. Cat. C airmisses are thus mere sightings, and if such happenings required reporting in any other methods of transport, the world would disappear under bits of paper.

Cat. B represents sightings where some change in course or height of one or both aircraft is required to avoid a possible collision, but no significant risk is involved.

Cat. A is where the aircraft come near enough before one or other pilot sees the risk to necessitate fairly urgent—or even drastic—action, and these do involve significant risk. Cat. A airmisses can properly be called Near Misses, and call for (and get) full investigation and remedial action to avoid recurrence.

Unfortunately many organs of the Press fail to distinguish between the categories, and lump the whole lot in as Near Misses, thus enormously exaggerating the real risk.

In 1970, there were 11 Cat. A Near Misses, 31 Cat. B, and 66 Cat. C reports involving transport aircraft. There is no record of the total number of civil and military flights which took place during the year, but a rough guess would be in the region of 2 million. There was no actual collision involving an airliner, and has not been one over the UK since these records started, so it is possible to say that existing methods have to date been adequate, since one cannot beat a zero record.

The British Air Line Pilots Association comments on the 1971 record were that it showed that 'the present air traffic control environment is totally unsuited to cope with the number of air traffic movements over Britain'.

A more unbiased conclusion must be that the existing patient and analytical work of the AMWG and consequent remedial actions to improve the system as defects show up in practice has proved satisfactory, taking into account the total picture on the basis of any cost/benefit/amenity considerations.

Index